Fooshee Benefaction

ÆDES CHRISTI
in Academia Oxoniensi

C.M.S. R.E. 1904.

A Penguin *Production*

GROUCHO

MARX

The Essential

GROUCHO

Edited by Stefan **KANFER**

'I believe his outrageous, unsentimental disregard for order will be equally funny a thousand years from now. In addition to all this, he makes me laugh' **Woody Allen**

PENGUIN BOOKS

THE ESSENTIAL GROUCHO

Julius Henry (Groucho) Marx was born in New York City
in 1890, the son of German immigrants. He had four
brothers: Leonard (Chico); Adolph, later known as Arthur
(Harpo); Milton (Gummo); and Herbert (Zeppo). The
brothers began their stage careers in various vaudeville
acts, sometimes with their mother Minnie. Groucho
played the guitar and sang outrageous songs – preparation
for the halcyon days when he broke audiences up with
'Lydia the Tattooed Lady' and 'Hello, I Must Be Going'.
The Marx Brothers made their Broadway debut in the
1924 musical *I'll Say She Is* and followed this with *The
Cocoanuts* (1925, filmed in 1929) and *Animal Crackers*
(1928, filmed in 1930). They went on to star in many other
classic films, including *Horse Feathers* (1932), *Duck Soup*
(1933), *A Night at the Opera* (1935) and *A Day at the Races*
(1937). *Love Happy* (1949) was the last film they made
together.

Of all the brothers, Groucho had the most successful inde-
pendent career. He made several other films, such as
Copacabana (1947), *A Girl in Every Port* (1952) and *Skidoo*
(1968), and hosted the television quiz show *You Bet Your
Life* between 1950 and 1961. He wrote several books,
including *Beds* (1930); an autobiography, *Many Happy
Returns!* (1942); *Groucho and Me* (1959); and *The Groucho
Letters* (1967). The Marx Brothers all had well-defined
screen personas, but Groucho's was always recognizable
with his cigar and bushy eyebrows; plastic versions of
his glasses and over-sized moustache are sold in toy and
costume shops all over the world to this day. His character
was also considered by audiences to be more human and
easy to relate to. He is one of the most frequently quoted
comedians of all time, with such memorable wise-cracks as

'Time flies like an arrow. Fruit flies like a banana' and 'If you want to see a comic strip, you should see me in the shower'. He died in 1977.

Stefan Kanfer is the author of nine books, including *A Journal of the Plague Years*; *Serious Business*; *Groucho: The Life and Times of Julius Henry Marx* (Allen Lane The Penguin Press, 2000); and the novels *Fear Itself* and *The Eighth Sin*. He was a writer and editor at *Time* magazine for over twenty years, and has written for most major periodicals. Before becoming a journalist, he wrote for the theatre and television, contributing material to Victor Borge and Alan Funt, among others. He has been a writer in residence at various colleges, and has received numerous awards for journalism and writing.

The
ESSENTIAL
GROUCHO

Writings by, for and about
Groucho Marx

Edited and with an Introduction by
STEFAN KANFER

PENGUIN BOOKS

PENGUIN BOOKS

Published by the Penguin Group
Penguin Books Ltd, 27 Wrights Lane, London w8 5TZ, England
Penguin Putnam Inc., 375 Hudson Street, New York, New York 10014, USA
Penguin Books Australia Ltd, Ringwood, Victoria, Australia
Penguin Books Canada Ltd, 10 Alcorn Avenue, Toronto, Ontario, Canada M4V 3B2
Penguin Books India (P) Ltd, 11, Community Centre,
Panchsheel Park, New Delhi – 110 017, India
Penguin Books (NZ) Ltd, Private Bag 102902, NSMC, Auckland, New Zealand
Penguin Books (South Africa) (Pty) Ltd, 5 Watkins Street,
Denver Ext 4, Johannesburg 2094, South Africa

Penguin Books Ltd, Registered Offices: Harmondsworth, Middlesex, England

First published in the USA by Vintage Books 2000
First published in Great Britain in Penguin Books 2000

2

Printed in England by Clays Ltd, St Ives plc

For Sari and Nate Kanfer

CONTENTS

Introduction   xi

"I know that you are true to the Army. I only hope it
  remains a standing Army."
  The Napoleon Sketch from *I'll Say She Is!*   3

"You can even get stucco—oh, how you can get stucco."
  Dialogue from *The Cocoanuts*   13

"One morning I shot an elephant in my pajamas."
  Dialogue from *Animal Crackers*   21

"You bet I'm shy. I'm a shyster lawyer."
  Dialogue from *Monkey Business*   28

"There'll be no diving for this cigar."
  Dialogue from *Horse Feathers*   32

"Go, and never darken my towels again!"
  Dialogue from *Duck Soup*   37

"I could rent you out as a decoy for duck hunters."
  Dialogue from the lost radio shows,
  Flywheel, Shyster, and Flywheel   46

"You haven't got a baboon in your pocket, have you?"
  Dialogue from *A Night at the Opera*   72

"Say, you're awfully large for a pill."
Dialogue from *A Day at the Races*   79

"I had dinner with my celebrated pen pal, T. S. Eliot."
From *The Groucho Letters*   87

"Right from the feedbag."
Covering Groucho   113

"I am sometimes jealous of my past."
From fugitive comic pieces and articles by Groucho Marx   126

"I'll never forget my wedding day . . . they threw vitamin pills."
Selections from *You Bet Your Life*   209

INTRODUCTION

Falstaff was louder and more flamboyant and outweighed Groucho Marx by some 250 pounds. Yet in one aspect these two comic forces were strikingly similar. According to Shakespeare, Sir John was not only witty himself but the cause of wit in others. According to a worldwide audience, so was Groucho.

Julius Henry Marx (1890–1977) was the third of Sam and Minnie Marx's six sons (the firstborn, Manfred, died in infancy). The German-Jewish immigrants raised their brood in the clamorous Upper East Side of New York, always a step or two from destitution—although they insisted that they were not poor, they just didn't have any money. Sam's inept tailoring drew few repeat customers; as for Minnie (née Schoenberg), she had brains, looks, ambition—but no outlet for her prodigious energy. All this was to change when she assumed the role for which she was born: Stage Mother.

Unlike Minnie's favorite, Leonard, who was to become Chico, Adolph (Harpo), Herbert (Zeppo), or Milton (Gummo), Julius was neither cute as a child nor prepossessing in early youth. Minnie favored her other four sons, and later on Groucho's slightly walleyed look put young ladies off. As the brothers grew, they split into pairs. The eldest, Chico and Harpo, went their own ways, finding trouble in school and adventure on the streets. Zeppo and Gummo were the babies of the family and sought company their own age. That left Groucho, the classic middle child, whose resentments were so marked that Minnie called him *die Eifersüchtige*—the Jealous One.

As such, he retreated into books, more interested in the tales of Horatio Alger than in any challenges to be found in Manhattan's uptown ghetto. Alone of the siblings, he excelled at his studies and fantasized that he might become a doctor. It was not to be. Minnie's parents were entertainers back in Germany, and even though they failed to catch on in the New World, something artistic resided in the genes. Minnie's brother Adolph was living proof. Restless in New York, he had quit the pants-pressing business, renamed himself Al Shean, and entered vaudeville. A few years later he was one-half of the hit comedy team Gallagher and Shean. The star made a great show when he stopped by to see his sister, flashing a diamond stickpin and scattering fistfuls of coins to the boys. Minnie got it into her head that she could take her sons along the same route. She hired a teacher to give Leonard piano lessons (although he learned only to "shoot" the keys with his right hand) and encouraged young Adolph to play a harp that his grandmother had brought from the old country. One epochal day Minnie listened to Julius singing along while Leonard rehearsed a piano piece. It occurred to her that the homeliest child had the most appealing voice. Tirelessly she hauled him around to auditions. When he caught on as a tenor, his fate was sealed. Minnie stopped the boy's formal education and entered him in the school of vaudeville. Following his example, three of the four remaining brothers took to the stage (Gummo wanted no part of performing). The Four Nightingales metamorphosed into the Marx Brothers, a wild comedy team that needed stern advice and drastic rewrites from Uncle Al.

Over the years the act acquired experience, discipline, and timing. It became so explosively funny that many comedians, including W. C. Fields and Jack Benny, dreaded to follow the Marx Brothers; they used up all the laughter in the theater. The quartet reached the top of the vaudeville bill rather late—Chico was pushing forty—but this was only the beginning. By the late 1920s almost everyone knew the Marxes by sight or reputation; they were famous not only for physical and verbal routines but for their unique stage names, dispensed by a cartoonist who ended everything with an *o*—kiddo, wacko, daddyo, et cetera. Harpo never spoke onstage, Chico assumed the accent of an Italian immigrant, and Zeppo played the juvenile lead, leaving a majority of the speeches to Groucho. As the centerpiece of the group, he made everyone funnier as he played with words. For special effects he used puns ("You're just a girl who's had some bad breaks. We can clean and oil those brakes, but you'll have to stay in the garage overnight"), grammatical misdirection ("One morning I shot an elephant in my pajamas. How he got in my pajamas I don't know"), and non sequiturs ("Either this man is dead or my watch has stopped"). He was celebrated for his ad-libs—Chico once tried to daunt him onstage by shouting, "The garbage man's outside!" to which Groucho instantly replied, "Tell him we don't want any." But most of the lines were carefully written and tested on out-of-town audiences before the Marx Brothers played the big time. When vaudeville palled, the group debuted on Broadway, then moved on to Hollywood. Their unfettered style won the hearts of critics and audiences who made them more celebrated than even Minnie had dared to hope.

Since it was obvious that Groucho was never going to be a physician, he sought a new goal: writing full-time. This also proved to be a chimera; he was too busy and too restless to sit at an Underwood. But he did attract the best comedy writers of his day, as collaborators, contributors, or fans. The time of Groucho's rise was, in John Updike's phrase, "a lighthearted era." It was the moment of George Gershwin (who enjoyed dressing up as Groucho for costume parties), Irving Berlin (who wrote the score for the Marx Brothers' first Broadway show, *The Cocoanuts*), S. J. Perelman (who wrote material for Groucho in the 1931 film *Monkey Business* and *Horse Feathers* the following year), James Thurber, Robert Benchley, and Dorothy Parker (Groucho's fellow contributors to *The New Yorker*), as well as others, as Groucho was wont to say, too humorous to mention. It was also the time of the surrealists, who saluted the Brothers in their art, and intellectuals who wrote essays singling out Groucho for his use of the absurd. In brief, he was part of the scene in every sense of the word—so much so that his name became the source of a now-clichéd pun about another Marx: Karl. As far away as Paris, a new graffito made its mark: *Je suis Marxiste, tendance Groucho.*

Still, neither fame nor applause nor salary was ever enough to satisfy Groucho's itch for recognition. He preferred the company of writers to performers (and to all three of his wives) and wanted to be of their company. Other comedians were content to recite lines and collect a paycheck. Not Groucho. With help or working solo he generated scenarios, plays, essays, articles, and even books. He learned from the comic masters of the period: Perelman, Benchley, Ring Lardner (a neighbor when Groucho lived on Long Island in the early thirties), George S. Kaufman (who wrote *The Cocoanuts* and *Animal Crackers*), and such second-tier stylists as Morrie Ryskind (Kaufman's co-writer on two Marx Brothers films), Norman Krasna (who co-wrote their Broadway show, *Time for Elizabeth*), and Arthur Sheekman (who co-wrote Groucho's radio program, *Flywheel, Shyster, and Flywheel*). The last became Groucho's shadow collaborator, anonymously editing and rewriting the pages that his friend produced—and he produced plenty. For Groucho was never without a market for his writing. Several newspaper editors went so far as to offer him the chance to become a regular humor columnist, but he turned them down. "I realize how difficult it is to be funny," he explained, "and I believe that the place for me to be funny is on the stage. There I do not have new material for every performance and my voice and mannerisms add to the comedy. Conducting a column I would not have these and I would have to be funny in cold type, and far too often to suit me. Yes, sir, this business of being funny is far too serious. Undertaking is much more the cheerful job of the two. And I do hear that humorists never die of old age—the strain is too much for them."

Groucho did die of old age, so he obviously made the right choice. Still, en route to the pantheon he found the time and inclination to write scores of amusing articles and five clothbound volumes. Much of this output fell short. *Beds*, for example, published in 1931 and reissued four decades later, was never successful. "Instead of buying my *Beds*," Groucho ruefully noted, "most people took to their own. During the next forty years people refused to have anything to do with *Beds*. Whole families slept standing up." Similarly, some of his articles misfired when they were first published and today seem musty and irrelevant. Yet there were enough fugitive pieces to constitute a bright posthumous volume, *Groucho Marx and Other Short Stories and Tall Tales*, compiled by Robert S. Bader. In addition, there are *The Groucho Letters*, a sheaf of correspondence between the comedian and some surprising cultural figures, including T. S. Eliot, E. B. White, Russell Baker, and the Warner brothers. In addition, there is Hector Arce's *The Secret Word Is Groucho*, featuring excerpts from the long-running radio and TV quiz show *You Bet Your Life*. Selections from these are all very well in their place, and their place is *The Essential Groucho*. But there is something more: the main reason why we still treasure Groucho today, more than twenty years after his death. From opening to fadeout, he was a performance artist, at his best palavering with Chico or a villain, or with the greatest straight woman in film history, Margaret Dumont. Happily, the scripts from his stage work and films are extant, and the best of Groucho's exchanges are reprinted here. Even without the large cigar, greasepaint mustache, inimitable lilt, and fluid slouch, they show why he remains one of the most influential figures in show business history.

When Gloria Stuart received an Academy Award nomination for Best Supporting Actress in the film *Titanic*, the eighty-something actress was interviewed about her life in Hollywood. As the wife of Arthur Sheekman, she had seen much of Groucho Marx through the years. Asked to summarize the comedian, she said, "He taught us all how to be irreverent." She meant the film community, but she could just as well have referred to the Western world. Onstage and in the cinema Groucho impudently kidded the medical, legal, and military professions, politics, the Academy, high society, and virtually every other bastion of power. These have never been the same since. Indeed, his influence has become so pervasive that students continue to mimic him, writers use his lines in more than twenty languages (often without credit), animators and editorial cartoonists and comedians regularly acknowledge their debt to the alpha mockingbird. His most famous phrase, "I don't want to join any club that would have me as a member" not only is useful in conversation but is the motto of the Groucho Club in London. (With Grouchovian perversity, the association has become one of the most exclusive in town.) His line "Outside of a dog a book is a man's best friend. Inside of a dog it's too dark to read" adorns the Vancouver, British Columbia, library, complete with credit chiseled in stone. Fair enough. For, more than any other comedian, Groucho loved reading and writing. That affection can be seen in the paragraphs he composed and in the routines his character provoked and inspired.

Unlike Elvis Presley, who died the same week, Julius Henry Marx left no house where his fans could pay homage. No U.S. commemorative stamp bears his likeness. His resting place is surprisingly modest and out

The

ESSENTIAL

GROUCHO

I'LL SAY SHE IS!

(1924)

―――――――――

The Napoleon Sketch was written by the cartoonist Will B. Johnstone and the vaudeville comedian Groucho Marx for the Brothers' first stage hit, I'll Say She Is! It contained the seeds of all that was to follow—the wordplay, double entendres, fraternal skirmishes, and absurdities that were to mark Groucho's career. Centerpiece of the free-form Broadway revue, it took the critics by surprise and New York by storm. Groucho played Napoleon, Chico was François, and Zeppo and Harpo were Alphonse and Gaston.

⌒

NAPOLEON SKETCH

FOOTMAN: The Empress! (*Empress walks downstairs left, followed by two pages. Everybody bows.*) The Emperor! (*Groucho bows*)

NAPOLEON: As you were. (*Everybody bows again*) Begone, peasants! Take French leave! (*Everybody exits*) (*Turns to footmen*) As for you, take that bib off—we don't eat for an hour yet.

EMPRESS: Napoleon, did you hurt yourself? You told me you would be in Egypt tonight. You promised me the Pyramids and Sphinx.

NAPOLEON: That remains to be seen, but where are my faithful advisers, François, Alphonse, and Gaston? Josephine, the whole thing Sphinx.

EMPRESS: Do you wish their advice?

NAPOLEON: Of course I do. They are always wrong. Let me think. *(Business of posing with hand in coat and taking snuff)* Ah! I love to sniff snuff.

EMPRESS: How often have I asked you not to use that horrible snuff?

NAPOLEON: Josephine, s'nuff.

FOOTMAN: Alphonse, First Gentleman-in-Waiting.

ALPHONSE: Napoleon! *(Passes Napoleon with outstretched arms to Empress)*

NAPOLEON: Alphonse!

FOOTMAN: François, Second Gentleman-in-Waiting.

FRANÇOIS: Napoleon! *(Passes Napoleon with outstretched arms to Empress)*

NAPOLEON: This devotion to me is touching, but it's not touching me. I must be quarantined.

FOOTMAN: Gaston, Third Gentleman-in-Waiting.

Gaston heads straight for the Empress.

NAPOLEON: Well, they are all taking the detour. Over there, Gas! Emperor of the world, what is there left for me to conquer?

ALPHONSE: Go to the North Pole—Africa.

FRANÇOIS: Go the end of the world.

NAPOLEON: What, Napoleon in Russia, and leave my Josephine alone with the Court?

EMPRESS: Napoleon, how can you doubt my love? *(Business of everybody kissing Empress)*

NAPOLEON: There is a lot of heavy lipping going on around here, but somehow or other I got shoved out of it. Forgive me, my Queen. I don't doubt your love. When I look into your big blue eyes, I know that you are true to the Army. I only hope it remains a standing Army. Fortunately France has no Navy, but then every man has qualms, even if they are only steamed qualms. Even an Emperor. *(Business with hat)*

EMPRESS: Ah! Ah! Napoleon.

NAPOLEON: But I must not tarry. I must be off. Josephine, if I leave here with these three snakes—chiselers—I must be off. I must be off to make Russia safe for sinus trouble. To make Russia safe for the five-year plan. That's how I bought this furniture.

EMPRESS: Napoleon, when you go, all France is with you.

NAPOLEON: Yes, and the last time I came home all France was with you, and a slice of Italy, too.

FRANÇOIS: He means me.

NAPOLEON: Oh, it's you.

EMPRESS: Napoleon, fight as you never fought before. Don't forget your flannels.

NAPOLEON: I shall not fire until I see the whites of their eggs. . . . There's a good yolk. Josephine, when one wears flannels, one can't forget. Alphonse . . . François . . . well, it's still breathing. He took a crack at it. I'll leave my Josephine in your arms. My honor is safe.

Harpo does baseball slide onto dress.

FRANÇOIS AND ALPHONSE: SAFE!

NAPOLEON: If you are going to get on, I'm going to get off. Get me a reservation for tomorrow night. It is like a free lunch counter. Three jolly woodpeckers. Can you play . . . *(To Gaston)* Hey, wait until I'm through. Hereafter, gentlemen, the line forms on the right. Farewell, my Queen. Beyond the Alps lies more Alps, and the Lord 'Alps those that 'Alps themselves. Vive la France! *(Music. Exit Left)*

ALPHONSE: Darling, I'll be right back. *(Exit Left)*

FRANÇOIS: Josie, I'll be hump back or half back. *(Exit Left)*

Harpo business with Empress. Exit Left.

ALPHONSE: Josephine!

EMPRESS: Alphonse!

ALPHONSE: Why are you crying?

EMPRESS: I thought you were never coming.

ALPHONSE: I thought Napoleon was never going.

EMPRESS: Are you sure he has gone?

ALPHONSE: Yes, he just kissed me good-bye.

EMPRESS: Me, too.

ALPHONSE: Josephine! *(Knock offstage)*

EMPRESS: Alphonse! Hide! Someone is coming.

Napoleon peeps in.

NAPOLEON: Ten seconds I've been gone, and she is still vertical, and no one is here. Ah! She loves me. Isn't she beautiful! *(Business of dancing)*

Enter footman.

EMPRESS: Alfred, bring champagne.

NAPOLEON: Get me a bologna sandwich. Never mind the bologna. Never mind the bread. Just bring the check.

EMPRESS: Oh! It's you. I thought you were at the front.

NAPOLEON: I was, but nobody answered the bell, so I came around here.

EMPRESS: Well, what are you looking for?

NAPOLEON: My sword—I lost my sword.

EMPRESS: There it is, dear, just where you left it.

NAPOLEON: How stupid of you. Why didn't you tell me? Look at that point. I wish you wouldn't open sardines with my sword. I am beginning to smell like a delicatessen. My Infantry is beginning to smell like the Cavalry. Farewell, my Queen, farewell. I'm going any minute now, farewell. It's ten cents a dance. I run on the hour and the half hour. Get a load of this footwork. Get me while I'm hot, Josie.

EMPRESS: Napoleon, remember, I expect you to return home victorious.

NAPOLEON: Our just is cause. We cannot lose. I am fighting for France, Liberty, and those three snakes hiding behind the curtain. Farewell, vis-à-vis Fifi D'Orsay. If my laundry comes, send it general delivery, care of Russia, and count it—I was a sock short lost week. My brassiere was missing too. The last time I had to use my mashie and you might sew on a button hither and yon. Hither is not bad, but yon is terrible. Farewell, my Queen. Vive la France. *(Music cue. Exit Left.)*

ALPHONSE: Josephine!

Knock offstage.

EMPRESS: Alphonse—hide.

FRANÇOIS: Josie, has he gone?

EMPRESS: Who?

FRANÇOIS: Anybody. Ah! Josie, you are so beautiful.

EMPRESS: Remember—

FRANÇOIS: But, Josie, I am just starting.

EMPRESS: But remember, I'm an Empress.

FRANÇOIS: Well, you don't Empress me very much. Why don't you marry me?

EMPRESS: What about Napoleon?

FRANÇOIS: I'll marry him too. He's got money. He's the guy I'm really after.

EMPRESS: Why, that's bigamy.

FRANÇOIS: Yes, and it's big o' me too.

EMPRESS: Please play. I love music.

François plays piano.

Knock on door. Enter Napoleon.

François hides.

NAPOLEON: I passed a groundhog coming in here. Farewell, my Queen, farewell.

EMPRESS: Napoleon, now what's wrong?

NAPOLEON: I lost my sword. I had a swell chance to stab one of those Russians. It was right near the gates of Moscow. If I find my sword I Moscow and get him. He promised to wait, but you can't depend on those Greasers. He was a Russian Serf. It Serfs me right. I'm sorry now Lincoln freed the Serfs, if that's the way they're going to act. I am getting disgusted with the whole war. If it rains tomorrow, I think I'll stay in bed. What are your plans, babe? The only thing that keeps me going is your devotion; it keeps me coming back too, I guess. It's women like you that make men like me like women like you. I guess I said something that time. Jo, you're as true as a three-dollar cornet, and believe me, that's nothing to blow about, and if you don't like it, you can trumpet. Where's my sword? Without my sword I'm a second lieutenant–letter carrier. I'm always holding the bag. I'll be an elevator starter by the time you get through with me. Ah! There's my sword, I wish you wouldn't open sardines with my sword. Oh, no, we had that, didn't we? Looks like I'm off again. The Russians are in full retreat, and I'm right in front of them.

EMPRESS: Ah! Darling, when you're away at night, I do nothing but toss and turn.

NAPOLEON: I don't mind the turning, but cut out the tossing. There has been a lot of talk about that lately. Farewell, my Queen. Caesar had his Brutus, Charles the First his Cromwell, and I've got rhythm—last two weeks in August. *(Music cue. Exit Left.)*

EMPRESS: Gaston! I thought you were never coming. Won't you please play for me?

Harpo plays the piano. Knock is heard—Harpo sits on couch—Empress sits on Harpo's lap to hide him—Napoleon enters.

NAPOLEON: Farewell, my Queen, farewell. One last kiss before I go. *(Kneels and kisses Harpo's hand, which is around Empress's waist)* My left flank has been turned—my rear end has been cut off, but I'll fight it out. Have you been plowing? Josephine, have you been hanging around a livery stable? I can't figure it out, as great as I am, I can't figure it out.

Business.

One half of you are getting awfully fresh. . . . *(Harpo puts finger to Empress's nose)* Any answer I give you would seem disrespectful.

EMPRESS: Napoleon, dear, I thought you had gone away. *(More business with hands on couch)*

NAPOLEON: I was detained. My horse overslept. My horse had his valves ground. When a fella needs a friend. I lost my sword and rubbers. I was in the midst of furious fighting. *(More business with hands on couch)* You're going to need a lot of money for gloves this winter. You have more hands than a pinochle deck.

EMPRESS: Napoleon, that's a wonderful uniform you are wearing. *(More business on couch)*

NAPOLEON: Josephine, you haven't got my horse under there, have you? Have you shifted your ballast, or is it my astigmatism? Where's my sword? *(Harpo and Empress point)*

NAPOLEON: Josephine, were there three swords? There seems to be a difference of opinion. Ah! There's my sword. *(More business on couch)* Come on, the whole three of you. Where are my rubbers?

EMPRESS: Here they are. *(Harpo puts feet out from under Empress's dress)*

NAPOLEON: Are those your feet? Maybe you better go to war and I'll stay here. You're getting an awful pair of gondolas, Josephine. They must have crossed you with an elephant. You are getting an awful pair of dogs, Josie. Oh! You are breaking them in for me? I wish you wouldn't wear them around the house. You know what happened to Empress Catherine of Russia. Well, she was headstrong and footstrong too, and they had to send for the Court physician. *(Business of putting on rubbers)* Ah! Ah! Not tonight, Josephine. They certainly feel good, all right. I don't know who is wearing them, but they certainly feel good. *(Cue for trumpet offstage)* Josephine, what are they playing? That old Southern melody—The Marseillaise in the Cold Cold Ground—the Lucky Strike Hour. Vive la France.

Music—Exit Left.

Napoleon returns.

NAPOLEON: I forgot to forget my sword.

EMPRESS: Oh, dear. I feel so faint. I must have music, sweet music. The harp. *(Empress rings bell. Footman enters.)* Bring in the harp. *(Harpo starts to play and Empress sings. Harpo stops and plays a few chords at the ends of phrases. After song, Harpo plays solo. At the end of solo, knock is heard.)*

EMPRESS: Hide! Hide!

NAPOLEON: *(From behind couch)* Josephine, it's me, the head man.

EMPRESS: Not yet.

NAPOLEON: Not yet, what? Josephine, it's me.

EMPRESS: I can't see you.

NAPOLEON: You never could.

EMPRESS: Don't be so fresh.

NAPOLEON: I can't help it. I'm wrapped in cellophane.

EMPRESS: François, will you keep quiet? Do you want Alphonse to hear you?

NAPOLEON: Women! Don't try to wool the pull over my eyes. Women! Who's been here?

EMPRESS: I have.

NAPOLEON: Alone?

EMPRESS: Alone.

NAPOLEON: Remember, you can feel some of the people all of the time, some of the people all of the time, all of the—oh! the hell with that. I just made that up. Lincoln copped it from me. Someone has been here. Ah! He's a harp.

EMPRESS: 'Tis my harp, and I was practicing.

NAPOLEON: I don't want you practicing with a harp. That's why I built the English Channel. Deep stuff. Don't you think that your perfidiousness is apparent to me? Do you think you can stand there and make a schlemiel out of Napoleon? Do you think it's fun being Napoleon? How would you like to be Napoleon and stand like this for one hundred and fifty years—a hundred and sixty? Someone has been here. I'm going to investigate. I'll smoke out these Siberian jackrabbits. *(Napoleon throws snuff)*

EMPRESS: I love but you.

Business of sneezing.

NAPOLEON: They say a man's home is his castle. Mine must be the Pennsylvania Station. Come out, come out, wherever you are.

EMPRESS: Napoleon, no one has been here, no one is here.

NAPOLEON: Why, if I thought there was I'd . . . *(Business of sneezing)* What was that—static?

EMPRESS: No, my hay fever.

More sneezing.

NAPOLEON: How many statics have you got? Officer of the Guard, remove the swine. *(Business of soldiers pulling Groucho)* Hey! You've got the wrong swine. If it wasn't so muddy, I'd take off. Come out here, I know you. *(To Harpo)* Take that off. I know you. *(Tries to remove sword from sheath)* Oh! I can't beat popular mechanics. *(Harpo spits in sword holder)* From Emperor to Cuspidor in two generations. So, my good Queen, while the Emperor has been winning victories on foreign fields, he has been losing on the home ground. So this is how you uphold the honor of the Bonapartes? Zounds on you, you Zanie. Zanes on you, you Zounie. Do you know what I'm going to do to you? Company fall in, right about-face, forward march! *(They exit)*

EMPRESS: Napoleon, what are you going to do to them?

NAPOLEON: Look at them down there in the courtyard. The firing squad will soon give you my answer. *(Business of Groucho doing a horse laugh)*

First shot offstage.

There goes Alphonse.

Second shot offstage.

There goes François.

Third shot offstage.

There goes Gaston.

After third shot, two soldiers run across stage in B.V.D.'s followed by Harpo. Harpo fires two more shots onstage at soldiers. Cue for curtain— Music cue.

THE COCOANUTS

(1929)

The Cocoanuts, *written by George S. Kaufman and the uncredited Morrie Ryskind, was the first full-fledged movie musical, complete with "down shots" of chorus lines, later used with great effect by Busby Berkeley. The film, lifted rather than adapted from the stage show, concerned the fortunes of an impoverished Florida hotelier (Groucho) who tries to recoup his failing fortunes. He has two schemes: selling worthless plots of land and romancing a millionairess (Margaret Dumont in her first appearance with the Marx Brothers). Setting the tone for all the movies to follow, Zeppo is a bland factotum, Harpo a manic girl chaser, and Chico a stooge who never seems to get things right, as in the "Bidding Scene," when he encumbers Groucho with help. The play was loaded with infallible material, laboriously tested out of town and on Broadway; understandably, Kaufman was appalled by Groucho's manic ad-libbing. But the grosses made it impossible to win an argument with the performer, and Groucho continued to improvise even when* The Cocoanuts *went before the cameras. Besides introducing the Brothers to a national audience, the musical is notable for another reason: Irving Berlin composed its score, and it is the only show in which he did not have a hit tune. Early on he had offered the song "Always," but Kaufman objected to the first line, "I'll be loving you, always." Perhaps recalling his own romantic interludes, the playwright suggested a more appropriate lyric: "I'll be loving you, Thursday." On that note, Berlin withdrew the number.*

BIDDING SCENE

Manning the front desk.

GROUCHO: Come over here, I want to see you. Now, listen to me. I'm not going to have that redheaded fellow running around the lobby. If you want to keep him up in the room, you'll have to keep him in a trap.

CHICO: You can't catch him.

GROUCHO: Who is he?

CHICO: He's my partner, but he no speak.

GROUCHO: Oh, that's your silent partner. Well, anyhow, you wired me about some property. I've thought it over. I can let you have three lots watering the front, or I can let you have three lots fronting the water. Now, these lots cost me nine thousand dollars and I'm going to let you have them for fifteen because I like you.

CHICO: I no buy nothing. I gotta no money.

GROUCHO: You got no money?

CHICO: I no gotta one cent.

GROUCHO: How're you going to pay for your room?

CHICO: That'sa your lookout.

GROUCHO: Oh, you're just an idle rumor?

CHICO: Well, you see, we come-a here to maka money. I reada in de paper, and it say: "Big boom in Florida." So we come. We're a coupla big booms, too!

GROUCHO: Well, I'll show you how you can make some *real* money. I'm going to hold an auction in a little while in Cocoanut Manor. You know what an auction is, eh?

CHICO: I come from Italy on the Atlantic-Auction.

GROUCHO: Well, let's go ahead as if nothing happened. I say I'm holding an auction at Cocoanut Manor. And when the crowd gathers
around, I want you to mingle with them. Don't pick their pockets, just
mingle with them—and—

CHICO: I'll find time for both.

GROUCHO: Well, maybe we can cut out the auction. Here's what I
mean. If someone says a hundred dollars, you say two—if someone
says two hundred dollars, you say three—

CHICO: Speaka up?

GROUCHO: That's right. Now, if nobody says anything, then you start it
off.

CHICO: How'm I going to know when nobody say nuthin'?

GROUCHO: Well, they'll probably notify you. You fool, if they don't say
anything, you'll hear 'em, won't you?

CHICO: Well, mebbe I no lissen.

GROUCHO: Well, don't tell 'em. Now then, if we're successful in dispos-
ing of these three lots, I'll see that you get a nice commission.

CHICO: How about some money?

GROUCHO: You can have your choice. Now, in arranging these lots, of
course, we use blueprints. You know what a blueprint is?

CHICO: Oysters!

GROUCHO: How is it that you never got double pneumonia?

CHICO: I go around by myself.

GROUCHO: I don't mean a whole lot. Just a little lot with nothing on it.

CHICO: Any time you gotta too much, you gotta whole lot. Look, I'll
explain it to you. Sometime you no gotta much; sometime you gotta
whole lot. You know that it's a lot. Somebody else maybe thinka it's

too much; it's a whole lot, too. Now, a whole lot is too much; too much is a whole lot; same thing.

GROUCHO: Come here, Rand McNally, and I'll explain this thing to you. Now look, this is a map and diagram of the whole Cocoanut section. This whole area is within a radius of approximately three-quarters of a mile. Radius? Is there a remote possibility that you know what a radius means?

CHICO: It'sa WJZ.

GROUCHO: Well—I walked right into that one. It's going to be a cinch explaining the rest of this thing to you—I can see that.

CHICO: I catcha on quick.

GROUCHO: That's a rodeo you're thinking of. Look, Einstein. Here's Cocoanut Manor. No matter what you say, this is Cocoanut Manor. Here's Cocoanut Manor. Here's Cocoanut Heights. That's a swamp—right over where the—where the road forks, that's Cocoanut Junction.

CHICO: Where have you got Cocoanut Custard?

GROUCHO: Why, that's on one of the forks. You probably eat with your knife, so you wouldn't have to worry about that. . . . Now, here's the main road, leading out of Cocoanut Manor. That's the road I wish you were on. Now over here—on this site we're going to build an Eye and Ear Hospital. This is going to be a sight for sore eyes. You understand? That's fine. Now, right here is the residential section.

CHICO: People live there, eh?

GROUCHO: No, that's the stockyard. Now all along here—this is the riverfront—those are all levees.

CHICO: That'sa the Jewish neighborhood.

GROUCHO: Well, we'll passover that. . . . You're a peach, boy! Now, here is a little peninsula, and here is a viaduct leading over to the mainland.

CHICO: Why a duck?

GROUCHO: I'm all right. How are you? I say, here is a little peninsula, and here's a viaduct leading over to the mainland.

CHICO: All right. Why a duck?

GROUCHO: I'm not playing Ask-Me-Another. I say, that's a viaduct.

CHICO: All right. Why a duck? Why a—why a duck? Why-a-no-chicken?

GROUCHO: I don't know why-a-no-chicken. I'm a stranger here myself. All I know is that it's a viaduct. You try to cross over there a chicken, and you'll find out why a duck. It's deep water, that's viaduct.

CHICO: That's why-a-duck?

GROUCHO: Look . . . Suppose you were out horseback riding and you came to that stream and wanted to ford over there, you couldn't make it. Too deep.

CHICO: But what do you want with a Ford when you gotta horse?

GROUCHO: Well, I'm sorry the matter ever came up. All I know is that it's a viaduct.

CHICO: Now, look . . . all righta . . . I catcha on to why-a-horse, why-a-chicken, why-a-this, why-a-that. I no catch on to why-a-duck.

GROUCHO: I was only fooling. I was only fooling. They're going to build a tunnel in the morning. Now, is that clear to you? Now I can go ahead. Look, I'm going to take you down and show you our cemetery. I've got a waiting list of fifty people at that cemetery just dying to get in. But I like you—

CHICO: Ah—you're-a my friend.

GROUCHO: I like you and I'm going to shove you in ahead of all of them. I'm going to see that you get a good steady position.

CHICO: That's good.

GROUCHO: And if I can arrange it, it will be horizontal.

CHICO: Yeah, I see—

GROUCHO: Now remember, when the auction starts, if anybody says one hundred dollars—

CHICO: I-a say-a two hundred—

GROUCHO: That's grand. Now, if somebody says two hundred—

CHICO: I-a say-a three hundred!

GROUCHO: That's great! Now you know how to get down there?

CHICO: No, I no understand.

GROUCHO: Listen. You go down there, down to that narrow path there until you come to the—to that little jungle there. You see it? Where those thatched palms are?

CHICO: Yes, I see.

GROUCHO: And then, there's a little clearing there, a little clearing with a wire fence around it. You see that wire fence there?

CHICO: All right. Why-a-fence?

GROUCHO: Oh no, we're not going to go through that again. You come along with me, and I'll fix you up. . . .

Groucho persuades Chico to act as his shill, bidding up plots of water-covered land. Alas, the junior con man is bad at arithmetic and worse at following instructions.

GROUCHO: Florida, folks, sunshine—perpetual sunshine—all year around. Let's get the auction started before we get a tornado. Right this way. Step forward. Step forward, everybody. Friends, you are now in Cocoanut Manor, one of the finest cities in Florida. Of course, we still need a few finishing touches. But who doesn't? This is the heart of the residential district. Every lot is a stone's throw from the station. As soon as they throw enough stones, we're going to build a station. Eight hundred beautiful residences will be built right here. Why, they are as good as up. Better. You can have any kind of home you want to. You can even get stucco—oh, how you can get stucco. Now is the time to buy, while the new boom is on. Remember that old saying, a new boom sweeps clean? And don't forget the guarantee—my personal guarantee: if those lots don't double in value in a year, I don't know what you can do about it. Now we'll take Lot Number Twenty—twentah—right at the corner of De Sota Avenue. Of course, you all know who De Sota was? He discovered a body of water. You've heard of the water they named after him. De Sota Water. Now, this lot has a twenty-foot frontage, a fourteen-foot backage, and a mighty fine garage. Now then, what am I offered for Lot Number Twenty? Anything at all. Anything at all to start it.

CHICO: Two hundred dollars.

GROUCHO: Ah—a gentleman bids two hundred dollars. Who'll bid three?

CHICO: Three hundred dollars.

GROUCHO: Well, the auction is practically over. Yes, it's all over but the shooting. I'll attend to that later.

CHICO: Four hundred dollars. Five hundred dollars.

GROUCHO: Do I hear six hundred?

CHICO: Six hundred-dollah.

GROUCHO: Sold for six hundred dollars. Wrap that up and put some poison on it. Well, I came out even on that one. That was a great success. Yeah, one more success like that and I'll sell my body to a medical institute. Now, we'll take Lot Number Twenty-one. There it is, over there, right where that cocoanut tree is. Now what am I offered for Lot Number Twenty-one?

CHICO: Two hundred dollars.

GROUCHO: Why, my friend, there's more than two hundred dollars' worth of milk in those cocoanuts—and *what* milk, milk from contented cow-co-nuts. Who will say three hundred?

CHICO: Four hundred dollars. Five hundred dollars. Six hundred—seven hundred—eight hundred. What th' heck do I care?

GROUCHO: What the heck do you care? But what about me? Sold to what the heck for eight hundred dollars. I hope all your teeth have cavities. And don't forget, abscess makes the heart grow fonder. . . . When he said via-duck, I should have smelt a rat. I did, but I didn't know who it was. . . . Now we will take Lot Number Twenty-two. What am I offered for Lot Number Twenty-two?

MAN: One hundred dollars.

CHICO: Two hundred dollars.

GROUCHO: Sold for one hundred dollars! Believe me, you have to get up early if you want to get out of bed.

ANIMAL CRACKERS

(1930)

Written by George S. Kaufman and the now-credited Morrie Ryskind, Animal Crackers began on Broadway in 1928. After a successful run the Brothers took the show on the road. A year later, adapted by the playwrights, it became their second motion picture in 1930. Something had intervened between stage and screen versions: the Depression, forcing a few new references to the stock market. Otherwise, the plot and characters remained unaltered. Once again Groucho is a fortune hunter, this time billing himself as the globe-trotter Captain Spaulding. And once again Zeppo is a bland presence, Harpo a wordless faun, and Chico a shrewd hustler playing dumb. Made at the dawn of the sound era, the film was a smash hit. Among many assets, Animal Crackers featured the Bert Kalmar–Harry Ruby song "Hurray for Captain Spaulding" ("The African explorer" / "Did someone call me schnorrer?"). Its melody was to introduce Groucho on radio and television for thirty-five years. The movie also contained a classic parody of Eugene O'Neill at his most portentous. Three scenes from the film follow: the first introduces Groucho to the heiress, the second pits him against Chico in a losing battle, and the third shows him at his most venal and lecherous, attempting to make love to Mrs. Rittenhouse and her companion while sending up the droning soliloquies of O'Neill's Strange Interlude.

i

MRS. RITTENHOUSE: And now, my friends, before we start the musical program, Captain Spaulding has kindly consented to tell us about his trip to Africa. Captain Spaulding . . .

GROUCHO: My friends, I am going to tell you of that great, mysterious, wonderful continent known as Africa. Africa is God's country and he can have it. Well, sir, we left N.Y. drunk and early on the morning of February second. After fifteen days on the water and six on the boat, we finally arrived on the shores of Africa. We at once proceeded three hundred miles into the heart of the jungle, where I shot a polar bear. This bear was six feet, seven inches in his stocking feet and had shoes on—

MRS. RITTENHOUSE: Pardon me just a moment, Captain, just a moment. I always thought polar bears lived in the frozen North.

GROUCHO: Oh, you did? Well this bear was anemic, and he couldn't stand the cold climate. He was a rich bear and he could afford to go away in the winter. You take care of your animals and I'll take care of mine. (Aside) Frozen North, my eye. (Back to the lecture) From the day of our arrival we led an active life. The first morning saw us up at six, breakfasted and back in bed at seven. This was our routine for the first three months. We finally got so we were back in bed by six-thirty. . . . I was sitting in front of the cabin when I bagged six tigers. . . . I bagged them to go away. . . . The principal animals inhabiting the African jungle are moose, elks, and Knights of Pythias. . . . You all know what a moose is. A moose runs around the floor, eats cheese, and is chased by the cats. The elks, on the other hand, live up in the hills and in the spring they come down for their annual convention. It is very interesting to watch them come down to the water hole. And you should see them run when they find that it's only a water hole. What they are looking for is an elkhol. One morning I shot an elephant in my pajamas. How he got in my pajamas, I don't know. Then we tried to remove the tusks. . . . But they were embedded so firmly we couldn't budge them. Of course in Alabama, the Tuscaloosa. But that is entirely ir-elephant to what I was talking about. We took some pictures of the native girls, but they weren't developed. But we're going back again in a couple of weeks.

ii

Installed as a local celebrity, Groucho negotiates with a musician.

GROUCHO: Say, I used to know a fellow that looked exactly like you by the name of Emanuel Ravelli. Are you his brother?

CHICO: I'm Emanuel Ravelli. . . .

GROUCHO: Well, no wonder you look like him. But I still insist there is a resemblance.

CHICO: Ha, Ha! He thinks I look alike.

GROUCHO: Well, if you do it's a tough break for both of you.

MRS. RITTENHOUSE: You are one of the musicians? But you were not due until tomorrow.

CHICO: Couldn't come tomorrow. That's too quick.

GROUCHO: Say, you're lucky they didn't come yesterday.

CHICO: We were busy yesterday, but we charge just the same.

GROUCHO: This is better than exploring. What do you fellows get an hour?

CHICO: For playing we getta ten dollars an hour.

GROUCHO: I see. What do you get for not playing?

CHICO: Twelve dollars an hour.

GROUCHO: Well, clip me off a piece of that.

CHICO: Now, for rehearsing, we make a special rate, that'sa fifteen dollars an hour. . . .

GROUCHO: And what do you get for not rehearsing?

CHICO: You couldn't afford it. You see, if we don't rehearse we don't play. And if we don't play that runs into money.

GROUCHO: How much would you want to run into an open manhole?

CHICO: Just the cover charge.

GROUCHO: Well, drop in sometime.

CHICO: Sewer!

GROUCHO: Well, we cleaned that up pretty well.

CHICO: Well, let's see how we stand . . .

GROUCHO: Flat-footed.

CHICO: Yesterday we didn't come. You remember yesterday we didn't come.

GROUCHO: Oh, I remember!

CHICO: That's three hundred dollars.

GROUCHO: Well, that's reasonable. I can see that, all right.

CHICO: Now today we did come, that's . . .

GROUCHO: That's a hundred you owe us. . . .

CHICO: Tomorrow we leave . . . that's worth about . . .

GROUCHO: A million dollars!

CHICO: Yeah, that's all right for me, but I got a partner.

iii

Groucho mixes romance, venality, and surrealism.

GROUCHO: Mrs. Rittenhouse, ever since I met you I've swept you off my feet. Something has been throbbing within me. Oh, it's been beating like the incessant tom-tom in the primitive jungle. There's something that I must ask you.

MRS. RITTENHOUSE: What is it, Captain?

GROUCHO: Would you wash out a pair of socks for me?

MRS. RITTENHOUSE: Why, Captain, I'm surprised.

GROUCHO: Well, it may be a surprise to you but it's been on my mind for weeks. It's just my way of telling you that I love you, that's all. I love you. I love you . . . There's never been . . .

MRS. RITTENHOUSE: Captain!

MRS. WHITEHEAD: I beg your pardon, am I intruding?

GROUCHO: Are you intruding? Just when I had her on the five-yard line. I should say you *are* intruding. Pardon me, I was using the subjunctive instead of the past tense. Yes, we're away past tents. We're living in bungalows now. This is a mechanical age, of course.

MRS. RITTENHOUSE: Mrs. Whitehead, you haven't met Captain Spaulding, have you?

MRS. WHITEHEAD: Why no, I haven't. How are you?

GROUCHO: How are *you*?

MRS. WHITEHEAD: I'm fine, thank you. And how are *you*?

GROUCHO: And how are *you*? That leaves you one up. Did anyone ever tell you you had beautiful eyes?

MRS. WHITEHEAD: No.

GROUCHO: *(Coy)* Well you have. *(To Mrs. Rittenhouse)* And so have you. *(To camera)* He shot her a glance . . . as a smile played around his lips. *(Back to the ladies)* In fact, I don't think I have seen four more beautiful eyes in my life. Well, three anyway. You've got beauty, charm, money. . . . You have got money, haven't you? Because if you haven't we can quit right now.

MRS. WHITEHEAD: The Captain is charming, isn't he?

MRS. RITTENHOUSE: I'm fascinated.

GROUCHO: I'm fascinated, too, right on the arm. . . . If I were Eugene O'Neill I could tell you what I really think of you two. You know, you're very fortunate that the Theatre Guild isn't putting this on. And so is the Guild. Pardon me, while I have a Strange Interlude. *(To camera as the ladies remain frozen in place)* Why you couple of baboons, what makes you think I'd marry either one of you? Strange how the wind blows tonight. It has a thin eerie voice. Reminds me of poor old Marsden. How happy I could be with either of these two if both of them just went away. . . . *(Back to action)* Well, what do you say, girls, what do you say? Will you marry me?

MRS. RITTENHOUSE: But, Captain, which one of us?

GROUCHO: Both of you. Let's all get married. This is my party. . . . *(To camera again)* Here I am talking of parties. I came down here for a party. What happens? Nothing. Not even ice cream. The gods look down and laugh. This would be a better world for children if the parents had to eat spinach. *(Back to action)* Well, what do you say, girls, what do you say? Are we all going to get married?

MRS. WHITEHEAD: All of us?

GROUCHO: All of us.

MRS. WHITEHEAD: But that's bigamy.

GROUCHO: Yes, and it's big o' me too. It's big of all of us. Let's be big for a change. I'm sick of these conventional marriages. One woman and one man was good enough for your grandmother, but who wants to marry your grandmother? Nobody, not even your grandfather. Think of the honeymoon. Strictly private. I wouldn't let another woman in on this. Well, maybe one or two. But no men. I may not go myself.

MRS. RITTENHOUSE: Are you suggesting companionate marriage?

GROUCHO: Well, it's got its advantages. You could live with your folks and I could live with your folks. And you could sell Fuller brushes. *(To camera)* Living with your folks. The beginning of the end. Drab, dead yesterdays shutting out beautiful tomorrows. Hideous stumbling footsteps creaking along the misty corridors of time. And in those corridors I see figures, strange figures, weird figures. Steel 186, Anaconda 74, American Can 138 . . . *(Back to the ladies)* Well, let's see, where were we? Oh yes, we were about to get married. Do you think we really ought to get married?

MRS. RITTENHOUSE: I think marriage is a very noble institution.

MRS. WHITEHEAD: It's the foundation of the American home.

GROUCHO: But the trouble is you can't enforce it. It was put over on the American people while our boys were over there. And while our girls were over here. You know, I've been waiting at the bottom of these stairs for years for just such a moment as this.

MRS. RITTENHOUSE: But, Captain, where are you going?

GROUCHO: I'm sorry, ladies, I'm sorry, but we'll have to postpone the wedding for a few days, maybe for a few years, I'm going to sow a couple of wild oats.

MONKEY BUSINESS

(1931)

Monkey Business (1931) and Horse Feathers (1932) were co-written by the humorist S. J. Perelman, who thereafter engaged in a lifelong skirmish with Groucho. Perelman never forgot or forgave the mistreatment he had received at the hands of the Brothers in general and Groucho in particular; he believed they had been rude and "megalomaniac to an unbelievable degree." For his part, Groucho felt that Perelman "could write a funny line," but was too affected and literary for the Barber in Peru— his name for the common ticket buyer. Groucho also resented the writer's refusal to acknowledge that he had worked on scenarios for the Marx Brothers until they became darlings of the intellectuals, whereupon he publicized their association in magazine pieces. The truth is that the two men were more alike than they admitted: Anglophilic, depressive, introspective, lovers of incongruity, and, above all, funny. Groucho as stowaway and, more improbably, as the head of a college were inspired ideas; neither man was willing to deny that.

⌒

A CONTRETEMPS WITH A GANGSTER, BRIGGS, AND HIS MOLL, LUCILLE

LUCILLE: You can't stay in that closet. (*Groucho steps out beside her*)

GROUCHO: Oh, I can't, can I? That's what they said to Thomas Edison, mighty inventor . . . Thomas Lindbergh, mighty flier, and Thomashefsky, mighty like a rose. *(He chucks her cheek)* Just remember, my little cabbage, that if there weren't any closets, there wouldn't be any hooks, and if there weren't any hooks, there wouldn't be any fish, and that would suit me fine. *(He returns to closet)*

LUCILLE: *(Leaning against the door)* Don't try to hide. I know you're in that closet.

GROUCHO: *(Stepping out behind her)* Did you see me go in the closet?

LUCILLE: No.

GROUCHO: Am I in the closet now?

LUCILLE: Well, no.

GROUCHO: Then how do you know I was in the closet? Your Honor, I rest my case. *(Throws himself down on the bed)*

LUCILLE: Come here, brown eyes.

GROUCHO: Oh, no. You're not going to get me off this bed.

LUCILLE: I didn't know you were a lawyer. You're awfully shy for a lawyer.

GROUCHO: You bet I'm shy. I'm a shyster lawyer.

LUCILLE: Well then, what do you think of an egg that would give me . . .

GROUCHO: I know, I know. You're a woman who's been getting nothing but dirty breaks. Well, we can clean and tighten your brakes, but you'll have to stay in the garage all night.

LUCILLE: I want excitement. I want to ha-cha-cha-cha. You don't realize it, but from the time he got the marriage license, I've led a dog's life.

GROUCHO: Are you sure he didn't get a dog's license?

LUCILLE: Oh, Alky can't make a fool of me. I want to go places. I want to do things. I want freedom, I want liberty, I want justice. . . .

GROUCHO: Madam, you're making history. In fact, you're making me, and I wish you'd keep my hands to yourself. . . . Madam, before I get through with you, you will have a clear case for divorce, and so will my wife. Now the first thing to do is to arrange for a settlement. You take the children, your husband takes the house. Junior burns down the house, you take the insurance, and I take you.

LUCILLE: But I haven't any children.

GROUCHO: That's just the trouble with this country. You haven't any children, and as for me . . . *(Dramatically)* I'm going back in the closet, where men are empty overcoats. *(He opens the door and steps in)*

LUCILLE: Oh, brown eyes!

She follows him into the closet and closes the door. Groucho emerges from the other door and leans against the wall. Lucille comes out after him and throws herself into his arms. Briggs comes in. Oblivious, Groucho backs up to Briggs and obliviously dances with him. He opens his eyes and winces. The music stops.

GROUCHO: Sir, this is an outrage, breaking into a man's home. I'm not in the habit of making threats, but there'll be a letter about this in the *Times* tomorrow morning.

BRIGGS: Yeah? But you won't read it, 'cause I'm gonna lay you out pretty.

GROUCHO: Oh, you're gonna lay me out pretty, eh? That's the thanks I get for freeing an innocent girl who, although she is hiding in the closet at this moment, has promised to become the mother of her children. And with that, sir, I bid you fond farewell. Good day, sir. Good day! *(Exits into closet)*

BRIGGS: Come out of there. I want to talk to you.

GROUCHO: *(Peeking out)* I'm sorry, but we're using the old-fashioned iceman, and we find him very satisfactory for keeping the house warm. *(Shuts door. Briggs opens it. Groucho emerges, crouched behind a dress, and makes for the door of the stateroom. As he gets there, Briggs catches him up and grabs the dress.)*

BRIGGS: Just as I thought, you're yellow — grabbing at a woman's skirts! *(Throwing down the dress)* I'm wise! I'm wise!

GROUCHO: You're wise, eh? Well, what's the capital of Nebraska? What's the capital of the Chase National Bank? Give up . . . ? Now, I'll try you on an easy one. How many Frenchmen can't be wrong?

BRIGGS: I know, but . . .

GROUCHO: You were warm and so was she. But don't be discouraged. With a little study you'll go a long ways, and I wish you'd start now.

BRIGGS: *(Showing his pistol)* Do you see this gat?

GROUCHO: Cute, isn't it? Santa Claus bring it for Christmas? I got a fire engine.

BRIGGS: Listen, mug, do you know who I am?

GROUCHO: Now don't tell me. Are you animal or vegetable? *(Briggs growls)* Animal.

BRIGGS: Get this. I'm Alky Briggs.

GROUCHO: And I . . . I'm the fella who talks too much. . . .

BRIGGS: Is there anything you've got to say before I drill ya?

GROUCHO: Yes, I'd like to ask you one question.

BRIGGS: Go ahead.

GROUCHO: Do you think that girls think less of a boy if he lets himself be kissed? I mean, don't you think that although girls go out with boys like me they always marry the other kind? Well, all right, if you're gonna kill me, hurry up. I have to take my tonic at two.

BRIGGS: Say, I can use a guy with your nerve. I think we could get along well together.

GROUCHO: Well, of course, the first year we might have our little squabbles, but then that's inevitable, don't you think?

HORSE FEATHERS

(1932)

For the Marx Brothers' third film, Paramount at last assigned a name producer (Herman Mankiewicz, co-writer of Citizen Kane*). The studio also hired an agile comedy director (Norman McLeod, who went on to work with Bob Hope and Bing Crosby, W. C. Fields, and Danny Kaye). Of the four scenarists (Bert Kalmar, Harry Ruby, S. J. Perelman, and Will John-stone), Perelman's punning touch is the most obvious. The satire of Prohibition, athletics, and the academy in general charts the tribulations of Quincy Adams Wagstaff (Groucho), new president of Huxley College, and his attempts to beat their rival Darwin College in the annual football game. In an inspired bit of casting, Zeppo plays Groucho's son, Chico an iceman, and Harpo a dogcatcher.*

⌒

PROFESSOR: And so, in retiring as president of this college, it is indeed a painful task to bid you all good-bye. And now, with the utmost plea-sure, may I present to you the man who is to guide the destinies of this great institution: Professor Quincy Adams Wagstaff. Professor, it is indeed an honor to welcome you to Huxley College.

GROUCHO: Never mind that. Hold this cane.

PROFESSOR: By the way, Professor, there is no smoking.

GROUCHO: That's what *you* said.

PROFESSOR: It would please the faculty if you would throw your cigar away.

GROUCHO: The faculty members might just as well keep their seats. There'll be no diving for this cigar. *(Clears throat)* Members of this faculty, faculty members, students of Huxley, Huxley students. I guess that covers everything. Well, I thought my razor was dull until I heard his speech, and that reminds me of a story that's so dirty I'm ashamed to think of it myself. As I look out over your eager faces I can readily understand why this college is flat on its back. The last college I presided over things were slightly different. I was flat on my back. Things kept going from bad to worse, but we all put our shoulders to the wheel, and it wasn't long before I was flat on my back again. Any questions? Any answers? Any rags, any bones, any bottles today? Any rags— Let's have some action around here. Who'll say seventeen seventy-six? That's the spirit, seventeen seventy-six. . . . No doubt you would like to know why I am here. I came to this college to get my son out of it. I remember the day he left to come here, a mere boy and a beardless youth. I kissed them both good-bye. By the way, where is my son? *(To coed)* Young lady, would you mind getting up so I can see the son rise? *(Coed gets off Zeppo's lap)* So, doing your homework in school, eh?

ZEPPO: Hello, old-timer.

PROFESSOR: My dear Professor, I'm sure the students would appreciate a brief outline of your plans for the future.

GROUCHO: What?

PROFESSOR: I said, the students would appreciate a brief outline of your plans for the future.

GROUCHO: You just said that. That's the trouble around here. Talk, talk, talk! Oh, sometimes I think I must go mad. Where will it all end? What is it getting you? Why don't you go home to your wife? I tell you what. I'll go home to your wife and outside of these improvements, she'll never know the difference. Pull over to the side of the road and let me see your marriage license.

PROFESSOR: Professor Wagstaff, now that you have stepped into my shoes—

GROUCHO: Oh, is that what I stepped in? I wondered what it was. If these are your shoes, the least you can do is have 'em cleaned.

PROFESSOR: The trustees have a few suggestions they would like to submit to you.

GROUCHO: I think you know what the trustees can do with their suggestions.

ZEPPO: Dad, let me congratulate you. I'm proud to be your son.

GROUCHO: My boy, you took the words right out of my mouth. I'm ashamed to be your father. You're a disgrace to our family name of Wagstaff, if such a thing is possible. What's all this talk I hear about you fooling around with the college widow? No wonder you can't get out of college. Twelve years in one college! I went to three colleges in twelve years and fooled around with three college widows. When I was your age, I went to bed right after supper. Sometimes I went to bed before supper. Sometimes I went without my supper and didn't go to bed at all. A college widow stood for something in those days. In fact, she stood for plenty.

ZEPPO: There's nothing wrong between me and the college widow.

GROUCHO: There isn't, huh? Then you're crazy to fool around with her!

ZEPPO: Aw, but you don't—

GROUCHO: I don't want to talk to you about this client, you snob. I'd horsewhip you if I had a horse. You may go now. Leave your name and address with the girl outside and if anything turns up we'll get in touch with you. Where're you going?

ZEPPO: Well, you just told me to go.

GROUCHO: So that's what they taught you in college! Just when I tell you to go, you leave me. You know you can't leave a schoolroom without raising your hand, no matter where you're going.

ZEPPO: Dad, this college has had a new president every year since eighteen eighty-eight.

GROUCHO: Yeah?

ZEPPO: And that's the year we won our last football game. Now, I like education as well as the next fellow—

GROUCHO: Well, move over and I'll talk to the next fellow.

ZEPPO: But a college needs something else besides education. And what this college needs is a good football team, and you can't have a good football team unless you have good football players.

GROUCHO: My boy, I think you've got something there, and I'll wait outside until you clean it up.

But later Groucho heeds Zeppo's advice. The Professor goes to a notorious speakeasy, hoping to meet some professional football players he can sneak onto the Huxley team. The saloon is guarded by Chico, who warily appraises the visitor from a peekhole in the front door.

CHICO: Who are you?

GROUCHO: I'm fine, thanks. Who are you?

CHICO: I'm fine, but you can't come in unless you give the password.

GROUCHO: Well, what is the password?

CHICO: Oh, no, you gotta tell me. Hey, I tell you what I do. I give you three guesses. It's the name of a fish.

GROUCHO: Is it Mary?

CHICO: 'At's no fish.

GROUCHO: Well, she drinks like one. Let me see, is it sturgeon?

CHICO: Hey, you crazy? Sturgeon's a doctor cuts you open when you're sick. Now, I give you one more chance.

GROUCHO: I got it! Haddock.

CHICO: 'At's funny, I gotta haddock, too.

GROUCHO: What do you take for a haddock?

CHICO: Well, sometimes I take-a aspirin, sometimes I take-a calomel.

GROUCHO: Say, I'd walk a mile for a calomel.

CHICO: You mean a chocolate calomel? I like that, too, but you no guess it. Hey, what's the matter? You no understand English? You can't come in here unless you say swordfish. Now, I give you one more guess.

GROUCHO: Swordfish, swordfish. I think I got it. Is it swordfish?

CHICO: Heh! That's it. You guess it.

GROUCHO: Pretty good, eh?

CHICO: Fine, you guess it all right.

They switch places as Chico exits as Groucho enters. Chico knocks.

GROUCHO: What do you want?

CHICO: I wanna come in.

GROUCHO: What's the password?

CHICO: Aw, you no fool me. Heh! Swordfish.

GROUCHO: No, I got tired of that. I changed it.

CHICO: Well, what's the password now?

GROUCHO: Say, I forgot it. I'd better come outside with you.

DUCK SOUP

(1933)

The Marx Brothers' fifth film was their last for Paramount. Arguably the team's best picture, it was inarguably the studio's biggest disappointment. For despite the efforts of a first-rate director, Leo McCarey, and a brilliant script by Bert Kalmar and Harry Ruby (with additional dialogue by Arthur Sheekman and Nat Perrin), the lunacies of a mythical country seemed irrelevant to the weirder events taking shape in Europe. The movie was almost forty years ahead of its time. In the era of Catch-22 and Vietnam protests, it suddenly seemed relevant. Audiences were newly beguiled by Groucho as Firefly, the head of Freedonia, Chico and Harpo as his spies, and Zeppo as the juvenile, in his last screen appearance. The film got an additional boost in 1986, when Woody Allen paid homage to Groucho in Hannah and Her Sisters: Allen's suicidal hero opts for life when he drops into a theater showing Duck Soup and experiences an epiphany: watching the comedian caper, he realizes that laughter is sufficient reason for going on. In 1998 the American Film Institute named Duck Soup one of America's One Hundred Greatest Pictures.

⌒

Groucho, the new head of Freedonia, is introduced to society by Mrs. Teasdale (Margaret Dumont). Louis Calhern plays Ambassador Trentino.

MRS. TEASDALE: As chairwoman of the reception committee, I extend the good wishes of every man, woman, and child of Freedonia.

GROUCHO: Never mind that stuff. Take a card.

MRS. TEASDALE: A card? What'll I do with a card?

GROUCHO: You can keep it. I've got fifty-one left. Now, what were you saying?

MRS. TEASDALE: As chairwoman of the reception committee, I welcome you with open arms.

GROUCHO: Is that so? How late do you stay open?

MRS. TEASDALE: I've sponsored your appointment because I feel you are the most able statesman in all Freedonia.

GROUCHO: Well, that covers a lot of ground. Say, you cover a lot of ground yourself. You'd better beat it. I hear they're going to tear you down and put up an office building where you're standing. You can leave in a taxi. If you can't leave in a taxi you can leave in a huff. If that's too soon, you can leave in a minute and a huff. You know you haven't stopped talking since I came here? You must have been vaccinated with a phonograph needle.

MRS. TEASDALE: The future of Freedonia rests on you. Promise me you'll follow in the footsteps of my husband.

GROUCHO: *(To camera)* How do you like that? I haven't been on the job five minutes and already she's making advances to me. *(To Mrs. Teasdale)* Not that I care, but where is your husband?

MRS. TEASDALE: Why, he's dead.

GROUCHO: I'll bet he's just using that as an excuse.

MRS. TEASDALE: I was with him to the very end.

GROUCHO: Huh! No wonder he passed away.

MRS. TEASDALE: *(Dramatically)* I held him in my arms and kissed him.

GROUCHO: Oh, I see. Then it was murder. Will you marry me? Did he leave you any money? Answer the second question first.

MRS. TEASDALE: He left me his entire fortune.

GROUCHO: Is that so? Can't you see what I'm trying to tell you? I love you.

MRS. TEASDALE: Oh, Your Excellency!

GROUCHO: You're not so bad yourself.

MRS. TEASDALE: Oh, I want to present to you Ambassador Trentino of Sylvania. Having him with us today is indeed a great pleasure.

TRENTINO: Thank you, but I can't stay very long.

GROUCHO: That's an even greater pleasure. *(To Trentino)* Now, how about lending this country twenty million dollars, you old skinflint?

TRENTINO: Twenty million dollars is a lot of money. I should have to take that up with my Minister of Finance.

GROUCHO: Well, in the meantime, could you let me have twelve dollars until payday?

TRENTINO: Twelve dollars?

GROUCHO: Don't be scared. You'll get it back. I'll give you my personal note for ninety days. If it isn't paid by then, you can keep the note.

TRENTINO: Your Excellency, haven't we seen each other somewhere before?

GROUCHO: I don't think so. I'm not sure I'm seeing you now. It must be something I ate . . .

MRS. TEASDALE: Your Excellency, the eyes of the world are upon you. Notables from every country are gathered here in your honor. This is a gala day for you.

GROUCHO: Well, a gal a day is enough for me. I don't think I could handle any more.

Installed as leader of Freedonia, Groucho summons his ministers to a cabinet meeting. There he imposes the new federal policies of chaos and absurdity.

GROUCHO: All right, the meeting is called to order.

MINISTER OF FINANCE: Your Excellency, here is the Treasury Department's report. I hope you'll find it clear.

GROUCHO: Clear? Huh! Why, a four-year-old child could understand this report. Run out and find me a four-year-old child. I can't make head or tail out of it. And now, members of the cabinet, we'll take up old business.

MINISTER OF COMMERCE: I wish to discuss the tariff.

GROUCHO: Sit down. That's new business. No old business? Very well. Then we'll take up new business.

MINISTER OF COMMERCE: Now, about that tariff.

GROUCHO: Too late. That's old business already. Sit down.

MINISTER OF WAR: Gentlemen, as your Secretary of War, I . . .

GROUCHO: The Secretary of War is out of order. Which reminds me, so is the plumbing.

MINISTER OF LABOR: The Department of Labor wishes to report that the workers of Freedonia are demanding shorter hours.

GROUCHO: Very well, we'll give them shorter hours. We'll start by cutting their lunch hour to twenty minutes. And now, gentlemen, we've got to start looking for a new Treasurer.

ANOTHER MINISTER: But you appointed one last week.

GROUCHO: That's the one I'm looking for.

MINISTER OF WAR: Gentlemen! Gentlemen! Enough of this. How about taking up the tax?

GROUCHO: How about taking up the carpet?

MINISTER OF WAR: I still insist we must take up the tax.

GROUCHO: He's right. You've got to take up the tacks before you can take up the carpet.

MINISTER OF WAR: I give all my time and energy to my duties and what do I get?

GROUCHO: You get awfully tiresome after a while.

MINISTER OF WAR: Sir, you try my patience!

GROUCHO: I don't mind if I do. You must come over and try mine sometime.

MINISTER OF WAR: That's the last straw! I resign. I wash my hands of the whole business.

GROUCHO: A good idea. You can wash your neck, too.

Although the hostile nation of Sylvania is ready to open fire, war is the last thing on Groucho's mind. The first thing is a romance with Freedonia's richest widow, Mrs. Teasdale.

GROUCHO: Here are the plans of war. They're as valuable as your life, and that's putting them pretty cheap. Watch them like a cat watches her kittens. Have you ever had kittens? No, of course not. You're too busy running around playing bridge. Can't you see what I'm trying to tell you? I love you. Why don't you marry me?

MRS. TEASDALE: Marry you?

GROUCHO: You take me, and I'll take a vacation. I'll need a vacation if we're going to get married. Married! I can see you right now in the kitchen, bending over a hot stove. But I can't see the stove.

MRS. TEASDALE: (*Wistful*) Rufus, what are you thinking of?

GROUCHO: Oh, I was just thinking of all the years I wasted collecting stamps. I suppose you'll think me a sentimental piece of fluff, but would you mind giving me a lock of your hair?

MRS. TEASDALE: (*Coy*) A lock of my hair? Why, I had no idea. . . .

GROUCHO: I'm letting you off easy. I was going to ask for the whole wig.

*Groucho's lovemaking intensifies in the presence of his rival for Mrs.
Teasdale's hand. Sylvanian Ambassador Trentino is every bit as venal as
Groucho but possesses a smoother line, finer wardrobe, and thicker
hide—until the final assault.*

TRENTINO: Gloria, I've waited for years. I can't be put off any longer. I
love you! I want you! Can't you see I'm at your feet? *(He goes down on
one knee)*

GROUCHO: When you get through with her feet, you can start on mine!
(To camera: If that isn't an insult, I don't know what is!) Gloria, I love
you! I realize how lonely you are.

TRENTINO: *(To Mrs. Teasdale)* Can't we go someplace where we can be
by ourselves?

GROUCHO: *(Also to Mrs. Teasdale)* What can this mug offer you? Wealth
and family? I can't give you wealth, but I—uh—we can have a little
family of our own.

MRS. TEASDALE: *(Melting)* Oh, Rufus!

GROUCHO: All I can offer you is a roofus over your head.

MRS. TEASDALE: Your Excellency, I really don't know what to say.

GROUCHO: I wouldn't know what to say either if I was in your place. *(To
Trentino)* Maybe you can suggest something. As a matter of fact, you
do suggest something. To me you suggest a baboon.

TRENTINO: What?

GROUCHO: I . . . I'm sorry I said that. It isn't fair to the rest of the
baboons.

TRENTINO: This man's conduct is inexcusable! Why I'll . . .

MRS. TEASDALE: Oh, gentlemen, gentlemen!

TRENTINO: I did not come here to be insulted!

He starts out, and Groucho goes after him.

MRS. TEASDALE: Oh!

TRENTINO: *(To Groucho)* You swine!

GROUCHO: Come again?

TRENTINO: You worm!

GROUCHO: Once more?

TRENTINO: You upstart!

GROUCHO: That's it! *(He slaps Trentino's face with his gloves; Mrs. Teasdale gasps)* Touché! *(He hands Trentino his card)*

TRENTINO: *(Tearing up the card)* Mrs. Teasdale, I'm afraid this regrettable occurrence may plunge our countries into war. *(Groucho starts fencing with Mrs. Teasdale's parasol)*

MRS. TEASDALE: Oh, this is terrible!

TRENTINO: I've said enough. I'm a man of few words.

GROUCHO: I'm a man of one word. Scram! *(Trentino exits)* The man doesn't live who can call a Firefly an upstart. Why, the *Mayflower* was full of Fireflys, and a few horseflies, too. The Fireflys were on the upper deck and the horseflies were on the Fireflys. *(He kisses Mrs. Teasdale's hand)* Good day, my sweet.

MRS. TEASDALE: Oh, Your Excellency, I must speak to you!

GROUCHO: I'll see you at the theater tonight. I'll hold your seat till you get there. After you get there, you're on your own.

A last-minute attempt at reconciliation is made.

MRS. TEASDALE: Your Excellency, the Ambassador's here on a friendly visit. He's had a change of heart.

GROUCHO: A lot of good that'll do him. He's still got the same face.

TRENTINO: I'm sorry we lost our tempers. I'm willing to forget if you are.

GROUCHO: Forget? You ask me to forget? A Firefly never forgets. Why, my ancestors would rise from their graves and I would only have to bury them again. Nothing doing. I'm going back to clean the crackers out of my bed. I'm expecting company.

TRENTINO: I am willing to do anything to prevent this war.

GROUCHO: It's too late. I've already paid a month's rent on the battle-field. . . .

MRS. TEASDALE: Won't you reconsider? Please relent for my sake.

GROUCHO: Well, maybe I am a little headstrong, but I came by it honestly. My father was a little Headstrong. My mother was a little Armstrong. The Headstrongs married the Armstrongs and that's why darkies were born. Heh! *(To Trentino)* It was silly of me to lose my temper on account of that little thing you called me.

TRENTINO: *(Good-naturedly)* Little thing I called you? Why, what did I call you?

GROUCHO: Gosh, I don't even remember what it was.

TRENTINO: Well, do you mean worm?

GROUCHO: No, that wasn't it.

TRENTINO: I know. Swine.

GROUCHO: Huh-uh. No, it was a seven-letter word.

TRENTINO: Oh, yes. Upstart.

GROUCHO: That's it! Upstart! *(He gets up angrily and slaps Trentino with his glove)*

TRENTINO: Mrs. Teasdale, this man is impossible! This is an outrage. My course is clear. This means war!

MRS. TEASDALE: Oh!

TRENTINO: You runt!

GROUCHO: I still like upstart the best.

TRENTINO: I shan't stay here a minute longer.

GROUCHO: Go, and never darken my towels again!

MRS. TEASDALE: Oh!

TRENTINO: My hat!

GROUCHO: My towels! *(Exeunt)*

FLYWHEEL, SHYSTER, AND FLYWHEEL

(1933)

The Marx Brothers' radio series Flywheel, Shyster, and Flywheel *was an attempt to capture their elan on the airwaves. Naturally the program had to get by without Harpo's mute shenanigans, but within the half-hour constraints it did well enough. Although some shows were strictly for the moment, others were used to try out new material or to reprise old routines that had worked well in movies. (The letter-writing sketch, for example, was originally featured in* Animal Crackers, *with Zeppo playing the part enacted by Chico on radio.) The first scripts were written by Nat Perrin and Arthur Sheekman, two of Groucho's favorites; later entries were done by George Oppenheimer and Tom McKnight. After twenty-six episodes* Flywheel *was canceled; its seven-thirty Eastern Standard Time slot failed to attract an audience large enough to justify the Marxes' two-thousand-dollar-per-week salaries. Subsequently the Brothers tried other moves from cinema to the broadcasting booth and the soundstage, only to meet with disappointment. It was not until 1947, when Groucho went solo on the quiz show* You Bet Your Life, *that Marx once again became the brand name it had been in the thirties.*

EPISODE 10, JANUARY 30, 1933

Phone rings.

MISS DIMPLE: Law offices of Flywheel, Shyster, and Flywheel. . . . Mr. Flywheel? Just a second; I'll call him. *(Calling out)* Mr. Flywheel! There's a man on the phone. He says he found the book you lost.

GROUCHO: Give me the phone, I'll talk to him. Hello. . . . Yes, this is Mr. Flywheel. . . . So you found my book, eh? . . . Oh, you needn't bother about bringing it over. You can read it to me over the phone. Start at page one fifty. That's where I left off. . . . Hello! Hello! Hmmm. *(Sneers)* He hung up on me. After I go to the trouble of putting aside legal business just to talk to him!

MISS DIMPLE: Legal business? Why, Mr. Flywheel, you were doing a crossword puzzle.

GROUCHO: Well, is doing a crossword puzzle illegal? Say, has that assistant of mine, Ravelli, been in this morning?

MISS DIMPLE: No, sir.

GROUCHO: He hasn't, eh? Well, when he gets here tell him to go down to the post office and have our inkwells filled. And while he's there, he can mail this letter.

MISS DIMPLE: But this letter has no stamp on it.

GROUCHO: Well, tell him to drop it in the box when nobody's looking.

MISS DIMPLE: But, Mr. Flywheel, a stamp only costs three cents.

GROUCHO: For three cents I'd deliver it myself.

MISS DIMPLE: Anyway, this letter is too heavy for one stamp. I think we'd better put two stamps on it.

GROUCHO: Nonsense. If we put two stamps on the letter, it'll be still heavier. On second thought, never mind the letter. It's just a little note to my friend Sam Jones, asking for a loan of two dollars. But poor old Sam probably has his own troubles. I hardly think he can spare it.

And even if he had it, I think he'd be a little reluctant to lend me the dough. He's kind of tight that way. Why, I don't think he'd let me have it if he thought I was going hungry. In fact, that guy wouldn't give me a nickel if I were starving. And he calls himself a friend . . . the cheap, four-flushing swine. I'll show him where to get off at. Take a letter to that snake and tell him I wouldn't touch his two dollars. And if he ever comes near this office again I'll break every bone in his body.

Chico heard whistling "Daffodils."

MISS DIMPLE: Oh, here comes Mr. Ravelli. *(Door opens)*

CHICO: Hello, boss. Hello, Miss Dimp.

GROUCHO: Don't try to change the subject. . . . Where have you been?

CHICO: I was in da barbershop, getting my hair cut.

GROUCHO: I see. Getting your hair cut during office hours.

CHICO: Well, my hair grows during office hours, don't it?

GROUCHO: When you're in the office, I want you to concentrate on your work. You can grow your hair at home.

Phone rings.

MISS DIMPLE: Flywheel, Shyster, and Flywheel. . . . Yes, Mr. Ravelli is here. . . . Who's calling? Who? . . . Mr. Ravelli, there's a man on the phone who wants to talk to you. He says his name is One-Round Gombatz.

CHICO: Oh, dat's my new prizefighter. I talk to him. Hello, One-Round. . . . How you feel? 'At'sa fine . . . Yeah? . . . 'At'sa fine. . . . Hmm . . . 'At'sa fine. . . . Good-bye. *(To Groucho)* Boss, I just gotta some bad news.

GROUCHO: Bad news? Well, 'at'sa fine!

CHICO: My new prizefighter, he don't feel so good today.

GROUCHO: You've got a fighter? Where'd you get him?

CHICO: It was easy. I was at da prizefights watchin' him fight, and da other guy knock him right into my lap.

GROUCHO: Oh, so that's how you picked him up.

CHICO: I no pick him up. Tree ushers, dey picked him up.

MISS DIMPLE: Oh, that's too bad. Did they have to carry him home?

CHICO: Not One-Round Gombatz. Dey don't have to carry him home. Dey carry him to da hospital.

GROUCHO: Ravelli, I'd be better off if they carried you there instead.

CHICO: No, boss. We're gonna make plenty of money wit One-Round Gombatz. He's gonna sign a contract wit me as soon as he learns to write his name.

GROUCHO: That's a good one. Who's going to sign your name?

CHICO: Gombatz. He's learning dat, too. Yeah, pretty soon, boss, we gonna own a fighter.

GROUCHO: We're going to own him? That's fine. Run down to the pawn-shop and see what we can get for him.

CHICO: I don't know what we can get for him, but he could use a set of false teeth. *(Knock at the door)*

MISS DIMPLE: Come in.

MRS. WILLOUGHBY: Excuse me. . . . I am Mrs. Willoughby.

GROUCHO: You come busting in here just to tell us that?

MRS. WILLOUGHBY: You misunderstand. I came to your office to trans-act some business.

GROUCHO: You want to use my office for your business?

MRS. WILLOUGHBY: No, no, no, gentlemen. I'm here for legal advice. . . . I've just been left a very large estate, with considerable money. I feel that before making some of the investments I have in mind, I ought to consult a lawyer.

CHICO: Lady. You come joosta to da right place. How'd you like to buy a prizefighter?

MRS. WILLOUGHBY: A prizefighter?

GROUCHO: Yes, madam. He punches like a mule, and if you don't believe it, I can have him punch you around a little—

MRS. WILLOUGHBY: No, no. I want to make some conservative investments. Some people have been trying to interest me in a wholesale grocery which I can buy for ten thousand dollars.

GROUCHO: What would you want with ten thousand dollars' worth of groceries? Why, you can get a regular dinner for sixty-five cents.

MRS. WILLOUGHBY: I'm talking about investments!

GROUCHO: Well, why didn't you say so? How much have you got to invest?

MRS. WILLOUGHBY: Oh, roughly about . . . two hundred thousand dollars.

GROUCHO: Two hundred thousand dollars? Ravelli, lock the door and tie her to that chair. Now, madam, I've got just the thing for you—a prizefighter.

MRS. WILLOUGHBY: I don't want a prizefighter!

CHICO: But, lady, he's a fine, clean fighter. Why, yesterday I bring him a big piece of spoiled meat, and before he eats it, he wipe it off good wit his sleeve.

GROUCHO: You brought our fighter spoiled meat? Why didn't you bring him good meat?

CHICO: Well, when I bring him good meat, he never leaves any for me.

MRS. WILLOUGHBY: I'm not interested in your prizefighter.

GROUCHO: Madam, if it's the price that stands in the way, you don't have to worry. You can buy our fighter on the installment plan. Ten dollars down, and ten dollars when he gets up.

MRS. WILLOUGHBY: I tell you, I don't want your fighter.

CHICO: Maybe she's right, boss. It'sa no use buying Gombatz unless she buys da referee, too.

MRS. WILLOUGHBY: Gentlemen, I'm afraid you're giving me bad advice.

GROUCHO: *Giving* you bad advice? Madam, you're gonna pay for it.

MRS. WILLOUGHBY: For the last time, gentlemen, I don't want a prize-fighter!

GROUCHO: All right, then, how about a pugilist?

MRS. WILLOUGHBY: Perhaps I'm not making myself clear. I distinctly said I don't want anything of that kind.

GROUCHO: Very well, let's forget about it. Mrs. Willoughby, how would you like to invest some money in a heavyweight boxer?

MRS. WILLOUGHBY: No, no, no, Mr. Flywheel! What I want is some high-grade, gilt-edge securities. Now, is that clear?

GROUCHO: Yes, perfectly clear. I'll get you some gilt-edge securities, but I warn you — it's going to be a prizefighter.

Music in strong.

MISS DIMPLE: *(on phone)* Hello, is this Morningville three three five five? . . . Mrs. Willoughby's residence? Well, hold the wire. Oh, Mr. Ravelli! I got that number for you.

CHICO: 'At'sa fine. I talk to 'em . . . Howadoyoudo. Is Mrs. Willoughby home? . . . She is? Well, as soon as she goes out, tell her I called. Good-bye. . . . What? . . . She wantsa talk to me? . . . Awright. . . . Hello, Mrs. Willoughby. How you feel? . . . Oh 'at'sa too bad. . . . You're a little pale? Aw, you crazy, you ain't a little pale. You look more like a big tub. Ha, ha, ha! Some joke, huh? . . . What? . . . Oh, your fighter? Well, don't worry about One-Round Gombatz. We got him a great fight for tomorrow night. He's gonna fight Cyclone Wilson. . . . Oh, sure, Gombatz, he's in great shape. They let him out of the hospital today. . . . Huh? Oh, don't worry. After the fight we send him back to the hospital. . . . You bet. Good-bye.

MISS DIMPLE: Oh, Mr. Ravelli, I meant to tell you. One-Round Gombatz is on his way over. Mr. Flywheel wants you to give him his instructions for tomorrow night's fight. (Knock on door) Oh! Here comes Mr. Gombatz now.

GOMBATZ: (punch-drunk goof) Hello dere, Mr. Ravelli.

CHICO: Hello, palooka.

GOMBATZ: (slow-witted anger) Say, what'sa idea of sayin "Hello, palooka"?

CHICO: Whatta you tink? Just because you're a palooka I don't say hello?

GOMBATZ: Aw, cut de wisecrackin an' gimme my tings. Mr. Flywheel said you'd gimme a new fightin outfit—shoes, an' trunks, an' all dat stuff.

CHICO: Awright, dope, awright. Here's you tings.

GOMBATZ: Wait a minute. Dere's only one shoe.

CHICO: Well, dat'sa Flywheel's idea. He told me to have your shoes half-soled, so I sold one shoe to da janitor.

GOMBATZ: An' look at dem red socks. Dey're too loud.

CHICO: Well, if da socks is loud, your feet won't fall asleep. Ha, ha, ha! Some joke. . . . Come on, now. Get to work.

GOMBATZ: Whatta you want me to do?

CHICO: I tink some road work she fix you up fine. You better run down to da beach.

GOMBATZ: Hey! Dat's too far. Dat's ten miles.

CHICO: What are you talking? Ten miles! Ain't I going dere with you?

GOMBATZ: Well?

CHICO: Well, den it's only five miles apiece.

GOMBATZ: Say-y-y! I never tought of dat! (*Door opens*)

CHICO: Shut up, palooka, here comes da big boss, Mr. Flywheel.

GOMBATZ: Hullo, Mr. Flywheel. I wanna tell you—

GROUCHO: Just a minute, Gombatz. I had a very tough day in court.

CHICO: What happened, boss?

GROUCHO: Oh, some pawnbroker accused my client of stealing an eight-day clock.

CHICO: Did you win the case?

GROUCHO: Well, we compromised. The pawnbroker got the clock and my client got the eight days.

GOMBATZ: Listen, Mr. Flywheel, I'm worried about dat fight. I don't tink I'm in good shape.

GROUCHO: You'll be in good shape. We'll let you fight in a corset. However, I'll soon find out if you're in good condition. Ravelli, get me a pair of boxing gloves. I want to take a sock at Gombatz.

CHICO: I ain't got no gloves, boss. But here's a chair you can hit him wit.

GOMBATZ: Hey, wait a minute. What'm I gonna get for dis fight?

GROUCHO: Gombatz, I was figuring it out this morning. It seems to me that for my share as manager . . . five thousand dollars would be reasonable. Then, of course, there are also other items. Training expenses, forty cents; movie tickets for me and my girl, a dollar and a half—but she paid for the tickets, so we'll make that just a dollar. Now let's see. That leaves you exactly two dollars and eighty cents.

CHICO: Hey, boss, what about me?

GROUCHO: He's right, Gombatz. I think Ravelli ought to get that two-eighty.

GOMBATZ: Say, I thought there was gonna be a tousand-dollar purse!

CHICO: Hey, palooka, for the money you're going to get, you won't need any purse.

GOMBATZ: You mean I ain't gonna get nuttin' outa dis fight?

GROUCHO: Now don't get excited. We bought something for you.

GOMBATZ: Yeah? What didja buy?

GROUCHO: We bought the referee. *(Knock on door)*

MISS DIMPLE: *(Whispering)* I think it's Mrs. Willoughby.

CHICO: I'm sick of talking to her. Miss Dimp, I'll go in de odder office. You tell her I ain't in.

MISS DIMPLE: But, Mr. Ravelli, she won't believe me if I tell her you're not in.

CHICO: Awright. Den I stay here and tell her myself. *(Door opens)*

MRS. WILLOUGHBY: Oh, gentlemen, I've been—

GROUCHO: *(With exaggerated cordiality)* Well, if it isn't dear, dear Mrs. Willoughby! You know, Willoughby, you're getting better looking every day.

MRS. WILLOUGHBY: *(Kittenish)* Oh, Mr. Flywheel. You exaggerate.

GROUCHO: Well, maybe I do. But you'll have to admit that your looks couldn't get any worse.

MRS. WILLOUGHBY: Please, let's not indulge in personalities. . . . Mr. Flywheel, I've been thinking about this curious investment you persuaded me to make. I mean that prizefighter.

GOMBATZ: You mean me?

CHICO: Shut up your face, Gombatz. She don't know what she's talking about.

MRS. WILLOUGHBY: It seems that all I do is lay out money for this pugilist. There's that hospital bill, money for trainers . . . and what about that five hundred dollars I gave you last week? I thought you were going to build a gymnasium.

GROUCHO: I thought I was going to build a gymnasium, too. But I didn't have a thing to wear to the fight, so I bought myself a couple of new suits instead.

MRS. WILLOUGHBY: That settles it. I'm through with the whole mess. I'm through with you. I'm through with this fighter. . . . I'm—

GROUCHO: Don't desert him, madam! One-Round Gombatz needs a woman's care. He's just a kid at heart. You ought to see him cutting out paper dolls.

MRS. WILLOUGHBY: Mr. Flywheel, I . . . *(Suddenly amazed by what she sees)* Oh! Mr. Ravelli! Did I see you put your hand in my overcoat pocket?

CHICO: I tink you did. But I bet you won't see me next time.

GROUCHO: Ravelli, didn't I tell you that if you stopped stealing I'd give you a dollar?

CHICO: I know, boss. But I wanted to save you da dollar.

MRS. WILLOUGHBY: Mr. Flywheel. I'm willing to forget what I spent on this fighter. That money I consider lost. But what about the other money—the five thousand you were going to invest more conservatively?

GROUCHO: Oh that? You have nothing to worry about, Mrs. Willoughby. I was lucky enough to get you in on a very sound investment with that five thousand dollars.

MRS. WILLOUGHBY: Well, I'm glad you've done at least one sensible thing. Now tell me, Mr. Flywheel, just what did you do with the money?

GROUCHO: Madam, I took that five thousand dollars and bet it on One-Round Gombatz.

Music in strong.

Open in fight auditorium, crowd yelling: "Knock him out!" "Oh, boy, what a sock!" et cetera.

PROMOTER: Hey, Slim, it looks like this fight won't last long. Run down to the dressing rooms and tell the boys on the next bout—Gombatz and Wilson—to get ready.

BOY: Okay, Mr. Jackson.

Yelling from fight fans continues for about five seconds, fading; boy knocks on door.

GROUCHO: *(from within)* Come in.

BOY: Gombatz-Wilson fight is next, Mr. Flywheel. You better get your man ready.

GROUCHO: Just a minute, son. You run down the hall and tell Cyclone Wilson to come in for a short rehearsal.

BOY: I don't know what you're talking about. But you'd better hurry up.

Door opens; distant cheering heard. Door shuts; cheering ends.

GROUCHO: *(Like a coach)* Just listen to that crowd cheering. They love you, Gombatz. They want you to win. . . . But win or lose, they hope you get killed. . . . Gombatz, in a little while you'll be out in front of that crowd, fighting. . . . Your little mother will be at home at the radio.

GOMBATZ: I ain't got no mother.

GROUCHO: Well, you've got a radio, haven't you? Just remember, Gombatz, we've done everything we could for you. We've paid the referee to give you the decision. We've paid the other fighter to let you win. Now, Gombatz, the rest is up to you. And don't forget, my boy—I've got great plans for you. If you win this fight, I'm going to let you fight my landlord. *(Knock on door)* Come in.

CHICO: Hullo, boss. Hullo, Gombatz.

GROUCHO: Oh, here you are, Ravelli. Late again. Didn't I tell you to get here early?

CHICO: Well, you see, boss, I left my house too late to come early.

GROUCHO: Well, why didn't you leave your house early?

CHICO: I couldn't. It was too late to leave early. Anyway, on da corner a fellow lost a nickel, and a whole bunch of kids were standing around looking for it.

GROUCHO: And I suppose you were standing there watching them!

CHICO: No. I was standing on da nickel.

ATTENDANT: Gombatz–Wilson fight next. Three minutes to go!

GROUCHO: Three minutes? Ravelli, get busy. Run over to Cyclone Wilson's dressing room and ask him to wear red fighting trunks so Gombatz will know him when they meet in the ring.

CHICO: Wilson? Hey, he ain't here yet. He's home sleepin.

GROUCHO: What? We've only got three minutes to go and Wilson isn't even up!

CHICO: Sure he's up. Tree o'clock in da morning I saw da janitor carry him up.

GROUCHO: Jumping Jupiter! Do you think he was drugged?

CHICO: Sure, he was drugged. Da janitor drugged him up tree flights of stairs.

GROUCHO: Quick! Gombatz, run out and find Jackson, the fellow who's promoting the fight.

GOMBATZ: Here comes Jackson.

JACKSON: Mr. Flywheel! I've got terrible news. Wilson has run out on us. . . . We can't find him anyplace.

CHICO: Don't worry, Mr. Jackson. Gombatz is much better when he fights alone.

JACKSON: I tell you, we got to get someone to fight Gombatz.

GROUCHO: I'd go in there and fight him myself, but I've got my glasses on. Ravelli, it's up to you.

CHICO: Hey, boss, you got anodder pair of glasses? I don't wanna fight him either.

GROUCHO: Come on! You're going in to fight for Wilson.

CHICO: Awright, I'll go in and fight for Wilson if somebody else go in and fight for me.

GROUCHO: Put on these gloves!

CHICO: I don't need da gloves, boss. My hands ain't cold.

ATTENDANT: Mr. Jackson, the crowd's hollering for the fight.

GROUCHO: Okay, we're ready. Gombatz, don't forget—you go down for a count of four in the third round. Ravelli, you go down for the count of three in the fourth round. No, you go down for the count of four . . . no, the count of three. . . . Well, never mind. The referee has all the instructions. Open the door. . . . Let's go.

As they start for ring, cheering is heard.

CHICO: Hey, boss, let's walk down de odder aisle. . . . Here comes Mrs. Willoughby.

MRS. WILLOUGHBY: Oh, Mr. Flywheel . . . I've been looking for you. The seat you got me is right behind a post.

GROUCHO: Well, come back tomorrow and we'll have the post torn down.

MRS. WILLOUGHBY: Now, what about that money wagered on Gombatz? My five-thousand-dollar bet?

GROUCHO: Your bet? Madam, you've made your bet, now lie in it.

MRS. WILLOUGHBY: But, Mr. Flywheel—

GROUCHO: Run along. I've got to look after these two bums. Now, Ravelli, you're going into that ring and you may never come out again. Before you step through those ropes, is there anything you want to say?

CHICO: Yes, boss, I'd like to ask a question. What building has tree hunnerd stories and no elevator?

GROUCHO: I give up, Ravelli. What building has three hundred stories and no elevator?

CHICO: A public library. Ha, ha, ha! Some joke.

GROUCHO: Come on! Get in that ring. And don't forget, you're supposed to take a beating. But while you're taking it, just remember . . . I'll be out there cheering. (*A couple of gongs*)

ANNOUNCER: Main bout. . . . Ten rounds to a dee-cision. . . . In this corner, One-Round Gombatz, the terror of the East Side. (*Cheers*) And in this corner, Emanuel Ravelli, the pride of the gashouse district. (*Cheers*)

GROUCHO: Wait a minute! Ravelli, is that a horseshoe I feel in your glove?

CHICO: Sure, I put it dere for good luck.

Gong sounds.

GROUCHO: All right, boys, go to it. If you need me, I'll be at the microphone.

Cheers, and cries of "Geev it to heem," "Put out the lights, they want to be alone!"

GROUCHO: (*At microphone*) Well, folks, here's Flywheel, bringing you a round-by-round account of the big fight. Zowie! There they go! Gombatz is leading, but Ravelli is close behind . . . chasing him around the ring. Ravelli's in a corner. . . . He's fighting back savagely . . . thus proving the old adage that if you get a rat in a corner, he'll fight back.

Boy, oh boy, oh boy, what a battle! . . . Folks, I'm going to put the mike in the ring so you can hear the grunting of the gladiators, to this.

Silence.

CHICO: Hey, Gombatz, what'sa matter wit you? You hit me dat time.

GOMBATZ: Well, what about you? You got me all covered with blood.

CHICO: I know, but it's my blood. *(Calling out)* Hey, Mr. Flywheel, I'm tired . . . stop the round.

GROUCHO: We can't, Ravelli. The timekeeper can't find his watch.

CHICO: Tell him to look in my back pocket.

GROUCHO: Hear that, folks? What a battle. . . . What a battle. . . . Gombatz looks great. . . . Gombatz is down. . . . He looks even better when he's down . . . listen to the count.

REFEREE: One . . . two . . .

Count continues.

GROUCHO: *(Calling)* Get up, Gombatz. Get up!

CHICO: *(Calling back)* Leave him lay dere, boss. He's got till ten to get up . . . and it's only half past nine now.

REFEREE: . . . six . . . seven . . .

GROUCHO: Get up, Gombatz! How am I going to explain to Mrs. Willoughby?

REFEREE: . . . nine . . . ten . . . OUT! The winner is Emanuel Ravelli!

Audience cheers.

GROUCHO: Ravelli, Ravelli, come here!

CHICO: Well, I guess I did pretty good, huh, boss?

GROUCHO: I thought you were supposed to throw the fight.

CHICO: I did trow it . . . *(Suddenly realizing)* Oh yeah, boss, I made a mistake. I trew it da wrong way. Say, here comes Mrs. Willoughby. I tink I better go back into da ring.

MRS. WILLOUGHBY: Mr. Flywheel, this is terrible! You've tossed away my five thousand dollars with your preposterous bet.

GROUCHO: Now just calm yourself, Mrs. Willoughby. I've got a very pleasant surprise for you. I didn't bet your five thousand dollars after all.

MRS. WILLOUGHBY: You didn't?

GROUCHO: No, I used the money to buy myself a little house in the country.

MRS. WILLOUGHBY: You bought a house with my money?

GROUCHO: Yes, you must come out and visit me sometime. But if I catch you stepping on the grass, I'll have you arrested.

Music in strong.

EPISODE 17, MARCH 20, 1933

Typewriting heard; phone rings.

MISS DIMPLE: Law offices of Flywheel, Shyster, and Flywheel . . . No, Mr. Flywheel isn't in. He won't be in for a few days. He's spending the weekend out in Long Island . . . at Mrs. Thorndyke's home. . . . Yes, his assistant, Mr. Ravelli, is visiting at the Thorndykes' too.

Fade out. Fade in on phone ringing.

MEADOWS: Hello, this is the Thorndyke residence. . . . No, Mrs. Thorndyke declines to be interviewed. Yes, that report is true. A very valuable painting was stolen from here last night. A Rembrandt. No, there has been no trace of it whatsoever. . . . No, this is not Mr. Thorndyke. This is the butler. Sorry, but that's all I can tell you on the phone. Good-bye. *(Turning away)* Oh, good morning, Mrs. Thorndyke.

MRS. THORNDYKE: Good morning, Meadows. Was that call for me?

MEADOWS: It was another newspaperman.

MRS. THORNDYKE: Did he have any news about the stolen painting?

MEADOWS: No, that's what he was after, madam.

MRS. THORNDYKE: Oh dear, that Rembrandt was the finest picture in my collection. Why, it cost over a hundred thousand dollars.

MEADOWS: Yes, madam.

MRS. THORNDYKE: And the humiliation! Being robbed when I'm entertaining so many prominent guests.

MEADOWS: Have the police found any clues at all, madam?

MRS. THORNDYKE: No, they seem completely baffled.

MEADOWS: May I suggest, madam, that you ask Mr. Flywheel and his assistant, Mr. Ravelli, to take over the case? They are lawyers, and surely they must have some understanding of the criminal mind and its workings.

MRS. THORNDYKE: A splendid suggestion, Meadows. I think I'll speak to Mr. Flywheel. Have you seen him this morning?

MEADOWS: Yes, he went horseback riding. Say, I believe he's coming in.

MRS. THORNDYKE: Why yes. (Calling out) Oh, good morning, Mr. Flywheel. . . . Why, what in the world are you looking for?

GROUCHO: I lost the bit you loaned me.

MRS. THORNDYKE: Oh, that's all right. I'll get you another bit.

GROUCHO: Well, that'll be two bits I owe you.

MRS. THORNDYKE: Mr. Flywheel, I hope you've not been distressed by last night's unfortunate occurrence.

GROUCHO: You mean the dinner you served? It wasn't much worse than the lunch.

MRS. THORNDYKE: No, I mean the painting that was stolen.

GROUCHO: Was there a painting stolen? I haven't seen a paper in three weeks. Are you sure you're in the right house? Where's my assistant, Ravelli?

CHICO: *(Entering)* Hey, here I am, boss!

GROUCHO: Ravelli, why didn't you inform me that there was a painting stolen? What do you think I hired you for?

CHICO: But, boss, I didn't know it.

GROUCHO: You should have asked me. I didn't know it either.

CHICO: Well, I'm sorry.

GROUCHO: Sorry, are you? Well, you're a contemptible cur. I repeat, sir, you're a contemptible cur. Oh, if I were a man, you'd resent that. . . . I can get along without you, you know. I got along without your father, didn't I? Yes, and your grandfather. Yes, and your uncle. Yes, Mrs. Thorndyke, and *your* uncle too. And my uncle as well.

MEADOWS: I beg pardon, madam.

MRS. THORNDYKE: What is it, Meadows?

MEADOWS: The police are here.

MRS. THORNDYKE: The police? Have them come in.

MEADOWS: Very good, madam.

GROUCHO: Oh, that's your game, Mrs. Thorndyke! Well, you can't shut me up.

MRS. THORNDYKE: But, Mr. Flywheel—

GROUCHO: Never mind, your attorney will hear about this. Ravelli, take a letter. I'll show this dame a thing or three. Ravelli, take dictation. . . . "Honorable Charles D. Vasserschlogel, c/o Vasserschlagel, Vasserschlegel, Vasserschlugel, and McCormick, semicolon."

CHICO: How do you spell semicolon?

GROUCHO: Make it a comma . . . "Dear Elsie:" No, never mind Elsie.

CHICO: Oh, you wanna I should scratch Elsie?

GROUCHO: Well, if you enjoy that sort of thing, it's quite all right with me. However, you'd better take it up with Elsie. Begin this way, Ravelli: "Honorable Charles D. Vasserschlogel, c/o Vasserschlagel, Vasserschlegel, Vasserschlugel, and McCormick. Gentlemen, question mark. In re yours of the fifth inst. yours to hand and in reply, I wish to state that the judiciary expenditures of this year, i.e., have not exceeded the fiscal year—brackets—this procedure is problematical. Quotes, unquotes, and quotes. Hoping this finds you, I beg to remain"—

CHICO: Hoping dis finds him where?

GROUCHO: Well, let him worry about that. Hang it all, don't be insolent, Ravelli. (Aside) Sneak! (Back to dictation) "Hoping this finds you, I beg to remain as of March twentieth, Cordially, respectfully, regards." That's all, Ravelli. Now, read me what you have.

CHICO: (Reading) "Honorable Charles D. Vasserschlogel, c/o Vasserschlagel, Vasserschlegel, and McCormick"—

GROUCHO: You left out a Vasserschlugel. Thought you could slip one over on me, didn't you, eh? All right, leave it out, and put in a windshield wiper instead. No, make it three windshield wipers and one Vasserschlugel. Go on with the reading.

CHICO: "Dear Elsie, scratch"—

GROUCHO: That won't do at all, Ravelli. That won't do at all. The way you've got it, you've got McCormick scratching Elsie. Turn that around and have Elsie scratch McCormick. You'd better turn McCormick around too, Ravelli. And see what you can do for me.

CHICO: Awright, I read some more. "Gentlemen, question mark . . ."

GROUCHO: Well, go on.

CHICO: After dat, boss, you said a lot of tings I don't tink was important, so I joosta left dem out.

GROUCHO: So you just left them out, eh? You just left them out? You left out the body of the letter, that's all. Yours not to reason why, Ravelli. You left out the body of the letter. All right, send it that way and tell them the body will follow. Closely followed by yours.

CHICO: Hey, boss, you want da body in brackets?

GROUCHO: No, it'll never get there in brackets. Put it in a box. Put in a box and mark it fragilly.

CHICO: Mark it what?

GROUCHO: Mark it fragilly. F-r-a-g—look it up, Ravelli. Look under *fragile*.

CHICO: Lemme see . . . "quotes, unquotes, quotes."

GROUCHO: That's three quotes.

CHICO: Yeah, I add another quote and make it a gallon.

GROUCHO: That's fine, Ravelli. That's going to make a dandy letter. I want you to make two carbon copies of that and throw the original away. And when you get through with that, throw the carbon copies away. Just send a stamp, airmail. That's all.

MRS. THORNDYKE: *(Approaching)* Mr. Flywheel—

GROUCHO: Now, what's the matter, Thorndyke?

MRS. THORNDYKE: I'm sorry you're so upset. I guess that stolen picture has upset everybody in the house.

CHICO: Picture stolen? Hey, you don't gotta worry, lady, everyting's gonna be all right. You just let me and my boss work on dis case for twenty-four hours, and den we'll call in somebody else.

GROUCHO: Madam, you think it's a mystery now. Wait till you see it tomorrow! Remember the Charley Ross disappearance? We worked on that case for twenty-four hours and they never did find him.

CHICO: Yeah. Dey couldn't find us for five years. . . .

GROUCHO: Hey, Mrs. Thorndyke!

MRS. THORNDYKE: Here I am, Mr. Flywheel. Have you found any trace of the picture thieves?

GROUCHO: You've nothing to worry about, madam. I hadn't been on the case five minutes and they stole my watch. It wasn't going, and now it's gone. Wait a minute! The watch fob's gone now, too. Well, I've still got the pocket. Anything I retain now is velvet except the coat and that's Prince Albert's.

MEADOWS: *(Approaching)* Pardon me, Mrs. Thorndyke.

MRS. THORNDYKE: Yes, Meadows?

MEADOWS: Here's the copy of the stolen painting, the duplicate that Mr. Flywheel asked me to get.

GROUCHO: Yes, Mrs. Thorndyke, the copy may help me solve the mystery. Let me take a look at that picture.

MEADOWS: There you are, sir.

GROUCHO: *(Examines it)* Hmm. Hmm. Say, it's signed Rembrandt. There's the criminal—Rembrandt.

MRS. THORNDYKE: Why, Mr. Flywheel! Rembrandt is dead!

GROUCHO: What! Rembrandt is dead? Then it's murder. Now we've got something. Ravelli, Ravelli!

CHICO: Whatta you want, boss?

GROUCHO: Come over here, Ravelli! Isn't there something that strikes you very funny about this picture?

CHICO: Yeah. *(Laughs heartily)*

GROUCHO: Come, come! It isn't as funny as all that. Did you ever see a tree like the one in this picture?

CHICO: Dat'sa no tree, dat's spinach.

GROUCHO: It can't be spinach, where's the egg?

CHICO: Well, it could be spinach. Look at all da sand around dere. Nope, you're right, boss, dat'sa coleslaw.

GROUCHO: Coleslaw? Did you ever see coleslaw like that?

CHICO: Sure, I got a coleslaw on my mout'.

GROUCHO: I don't want any of your lip. Say, this is a left-handed painting. Look at the signature.

CHICO: You're right. It's in da right-hand corner.

GROUCHO: This is either a left-handed painting or a vegetable dinner. Now, in order to solve the mystery, all we got to do is to find the left-handed person who painted it. In a case like this, the first thing we got to do is to find a motive. Now, what could have been the motive of the guys who swiped the Rembrandt?

CHICO: I got it, boss. Robbery! *(Music in strong)* Mrs. Thorndyke is giving a five-tousand-dollar reward for anybody who finds dat painting.

GROUCHO: Well?

CHICO: I got an idea how to find it. Of course, in a case like dis, what's so mysterious—you gotta to do like a Sherlock Holmes. You gotta get whatta dey calla da clues. Now you go about it like-a dis—you say to yourself, What have you? And de answer come right back. Someting was stolen. Den you say to yourself, What was stolen? And de answer come right back, A painting.

GROUCHO: Say, what are you, a ventriloquist?

CHICO: Now, you say to yourself, Who stole-a da painting? And de answer come right back, Somebody in dis house. So far I'm right, eh, boss?

GROUCHO: Well, it's pretty hard to be wrong if you keep answering yourself all the time.

CHICO: Now, you take da clue, and you put 'em together. And whatta we got? A painting was stolen. Where was it stolen? In dis house. Who stole it? Somebody in dis house. Now, to find de painting, all we got to do is to go to everybody in dis house, and we ask dem if dey took it. Dat's what you call a brain—eh, boss?

GROUCHO: You know, I could rent you out as a decoy for duck hunters. You say you're going to go to everybody in this house and ask them if they took it, eh? Suppose nobody in the house took the painting?

CHICO: Den we go to da house next door.

GROUCHO: Well, suppose there isn't any house next door?

CHICO: Well, den of course, we got to build one.

GROUCHO: Well, now you're talking. What kind of a house do you think we ought to put up?

CHICO: Well, I tell you what my idea is. I tink we builda someting nice and small and comfortable.

GROUCHO: That's the way I feel about it. I don't want anything elaborate. Just a little place that I can call home and tell the wife I won't be home for dinner.

CHICO: Look here, boss, I draw some plans on da table. What you say we build right about here?

GROUCHO: No, I think I'd like something over here, if I could get it. I don't like Junior crossing the tracks on his way to the reform school. As a matter of fact, I don't like Junior at all.

CHICO: All right, we gotta someting over here. And believe me, dat'sa very convenient. Oh, very convenient. Look, all you have to do is to open da door, step outside, and dere you are.

GROUCHO: There you are? There you are where?

CHICO: Outside.

GROUCHO: Well, suppose you want to get back in again?

CHICO: You had no right to go out.

GROUCHO: Well, that's a quarter I owe you. Now all we've got to do is to find the painting.

CHICO: Ah, dat's where my detective brain comes in. Now we gotta hurry up and build da house because I tink the painting is inside.

GROUCHO: Maybe it's me. Maybe I'm not getting enough sleep these days. Let me take a look at those plans. Say, maybe that's the painting down in the cellar.

CHICO: Dat's no cellar. Dat's da roof.

GROUCHO: That's the roof, way down there?

CHICO: Sure, you see we keep da roof in da basement, so when da rain comes, da chinemy he'sa no get wet. Now, what do you say? Are you ready to sign da lease?

GROUCHO: Well, it's a little abrupt. I'd like to discuss it with my husband. Could you come back this evening?

CHICO: Are you married?

GROUCHO: Didn't you see me sewing on little things? Why, I've got a girl as big as you are.

CHICO: Well, get me one.

GROUCHO: How about the painting, Ravelli?

CHICO: Oh, we take care of dat. I tink da kitchen should be white, da dining room should be green—

GROUCHO: No, no, the painting. The painting.

CHICO: Dat's what I say, da painting. Da kitchen should be white, da dining room—

GROUCHO: No, I'm not talking about the kitchen. I mean the painting. The painting that was stolen. Don't you remember there was a painting stolen? A valuable oil painting? Don't you remember that?

CHICO: No, I'm a stranger around here.

GROUCHO: Who do you think I am? One of the early settlers? Don't you remember that Mrs. Thorndyke lost a valuable Rembrandt oil painting worth a hundred thousand dollars? Don't you remember that?

CHICO: No. But I've seen you someplace before.

GROUCHO: Well. I don't know where I was, but I won't go there again.

CHICO: Hey, boss, it comes to me like a flash. You know what happened to dis painting? Dis painting wasn't stolen.

GROUCHO: No?

CHICO: Dis painting disappear. And you know what make it disappear? Moths. Moths eat it. Left-handed moths. Dat's my solution.

GROUCHO: Well, I wish you were in it. You say that left-handed moths ate the painting, eh? You know, I'd buy you a parachute if I thought it wouldn't open.

CHICO: I got a pair of shoes.

GROUCHO: Well, let's get out of here. I've taken an awful lacing here tonight. We solved it, though. You solved it. Let's go and get the reward. The painting was eaten by a left-handed moth. I don't know how I overlooked it.

CHICO: You know, we did a good day's work.

GROUCHO: How do you feel, tired? Maybe you ought to lie down for a couple of years?

CHICO: Naw, I stick it out.

MRS. THORNDYKE: Oh, Mr. Flywheel, Mr. Flywheel!

CHICO: Hey, it'sa Mrs. Thorndyke. We ask her for da reward.

MRS. THORNDYKE: Gentlemen, something amazing has happened.

CHICO: We don't care about dat. We joosta found out what happened to da picture. Da moths ate your picture, so you can give us the five-tousand-dollar reward.

MRS. THORNDYKE: Give you five thousand dollars' reward! Why, the picture was just found under your bed. Mr. Ravelli, I hate to say this, but I suspect you stole the Rembrandt.

CHICO: Awright, den I take tree tousand dollars' reward.

Music in strong.

A NIGHT AT THE OPERA

(1935)

A Night at the Opera *and* A Day at the Races *were made for the Brothers' new studio, Metro-Goldwyn-Mayer, and propelled them to global prominence. In the first feature Groucho played Otis B. Driftwood, a fast-talking promoter. It was these high-budget, well-cast features that made maximum use of Margaret Dumont and caused her to be dubbed the Fifth Marx Brother. Alas, this brace of films represented the peak of the team's performances. The legendary producer Irving Thalberg died during the preparation of* Races, *and Louis B. Mayer, who disliked Groucho, let it be known that he was not a fan of the comedian's iconoclastic style. Nearly everybody else was;* Opera *and* Races *were two of MGM's biggest grossers in the thirties, and they remain perennial favorites in video rental stores.*

Seated at a fancy restaurant, the wealthy parvenu Mrs. Claypool is about to lose her composure when she finds Otis B. Driftwood having dinner with another lady. He attempts to mollify her, as only Groucho can.

MRS. CLAYPOOL: Three months ago you promised to put me into society. In all that time, you've done nothing but draw a very handsome salary.

GROUCHO: You think that's nothing, huh? How many men do you suppose are drawing handsome salaries nowadays? Why you can count them on the fingers of one hand, my good woman.

MRS. CLAYPOOL: I'm not your good woman!

GROUCHO: Don't say that, Mrs. Claypool. I don't care what your past has been. To me you'll always be my good woman, because I love you. There, I didn't mean to tell you, but you, you dragged it out of me. I love you.

MRS. CLAYPOOL: It's rather difficult to believe that when I find you dining with another woman.

GROUCHO: That woman? Do you know why I sat with her?

MRS. CLAYPOOL: No—

GROUCHO: Because she reminded me of you.

MRS. CLAYPOOL: Really?

GROUCHO: Of course! That's why I'm sitting here with you, because you remind me of you. Your eyes, your throat, your lips, everything about you reminds me of you, except you. How do you account for that? *(To the audience)* If she figures that one out, she's good.

MRS. CLAYPOOL: Mr. Driftwood, I think we'd better keep everything on a business basis.

GROUCHO: How do you like that? Every time I get romantic with you, you want to talk business. I don't know, there's something about me that brings out the business in every woman. All right, we'll talk business. You see that man over there eating spaghetti?

MRS. CLAYPOOL: No.

GROUCHO: Well, you see the spaghetti, don't you? Now, behind that spaghetti is none other than Herman Gottlieb, Director of the New York Opera Company. Do you follow me?

MRS. CLAYPOOL: Yes.

GROUCHO: Well, stop following me, or I'll have you arrested. Now, I've arranged for you to invest two hundred thousand dollars in the New York Opera Company.

MRS. CLAYPOOL: I don't understand.

GROUCHO: Don't you see? You'll be a patron of the opera. You'll get into society. Then you can marry me and they'll kick you out of society. And all you've lost is two hundred thousand dollars.

Anxious to sign up an unknown opera tenor, the self-appointed promoter Groucho has to deal with the singer's self-appointed agent, Chico. The con men try to top each other, wrangling over the fine points of a contract and tearing off the displeasing clauses until only scraps are left.

GROUCHO: What's his name?

CHICO: What do you care? I can't pronounce it. What do you want with him?

GROUCHO: I want to sign him up for the New York Opera Company. Do you know that America is waiting to hear him sing?

CHICO: Well, he can sing loud, but he can't sing that loud.

GROUCHO: Well, I think I can get America to meet him halfway. Could he sail tomorrow?

CHICO: You pay him enough money, he could sail yesterday. How much you pay him?

GROUCHO: Well, I don't know. Let's see—a thousand dollars a night. I'm entitled to a small profit. How about ten dollars a night?

CHICO: Ten dollars! I'll take it.

GROUCHO: All right, but remember I get ten percent for negotiating the deal.

CHICO: Yes, and I get ten percent for being the manager. How much does that leave?

GROUCHO: Well, that leaves him—uh—eight dollars.

CHICO: Eight dollars, eh? Well, he senda five dollars home to his mother.

GROUCHO: Well, that leaves him three dollars.

CHICO: Three dollars. Can he live in New York on three dollars?

GROUCHO: Like a prince. Of course, he won't be able to eat, but he can live like a prince. However, out of that three dollars, you know, he'll have to pay income tax.

CHICO: Oh, his income tax, eh?

GROUCHO: Yes. You know, there's a federal tax and a state tax and a city tax and a street tax and a sewer tax.

CHICO: How much does this come to?

GROUCHO: Well, I figure if he doesn't sing too often he can break even.

CHICO: All right, we take it.

GROUCHO: All right, fine. Now—uh—here are the contracts. You just put his name at the top and—uh—you just sign it at the bottom. . . .

CHICO: You read it.

GROUCHO: All right. I'll read it to you. Can you hear?

CHICO: Did you say anything?

GROUCHO: Well, I haven't said anything worth hearing.

CHICO: Well, that's why I didn't hear anything.

GROUCHO: Well, that's why I didn't say anything.

CHICO: Can you read?

GROUCHO: I can read but I can't see it. I don't seem to have it in focus here. If my arms were a little longer, I could read it. You haven't got a baboon in your pocket, have you? Here—here—here we are. I've got it. Now, pay particular attention to this first clause because it's the most important. Says the—uh—the party of the first part shall be known in this contract as the party of the first part. How do you like that? That's pretty neat, eh?

CHICO: No, that's no good.

GROUCHO: What's the matter with it?

CHICO: I don't know. Let's hear it again.

GROUCHO: It says the—uh—the party of the first part should be known in this contract as the party of the first part.

CHICO: That sounds a little better this time.

GROUCHO: Well, it grows on you. Would you like to hear it once more?

CHICO: Uh—just the first part.

GROUCHO: What do you mean? The party of the first part?

CHICO: No, the first part of the party of the first part.

GROUCHO: All right. It says the—uh—the first part of the party of the first part, should be known in this contract as the first part of the party of the first part, should be known in this contract— Look, why should we quarrel about a thing like this? We'll take it right out, eh? *(They rip pieces out of the contract)*

CHICO: Yeah, it's too long anyhow. Now, what have we got left?

GROUCHO: Well, I've got about a foot and a half. Now, it says—uh—the party of the second part shall be known in this contract as the party of the second part.

CHICO: I don't know about that.

GROUCHO: Now, what's the matter?

CHICO: I no like the second party either.

GROUCHO: Well, you should have come to the first party. We didn't get home till around four in the morning. I was blind for three days.

CHICO: Hey, look! Why can't the first part of the second party be the second part of the first party? Then you've got something.

GROUCHO: Well . . . rather than go through all that again, what do you say? *(They rip another segment from their contracts)*

CHICO: Fine.

GROUCHO: Now—uh—I've got something here you're bound to like. You'll be crazy about it.

CHICO: No, I don't like it.

GROUCHO: You don't like what?

CHICO: Whatever it is—I don't like it.

GROUCHO: Well, don't let's break up an old friendship over a thing like that. Ready? *(They rip again)*

CHICO: Okay. Now, the next part, I don't think you're going to like.

GROUCHO: Well, your word's good enough for me. Now, then, is my word good enough for you?

CHICO: I should say not.

GROUCHO: Well, that takes out two more clauses. *(Out they go)* Now, the party of the eighth part—

CHICO: No.

GROUCHO: No?

CHICO: No. That's no good. No. *(More ripping)*

GROUCHO: The party of the ninth—

CHICO: No, that's no good too. Hey, how is it my contract is skinnier than yours?

GROUCHO: Well, I don't know. You must have been out on a tear last night. But, anyhow, we're all set now, aren't we? Now, just you put your name right down there and then the deal is—is—uh—legal.

CHICO: I forgot to tell you. I can't write.

GROUCHO: Well, that's all right. There's no ink in the pen, anyhow. But listen, it's a contract, isn't it?

CHICO: Oh sure. Hey wait—wait! What does this say here? This thing here?

GROUCHO: Oh, that? Oh, that's just the usual clause. That's in every contract. That just says—uh—if any of the parties participating in this contract is shown not to be in their right mind, the entire agreement is automatically nullified.

CHICO: Well, I don't know.

GROUCHO: It's all right. That's in every contract. That's what they call a sanity clause.

CHICO: Ah, you fool wit me. There ain't no Sanity Claus!

A DAY AT THE RACES

(1937)

―――――――――――――――

In A Day at the Races, Groucho and Margaret Dumont meet once again. The wealthy hypochondriac Mrs. Emily Upjohn has been languishing at the Standish sanitarium. She sum mons her favorite medical man, Hugo Z. Hackenbush ("I didn't know there was anything wrong with me until I met him"), unaware that he is an animal doctor. Groucho immediately arouses the suspicion of the sanitarium's medical staff, led by Drs. Whitmore and Wilmerding.

⌒

MRS. UPJOHN: Surely, you don't question the doctor's ability?

WHITMORE: No, not exactly. But running a sanitarium calls for a man with peculiar talents.

GROUCHO: You don't have to look any further. I've got the most peculiar talents of any doctor you ever met. *(To Whitmore)* Why don't you go out and bring in something? Preferably your resignation?

WHITMORE: Tell me, Dr. Hackenbush, just what was your medical background?

GROUCHO: Medically?

WHITMORE: Yes.

GROUCHO: Well, at the age of fifteen I got a job in a drugstore, filling prescriptions.

WHITMORE: Don't you have to be twenty-one to fill prescriptions?

GROUCHO: Well, that's for grown-ups. I just filled them for children.

WHITMORE: No, no, doctor. I mean, where did you get your training as a physician?

GROUCHO: Oh, well, to begin with, I took four years at Vassar.

MRS. UPJOHN: Vassar! But that's a girls' college.

GROUCHO: I found that out the third year. I'd've been there yet but I went out for the swimming team.

WHITMORE: The doctor seems reluctant to discuss his medical experiences.

GROUCHO: Well, medically, my experiences have been most unexciting, except during the flu epidemic.

WHITMORE: Ah, and what happened?

GROUCHO: I got the flu.

MRS. UPJOHN: Oh, doctor, I think it's time for my pill.

GROUCHO: *(Privately, to Mrs. Upjohn)* Ixnay on the opeday.

MRS. UPJOHN: Now, you told me to take them regularly.

WHITMORE: Just a minute, Mrs. Upjohn, that looks like a horse pill to me.

GROUCHO: Oh, you've taken them before?

MRS. UPJOHN: Are you sure, doctor, you haven't made a mistake?

GROUCHO: You have nothing to worry about. The last patient I gave one of those to won the Kentucky Derby.

WHITMORE: Uh, may I examine this, please? Do you actually give those to your patients? Isn't that awfully large for a pill?

GROUCHO: No. It was too small for a basketball and I didn't know what to do with it. Say, you're awfully large for a pill yourself.

WHITMORE: Wilmerding, just what is your opinion?

WILMERDING: It must take a lot of water to swallow that.

GROUCHO: Nonsense. You can swallow that with five gallons.

WHITMORE: Isn't that a lot of water for a patient to take?

GROUCHO: Not if the patient has a bridge in her mouth. You see, the water flows under the bridge and the patient walks over the bridge and meets the pill on the other side.

Standish is about to go broke. Tony (Chico), the sanitarium's good-hearted bus driver and part-time con artist, comes up with a scheme to get the institution out of the red. He will bet every dollar in his possession on a little-known but speedy horse, Sun-Up. The trouble is, he hasn't got a dollar—until he arranges to meet Groucho at the track. Assuming the guise of an ice cream peddler, Chico goes to work.

CHICO: Get your ice cream.

GROUCHO: Two dollars on Sun-Up.

CHICO: Hey. Hey, boss. Come here. You wanta something hot?

GROUCHO: Not now. I just had lunch. Anyhow, I don't like hot ice cream. . . . (*At the betting window*) Two dollars on Sun-Up.

CHICO: Hey, come here. I no sell ice cream. That's a fake to foola the police. I sella tips on the horses. . . . Sun-Up is the worse horse on the track.

GROUCHO: I notice he wins all the time.

CHICO: Aw, that's just because he comes in first.

GROUCHO: Well, I don't want them any better than first.

CHICO: Hey, boss, come here. Come here. Suppose you bet on Sun-Up. What you gonna get for your money? Two to one. One dollar and you remember me all your life.

GROUCHO: That's the most nauseating proposition I've ever had.

CHICO: Come on, come on, you look like a sport. Come on, boss. . . . Thank you.

GROUCHO: What's this?

CHICO: That'sa the horse.

GROUCHO: How'd he get in here?

CHICO: *(Selling)* Get your ice cream. Tootsie-fruitsie ice cream.

GROUCHO: *(Consulting the book)* Z-V-B-X-R-P-L. I had the same horse when I had my eyes examined. Hey, ice cream: What about this optical illusion you just slipped me? I don't understand it.

CHICO: Oh, that's not the real name of the horse, that's the name of the horse's code. Look in your codebook.

GROUCHO: What do you mean, code?

CHICO: Yeah, look in the codebook. That'll tell you what horse you got.

GROUCHO: Well, I haven't got a codebook.

CHICO: You no gotta codebook?

GROUCHO: You know where I can get one?

CHICO: Well, just by accident I think I got one here. Here you are.

GROUCHO: How much is that?

CHICO: That's free.

GROUCHO: Oh, thanks.

CHICO: Just a one-dollar printing charge.

GROUCHO: Well, give me one without printing. I'm sick of printing.

CHICO: Aw, come on, you want to win.

GROUCHO: I want to win but I don't want the savings of a lifetime wiped out in a twinkling of an eye.

CHICO: Thank you very much. *(Calling out)* Ice cream.

GROUCHO: Z-V-B-X-R-P-L. Page thirty-four. Hey, ice cream, I can't make head or tail out of this.

CHICO: Oh, that's all right, look in the master codebook . . . that'll tell you where to look.

GROUCHO: Master code? I haven't got any master codebook.

CHICO: You no gotta master codebook?

GROUCHO: No . . . do you know where I can get one?

CHICO: Well, just by accident I think I got one right here . . . huh—here you are . . .

GROUCHO: Lot of quick accidents around here for a quiet neighborhood. Just a minute. Is there a printing charge on this?

CHICO: No.

GROUCHO: Oh, thanks.

CHICO: Just a two-dollar delivery charge.

GROUCHO: What do you mean? I'm standing right next to you.

CHICO: Well, for such a short distance I make it a dollar.

GROUCHO: Couldn't I move over here and make it fifty cents?

CHICO: Yes, but I'd move over here and make it a dollar just the same.

GROUCHO: Say, maybe I better open a charge account . . . huh?

CHICO: You gotta some references?

GROUCHO: Well, the only one I know around here is you.

CHICO: That's no good . . . you'll have to pay cash.

GROUCHO: You know a little while ago I could have put the two dollars on Sun-Up and have avoided all this.

CHICO: Yeah, I know . . . throw your money away. . . . Thank you very much.

GROUCHO: Now I'm all set, huh?

CHICO: Yes, sir. Get your tootsie-fruitsie ice cream.

GROUCHO: Master code . . . plain code . . . Z-V-B-X-R-P-L. . . . The letter Z stands for *J* unless the horse is a filly. Hey, tootsie-fruitsie. . . . Is the horse a filly?

CHICO: I don't know . . . look in your Breeder's Guide. Get your ice cream . . . tootsie . . .

GROUCHO: What do you mean, Breeder's Guide? I haven't got a Breeder's Guide.

CHICO: You haven't got a Breeder's Guide?

GROUCHO: Not so loud. . . . I don't want it to get around that I haven't got a Breeder's Guide. . . . Even my best friends don't know I haven't got a Breeder's Guide.

CHICO: Well, boss, I feel pretty sorry for you walking around without a Breeder's Guide . . . why you're just throwing your money away buying those other books without a Breeder's Guide.

GROUCHO: Where can I get one? As though I didn't know.

CHICO: One is no good . . . you got to have the whole set. . . . Get your tootsie-fruitsie . . .

GROUCHO: Hey, you know, all I wanted was a horse, not a public library. . . . How much is the set?

CHICO: One dollar.

GROUCHO: One dollar?

CHICO: Yeah . . . four for five.

GROUCHO: Well, all right . . . give me the four of them. There's no use throwing away money, eh?

CHICO: Here you are . . . *(At betting window)* Six dollars on Sun-Up.

GROUCHO: *(Consulting book)* ZVBXRPL is Burns.

CHICO: Some day the code gives you the name of the jockey instead of the horse. Now you find out who Jockey Burns is riding and that's the horse you bet on. It's easy. Get your ice cream, tootsie-fruitsie . . .

GROUCHO: Oh, I'm getting the idea of it. I didn't get it for a long time, you know. It's pretty tricky when you don't know it, isn't it, huh?

CHICO: It's not that book. . . . Nope . . . nope, it's not that book. . . . No, you haven't got that book.

GROUCHO: You've got it, huh? I'll get it in a minute, though, won't I?

CHICO: Get your ice cream . . . tootsie-fruitsie . . .

GROUCHO: I'm getting a fine tootsie-fruitsing right here.

CHICO: Get your ice cream.

GROUCHO: How much is it?

CHICO: One dollar.

GROUCHO: And that's the last book I'm buying.

CHICO: Sure you don't need no more . . .

GROUCHO: Here's a ten-dollar bill, and shoot the change, will you? They're going to the post.

CHICO: I gotta no change. . . . I'll have to give you nine more books, you don't mind, huh, boss? You take the nine more books.

GROUCHO: Say, you don't handle any bookcases there, do you? . . . Tell me, what horse have I got? Hurry up, will you?

CHICO: I'll find it, here it is, here it is. . . . Right here . . .

GROUCHO: I just hear the fellow blowing his horn.

CHICO: Here it is, here. . . . Jockey Burns—hundred and fifty-two . . . that's Rosie. . . . Oh, boy, look . . . forty to one!

GROUCHO: Forty to one. . . . Am I going to give that bookie a whipping. . . . I was going to bet on Sun-Up at ten to one. (At betting window) Say there . . . big boy, two dollars on Rosie, huh?

BOOKIE: Sorry, that race is over . . .

GROUCHO: Over . . . who won?

BOOKIE: Sun-Up.

CHICO: *(At window, collecting winnings)* Gooda-by, boss *(Counts bills)* Ten . . . twenty . . . thirty . . .

GROUCHO: *(Picked clean, he pushes Tony's cart)* Get your tootsie-fruitsie nice ice cream . . . nice tootsie-fruitsie ice cream . . .

THE GROUCHO LETTERS

(1967)

In 1964 an official at the Library of Congress learned that Groucho had corresponded at some length with T. S. Eliot. Intrigued, he asked the comedian if the library could be the custodian of his letters. Groucho, reminding the world that he had never finished grade school, was only too glad to comply. Three years later a selection of those missives were included in The Groucho Letters.

When the Marx Brothers were about to make a movie called A Night in Casablanca, *there were threats of legal action from Warner Bros., who, five years before, had made a picture called* Casablanca *starring Humphrey Bogart and Ingrid Bergman. Whereupon Groucho, speaking for his brothers and himself, dispatched the following letters:*

Dear Warner Brothers:

Apparently there is more than one way of conquering a city and holding it as your own. For example, up to the time that we contemplated making this picture, I had no idea that the city of Casablanca belonged exclusively to Warner Brothers. However, it was only a few days after our announcement appeared that we received your long, ominous legal document warning us not to use the name Casablanca.

It seems that in 1471, Ferdinand Balboa Warner, your great-great-grandfather, while looking for a shortcut to the city of Burbank, had stumbled on the shores of Africa and, raising his alpenstock (which he later turned in for a hundred shares of common), named it Casablanca.

I just don't understand your attitude. Even if you plan on rereleasing your picture, I am sure that the average movie fan could learn in time to distinguish between Ingrid Bergman and Harpo. I don't know whether I could, but I certainly would like to try.

You claim you own Casablanca and that no one else can use that name without your permission. What about "Warner Brothers"? Do you own that, too? You probably have the right to use the name Warner, but what about Brothers? Professionally, we were brothers long before you were. We were touring the sticks as the Marx Brothers when Vitaphone was still a gleam in the inventor's eye, and even before us there had been other brothers—the Smith Brothers; the Brothers Karamazov; Dan Brothers, an outfielder with Detroit; and "Brother, Can You Spare a Dime?" (This was originally "Brothers, Can You Spare a Dime?" but this was spreading a dime pretty thin, so they threw out one brother, gave all the money to the other one and whittled it down to "Brother, Can You Spare a Dime?")

Now, Jack, how about you? Do you maintain that yours is an original name? Well, it's not. It was used long before you were born. Offhand, I can think of two Jacks—there was Jack of "Jack and the Beanstalk" and Jack the Ripper, who cut quite a figure in his day.

As for you, Harry, you probably sign your checks, sure in the belief that you are the first Harry of all time and that all other Harrys are impostors. I can think of two Harrys that preceded you. There was Lighthouse Harry of Revolutionary fame and a Harry Appelbaum who lived on the corner of Ninety-third Street and Lexington Avenue. Unfortunately, Appelbaum wasn't too well known. The last I heard of him, he was selling neckties at Weber and Heilbroner.

Now about the Burbank studio. I believe this is what you brothers call your place. Old Man Burbank is gone. Perhaps you remember him. He was a great man in a garden. His wife often said Luther had ten green thumbs. What a witty woman she must have been! Burbank was the wizard who crossed all those fruits and vegetables until he had the poor plants in such a confused and jittery condition that they could never decide whether to enter the dining room on the meat platter or the dessert dish.

This is pure conjecture, of course, but who knows—perhaps Burbank's survivors aren't too happy with the fact that a plant that grinds out pictures on a quota settled in their town, appropriated Burbank's name, and uses it as a front for their films. It is even possible that the Burbank family is prouder of the potato produced by the old man than they are of the fact that from your studio emerged *Casablanca* or even *Gold Diggers of 1931.*

This all seems to add up to a pretty bitter tirade, but I assure you it's not meant to. I love Warners. Some of my best friends are Warner Brothers. It is even possible that I am doing you an injustice and that you, yourselves, know nothing at all about this dog-in-the-Wanger attitude. It wouldn't surprise me at all to discover that the heads of your legal department are unaware of this absurd dispute, for I am acquainted with many of them and they are fine fellows with curly black hair, double-breasted suits, and a love of their fellow man that out-Saroyans Saroyan.

I have a hunch that this attempt to prevent us from using the title is the brainchild of some ferret-faced shyster, serving a brief apprenticeship in your legal department. I know the type well—hot out of law school, hungry for success, and too ambitious to follow the natural laws of promotion. This bar sinister probably needled your attorneys, most of whom are fine fellows with curly black hair, double-breasted suits, et cetera, into attempting to enjoin us. Well, he won't get away with it! We'll fight him to the highest court! No pasty-faced legal adventurer is going to cause bad blood between the Warners and the Marxes. We are all brothers under the skin and we'll remain friends till the last reel of *A Night in Casablanca* goes tumbling over the spool.

Sincerely,
Groucho Marx

For some curious reason, this letter seemed to puzzle the Warner Bros. legal department. They wrote—in all seriousness—and asked if the Marxes could give them some idea what their story was about. They felt that something might be worked out. So Groucho replied:

Dear Warners:

There isn't much I can tell you about the story. In it I play a Doctor of Divinity who ministers to the natives and, as a sideline, hawks can openers and pea jackets to the savages along the Gold Coast of Africa.

When I first meet Chico, he is working in a saloon, selling sponges to barflies who are unable to carry their liquor. Harpo is an Arabian caddie who lives in a small Grecian urn on the outskirts of the city.

As the picture opens, Porridge, a mealymouthed native girl, is sharpening some arrows for the hunt. Paul Hangover, our hero, is constantly lighting two cigarettes simultaneously. He apparently is unaware of the cigarette shortage.

There are many scenes of splendor and fierce antagonisms, and Color, an Abyssinian messenger boy, runs Riot. Riot, in case you have never been there, is a small nightclub on the edge of town.

There's a lot more I could tell you, but I don't want to spoil it for you. All this has been okayed by the Hays Office, *Good Housekeeping,* and the survivors of the Haymarket Riots; and if the times are ripe, this picture can be the opening gun in a new worldwide disaster.

Cordially,
Groucho Marx

Instead of mollifying them, this note seemed to puzzle the attorneys even more. They wrote back and said they still didn't understand the story line and they would appreciate it if Mr. Marx would explain the plot in more detail. So Groucho obliged with the following:

Dear Brothers:

Since I last wrote you, I regret to say there have been some changes in the plot of our new picture, *A Night in Casablanca.* In the new version I play Bordello, the sweetheart of Humphrey Bogart. Harpo and Chico are itinerant rug peddlers who are weary of laying rugs and enter a monastery just for a lark. This is a good joke on them, as there hasn't been a lark in the place for fifteen years.

Across from this monastery, hard by a jetty, is a waterfront hotel, chock-full of apple-cheeked damsels, most of whom have been barred by the Hays Office for soliciting. In the fifth reel, Gladstone makes a speech that sets the House of Commons in an uproar and the King promptly asks for his resignation. Harpo marries a hotel detective; Chico operates an ostrich farm. Humphrey Bogart's girl, Bordello, spends her last years in a Bacall house.

This, as you can see, is a very skimpy outline. The only thing that can save us from extinction is a continuation of the film shortage.

Fondly,
Groucho Marx

After that, the Marxes heard no more from the Warner Bros.' legal department.

Despite T. S. Eliot's notorious anti-Semitism ("The rats are underneath the piles/ the jew is underneath the lot"), he was an avid Groucho Marx fan. Like any humble filmgoer, the Nobel laureate wrote to Groucho in 1961, requesting an autographed photo. The astonished Groucho sent off a flattering studio shot. But that was not what Eliot wanted; he wished for a likeness of the screen Groucho, complete with jutting cigar, painted mustache, and suggestive eyebrows. Off went a second picture, and this one met with the poet's approval.

FROM T. S. ELIOT

26TH APRIL, 1961

Dear Groucho Marx,

This is to let you know that your portrait has arrived and has given me great joy and will soon appear in its frame on my wall with other famous friends such as W. B. Yeats and Paul Valéry. Whether you really want a photograph of me or whether you merely asked for it out of politeness, you are going to get one anyway. I am ordering a copy of one of my better ones and I shall certainly inscribe it with my gratitude and assurance of admiration. You will have learned that you are my most coveted pinup, I shall be happy to occupy a much humbler place in your collection.

And incidentally, if and when you and Mrs. Marx are in London, my wife and I hope that you will dine with us.

> Yours sincerely,
> T. S. Eliot

P.S. I like cigars too but there isn't any cigar in my portrait either.

> JUNE 19, 1961

Dear T.S.:

Your photograph arrived in good shape and I hope this note of thanks finds you in the same condition.

I had no idea you were so handsome. Why you haven't been offered the lead in some sexy movies I can only attribute to the stupidity of the casting directors.

Should I come to London I will certainly take advantage of your kind invitation and if you come to California I hope you will allow me to do the same.

> Cordially,
> Groucho Marx

> JANUARY 25, 1963

Dear Mr. Eliot:

I read in the current *Time* magazine that you are ill. I just want you to know that I am rooting for your quick recovery. First because of your contributions to literature and, then, the fact that under the most trying conditions you never stopped smoking cigars.

Hurry up and get well.

> Regards,
> Groucho Marx

23RD FEBRUARY, 1963

Dear Groucho Marx,

It seems more of an impertinence to address Groucho Marx as "Dear Mr. Marx" than it would be to address any other celebrity by his first name. It is out of respect, my dear Groucho, that I address you as I do. I should only be too happy to have a letter from Groucho Marx beginning "Dear T.S.E." However, this is to thank you for your letter and to say that I am convalescing as fast as the awful winter weather permits, that my wife and I hope to get to Bermuda later next month for warmth and fresh air and to be back in London in time to greet you in the spring. So come, let us say, about the beginning of May.

Will Mrs. Groucho be with you? (We think we saw you both in Jamaica early in 1961, about to embark in that glass-bottomed boat from which we had just escaped.) You ought to bring a secretary, a public relations official and a couple of private detectives, to protect you from the London press; but however numerous your engagements, we hope you will give us the honour of taking a meal with us.

Yours very sincerely,
T. S. Eliot

P.S. Your portrait is framed on my office mantelpiece, but I have to point you out to my visitors as nobody recognises you without the cigar and rolling eyes. I shall try to provide a cigar worthy of you.

16TH MAY, 1963

Dear Groucho,

I ought to have written at once on my return from Bermuda to thank you for the second beautiful photograph of Groucho, but after being in hospital for five weeks at the end of the year, and then at home for as many under my wife's care, I was shipped off to Bermuda in the hope of getting warmer weather and have only just returned. Still not quite normal activity, but hope to be about when you and Mrs. Groucho turn up. Is there any date known? We shall be away in Yorkshire at the end of June and the early part of July, but are here all the rest of the summer.

Meanwhile, your splendid new portrait is at the framers. I like them both very much and I cannot make up my mind which one to take home and which one to put on my office wall. The new one would impress visitors more, especially those I want to impress, as it is unmistakably Groucho. The only solution may be to carry them both with me every day.

Whether I can produce as good a cigar for you as the one in the portrait appears to be, I do not know, but I will do my best.

> Gratefully,
> Your admirer,
> T.S.

JUNE 11, 1963

Dear Mr. Eliot:

I am a pretty shabby correspondent. I have your letter of May 16th in front of me and I am just getting around to it.

The fact is, the best laid plans of mice and men, etc. Soon after your letter arrived I was struck down by a mild infection. I'm still not over it, but all plans of getting away this summer have gone by the board.

My plan now is to visit Israel the first part of October when all the tourists are back from their various journeys. Then, on my way back from Israel, I will stop off in London to see you.

I hope you have fully recovered from your illness, and don't let anything else happen to you. In October, remember you and I will get drunk together.

> Cordially,
> Groucho

24TH JUNE, 1963

Dear Groucho,

This is not altogether bad news because I shall be in better condition for drinking in October than I am now. I envy you going to Israel and I wish I could go there too if the winter climate is good as I have a keen admiration for that country. I hope to hear about your visit when I see you and I hope that, meanwhile, we shall both be in the best of health.

One of your portraits is on the wall of my office room and the other one on my desk at home.

Salutations,
T.S.

OCTOBER 1, 1963

Dear Tom:

If this isn't your real name, I'm in a hell of fix! But I think I read somewhere that your first name is the same as Tom Gibbons', a prizefighter who once lived in St. Paul.

I had no idea you were seventy-five. There's a magnificent tribute to you in *The New York Times* book review section of the September 29th issue. If you don't get *The New York Times* let me know and I'll send you my copy. There is an excellent photograph of you by a Mr. Gerald Kelly. I would say, judging from this picture, that you are about sixty and two weeks.

There was also a paragraph mentioning the many portraits that are housed in your study. One name was conspicuous by its absence. I trust this was an oversight on the part of Stephen Spender.

My illness which, three months ago, my three doctors described as trivial, is having quite a run in my system. The three medics, I regret to say, are living on the fat of the land. So far, they've hooked me for eight thousand bucks. I only mention this to explain why I can't get over there in October. However, by next May or thereabouts, I hope to be well enough to eat that free meal you've been promising me for the past two years.

My best to you and your lovely wife, whoever she may be.

I hope you are well again.

Kindest regards,
Groucho

16TH OCTOBER, 1963

Dear Groucho,

Yours of October 1st to hand. I cannot recall the name of Tom Gibbons at present, but if he helps you to remember my name that is all right with me.

I think that Stephen Spender was only attempting to enumerate oil and water colour pictures and not photographs—I trust so. But, there are a good many photographs of relatives and friends in my study, although I do not recall Stephen going in there. He sent me what he wrote for *The New York Times* and I helped him a bit and reminded him that I had a good many books, as he might have seen if he had looked about him.

There is also a conspicuous and important portrait in my office room which has been identified by many of my visitors together with other friends of both sexes.

I am sorry that you are not coming over here this year, and still sorrier for the reason for it. I hope, however, that you will turn up in the spring if your doctors leave you a few nickels to pay your way. If you do not turn up, I am afraid all the people to whom I have boasted of knowing you (and on being on first name terms at that) will take me for a four flusher. There will be a free meal and free drinks for you by next May. Meanwhile, we shall be in New York for the month of December and if you should happen to be passing through there at that time of year, I hope you will take a free meal there on me. I would be delighted to see you wherever we are and proud to be seen in your company. My lovely wife joins me in sending you our best, but she didn't add "whoever he may be"—she knows. It was I who introduced her in the first place to the Marx Brothers films and she is now as keen a fan as I am. Not long ago we went to see a revival of *The Marx Brothers Go West*, which I had never seen before. It was certainly worth it.

Ever yours,
Tom

P.S. The photograph is on an oil portrait, done 2 years ago, not a photograph direct from life. It is very good-looking and my wife thinks it is a very accurate representation of me.

NOVEMBER 1, 1963

Dear Tom:

Since you are actually an early American (I don't mean that you are an old piece of furniture, but you are a fugitive from St. Louis), you should have heard of Tom Gibbons. For your edification, Tom Gibbons was a native of St. Paul, Minnesota, which is only a stone's throw from Missouri. That is, if the stone is encased in a missile. Tom was, at one time, the light-heavyweight champion of the world, and although outweighed by twenty pounds by Jack Dempsey, he fought him to a standstill in Shelby, Montana.

The name Tom fits many things. There was once a famous Jewish actor named Thomashevsky. All male cats are named Tom—unless they have been fixed. In that case they are just neutral and, as the upheaval in Saigon has just proved, there is no place any more for neutrals.

There is an old nursery rhyme that begins "Tom, Tom, the piper's son," etc. The third President of the United States' first name was Tom . . . in case you've forgotten Jefferson.

So, when I call you Tom, this means you are a mixture of a heavyweight prizefighter, a male alley cat, and the third President of the United States.

I have just finished my latest opus, *Memoirs of a Mangy Lover*. Most of it is autobiographical and very little of it is fiction. I doubt whether it will live through the ages, but if you are in a sexy mood the night you read it, it may stimulate you beyond recognition and rekindle memories that you haven't recalled in years.

Sex, as an industry, is big business in this country, as it is in England. It's something everyone is deeply interested in even if only theoretically. I suppose it's always been this way, but I believe that in the old days it was discussed and practiced in a more surreptitious manner. However, the new school of writers have finally brought the bedroom and the lavatory out into the open for everyone to see. You can blame the whole thing on Havelock Ellis, Krafft-Ebing and Brill, Jung and Freud. (Now there's a trio for you!) Plus, of course, the late Mr. Kinsey who, not satisfied with hearsay, trundled from house to house, sticking his nose in where angels have always feared to tread.

However I would be interested in reading your views on sex, so don't hesitate. Confide in me. Though admittedly unreliable, I can be trusted with matters as important as that.

If there is a possibility of my being in New York in December, I will certainly try to make it and will let you know in time.

My best to you and Mrs. Tom.

Yours,
Groucho

3RD JUNE, 1964

Dear Groucho,

This is to let you know that we have arranged for a car from International Car Hire (a firm of whom we make a good deal of use) to collect you and Mrs. Groucho at 6:40 P.M. on Saturday from the Savoy, and to bring you to us for dinner and take you home again at the end of the evening. You are, of course, our guests entirely, and we look forward to seeing you both with great pleasure.

The picture of you in the newspapers saying that, amongst other reasons, you have come to London to see me has greatly enhanced my credit in the neighbourhood, and particularly with the greengrocer across the street. Obviously I am now someone of importance.

Ever yours,
Tom

TO GUMMO MARX

JUNE, 1964

Dear Gummo:

Last night Eden and I had dinner with my celebrated pen pal, T. S. Eliot. It was a memorable evening.

The poet met us at the door with Mrs. Eliot, a good-looking, middle-aged blonde whose eyes seemed to fill up with adoration every time she looked at her husband. He, by the way, is tall, lean, and rather stooped over; but whether this is from age, illness, or both, I don't know. At any rate, your correspondent arrived at the Eliots' fully prepared, for a literary evening. During the week I had read *Murder in the Cathedral* twice; "The Waste Land" three times, and just in case of a conversational bottleneck, I brushed up on *King Lear*.

Well, sir, as cocktails were served, there was a momentary lull—the kind that is more or less inevitable when strangers meet for the first time. So, apropos of practically nothing (and "not with a bang but a whimper") I tossed in a quotation from "The Waste Land." That, I thought, will show I've read a thing or two besides my press notices from vaudeville.

Eliot smiled faintly—as though to say he was thoroughly familiar with his poems and didn't need me to recite them. So I took a whack at *King Lear*. I said the king was an incredibly foolish old man, which God knows he was; and that if he'd been my father I would have run away from home at the age of eight—instead of waiting until I was ten.

That, too, failed to bowl over the poet. He seemed more interested in discussing *Animal Crackers* and *A Night at the Opera*. He quoted a joke—one of mine—that I had long since forgotten. Now it was my turn to smile faintly. I was not going to let anyone—not even the British poet from St. Louis—spoil my Literary Evening. I pointed out that King Lear's opening speech was the height of idiocy. Imagine (I said) a father asking his three children: Which of you kids loves me the most? And then disowning the youngest—the sweet, honest Cordelia—because, unlike her wicked sister, she couldn't bring herself to gush out insincere flattery. And Cordelia, mind you, had been her father's favorite!

The Eliots listened politely. Mrs. Eliot then defended Shakespeare; and Eden, too, I regret to say, was on King Lear's side, even though I am the one who supports her. (In all fairness to my wife, I must say that, having played the Princess in a high school production of *The Swan*, she has retained a rather warm feeling, for all royalty.)

As for Eliot, he asked if I remembered the courtroom scene in *Duck Soup*. Fortunately I'd forgotten every word. It was obviously the end of the Literary Evening, but very pleasant none the less. I discovered that Eliot and I had three things in common: (1) an affection for good cigars and (2) cats; and (3) a weakness for making puns—a weakness that for many years I have tried to overcome. T.S., on the other hand, is an unashamed—even proud—punster. For example, there's his Gus, the Theater Cat, whose "real name was Asparagus."

Speaking of asparagus, the dinner included good, solid English beef, very well prepared. And, although they had a semibutler serving, Eliot insisted on pouring the wine himself. It was an excellent wine and no maître d' could have served it more graciously. He is a dear man and a charming host.

When I told him that my daughter Melinda was studying his poetry at Beverly High, he said he regretted that, because he had no wish to become compulsory reading.

We didn't stay late, for we both felt that he wasn't up to a long evening of conversation—especially mine.

Did I tell you we called him Tom?—possibly because that's his name. I, of course, asked him to call me Tom too, but only because I loathe the name Julius.

Yours,
Tom Marx

thing is too much for me. At any rate, temporarily I am throwing the whole thing in the lap of Dr. Morris Fishbein.

The next letter was from the proprietor of a Beverly Hills liquor store, and a gloomier prophet I have rarely read. He warned me that liquor prices were going sky high and that I had better lay away 30 or 40 cases of hard booze before war is officially declared. Since my drinking these days is confined to swallowing a thimbleful of cooking sherry each night before dinner, his letter left me in a fairly calm condition.

The third letter was from the Continental Can Company pleading with me to send in my proxy on my IGO shares of stock which, incidentally, have gone down seven points since I bought them. The letter pointed out, rather querulously I thought, that I was a stockholder in a giant and growing corporation, but that its officers were helpless to proceed with the business at hand unless I was willing to cooperate and send in my proxy, and pronto. The whole company, they implied, was going to hell. Thousands of stockholders were sitting in a drafty auditorium in Wilmington, Delaware, unable to unseat the present officials unless they were morally strengthened by my proxy.

The next letter was from the Electric Bond and Share Company (in case you've forgotten, this is the uptown equivalent of Goldman Sachs). In 1929 this outfit reduced my bank account by $38,000. Unfortunately, through some confusion in the bookkeeping department, I find myself 21 years later, still the owner of one-half share. In case you are not too familiar with current Wall Street prices, an entire share can be purchased for $1.10. They, too, were after my proxy. I have tried many times to dispose of this shrunken security. One year in desperation I even sent them the half share, special delivery and registered, but a few days later it came back—this time to make matters worse, with six cents postage due. One year I destroyed the God-damned stock but it didn't faze EB&S one bit. I am on their books and apparently they are determined to keep me there—at least until the next market crash.

The next was a letter from AFRA. They pointed out that I was some months behind in my dues and unless the money was forthcoming in the near future they were planning on pulling out the musicians, stage hands, cameramen, electricians, studio policemen, and an ex-vice president of radio who stands in front of NBC giving away free ducats for Spade Cooley.

So, Fred, I say to hell with the U.S. mails. I would be deeply indebted to you if you would write your congressman asking him to vote against any further appropriations for the post office. Without funds this monster would soon wither away and die and I could then spend my declining years with an empty wastebasket and a light heart.

Regards,
Groucho

Goodman Ace was another friend from vaudeville days. He and Groucho had first met in Kansas City, where Ace was a drama critic. From the Midwest the journalist moved on to Hollywood, where he became a gagwriter for radio programs like The Big Show *and, later, for Perry Como's TV program. From time to time he interested himself in the careers of Groucho's children.*

TO GOODMAN ACE

JANUARY 18, 1951

Dear Goodman:

Your letter received and you certainly have your problems. For a miserable pittance I'll promise not to show it to Wald and Krasna.

Miriam had told me that she had spoken to you and that you were not going to do the *Big Show* the week I'm on. I then instructed Gummo to call McConnell and to tell them that without you I would not appear. Either you are a shifty crook, or you just don't remember what you say from time to time.

I had a very pleasant morning today. To begin with, it was raining. After reading the war news I went to my lawyer's, who immediately opened up with the news that the government didn't see eye to eye with your correspondent about some tax items back in 1946 and 1947 when I was a comparatively young man. This doesn't involve much, but what makes it even more pleasant is that the returns as yet have not come in for 1948 and 1949.

I only cite these annoyances to show you that it isn't necessary to have relatives in Kansas City to be unhappy. Frankly the whole thing doesn't disturb me too much and I snap my fingers at the Revenue Department. However, when you arrive on February 4th and you knock on my front door, if there's no answer you can always reach me at the Federal jail down near the Union depot.

Thanks for the dress for Melinda. She said she would thank you personally when you arrive. That is, if you are still working on the *Big Show*. If not you can look elsewhere for your thanks. Most people that I speak to like the *Big Show* and most of them agree with me that it's too long by at least 30 minutes. I read the rating in *Variety* and if these ratings are to be taken seriously, I question whether it will continue into the next season. My predictions are usually accurate. I was the fellow who said there would be no market crash in 1929.

I await your arrival with a remarkable amount of composure.

Love from all,
Groucho

P.S. I saw Joe DiMaggio last night at Chasen's and he wasn't wearing his baseball suit. This struck me as rather foolish. Suppose a ball game broke out in the middle of the night? By the time he got into his suit the game would be over.

Phil Silvers was a comedian who had come out of burlesque, only to struggle for years as a second banana in bottom-of-the-bill screen comedies. Groucho always admired the man's humor and tenacity, and encouraged him to stay in the business. When Silvers finally made the big time starring as Sergeant Bilko in a long-running TV sitcom, no one was more delighted than his mentor.

TO PHIL SILVERS

NOVEMBER 15, 1951

Dear Phil:

I won't bore you with the details of how happy I am over your success. You've had it coming. You have been scrambling around near the top for many a year and now at long last you've broken through. The critics called you a major comic. Well, it couldn't have happened to a nicer guy.

But I must warn you. In a musical, as you know, there are temptations. Thirty or forty beautiful babes in back of you kicking up high — so high that they frequently display sections of their anatomy that in other circles are carefully reserved for the man they ultimately marry. Phil, steer clear of these man-traps. Marry, if you must, but don't marry a chorus girl. As the years roll by you will discover their high kicks grow proportionately lower, and their busts sag just as much as the busts of girls who have never seen the inside of a dressing room.

You may ask then what is the difference? As a veteran of three Broadway musicals, I can quickly tell you chorus girls are notoriously pampered and insolvent. No matter where you take them, they order champagne and chicken à la king. This can be very embarrassing if you are in the Automat.

However, if you must marry, I suggest you look in other fields. In a city as big as New York I am sure there are pants manufacturers, wholesale delicatessen dealers, and various other merchants who have daughters who conceivably have virtues even more indispensable to a nearsighted major comic than a talent for high kicking.

So steer clear of these coryphées. This doesn't necessarily mean that you have to snub them. Remember they too are people, even though they spend most of their waking hours grinding and bumping. I suggest that when you arrive at the theater give them a hearty but dignified greeting. You might even toss in a low, courtly bow. Under no circumstances shake their hands, for the slightest physical contact can lead to disaster.

If there are not too many in the group, you might inquire solicitously about their health. If you are in a particularly gracious mood, you might even give them a brief resume of your physical condition. The social amenities out of the way, walk quickly to your dressing room, and unless there is a fire backstage, don't emerge until the callboy has notified you that it is time to make your entrance. Your behavior on the road we can discus at some future date. You realize, of course, that once you get to Altoona, Sioux City, and other way stations, you may have to modify your attitude, but judging from the reviews this is a problem that need not concern you for some time.

So look smart, be smart, and remember . . . in Union there is alimony.

Love,
Groucho

Groucho took Norman Krasna under his wing when the aspiring writer was twenty-two and watched him ascend to successful Broadway playwright and Oscar-winning scenarist. In the 1940s the pair collaborated on Time for Elizabeth. *Groucho's only attempt at legitimate stage comedy bombed in New York in 1948, but the critical panning seemed only to cement a friendship that lasted to the end of his life.*

TO NORMAN KRASNA

BEVERLY HILLS, SEPTEMBER 3, 1961

Dear Norman:

I'm worried about Harry Ruby. He's taken to writing his letters in verse. Being a song writer that in itself would be understandable if he'd properly confine his subjects to such matters as moon in June, dolls who are both glamorous and amorous, or even—since he's still an incurable baseball nut—to Dizzy Dean's earned-run average.

But no; Ruby is now writing verses about verses. Explaining that "Writing Poetry Is for Those/Who Can't Express Themselves in Prose," he goes on to say:

> When I consult Roget or March
> For Words to weave upon my loom,
> My eyebrows testily I arch
> And order junior from the room.
> I run my fingers through my hair,
> I pace the floor and curse my luck
> As I imagine Baudelaire
> And Shelley did when they were stuck.

But that, Norman, is not all. The man who wrote the memorable "Hurray for Captain Spaulding" now comes up with:

> It isn't for the dead I grieve,
> It's for the living whom the dead bereave.

And

> This creed Death uses for his text:
> "No one is better than the next";
> So Death is, quite ironically,
> The only true democracy.

See what I mean? My best to you and the family.

Groucho

P.S. I was needlessly alarmed. Last night Ruby and I went to the ball game. When he yelled for the Dodgers, it was in 100 percent prose.

Joseph McCarthy, leader of the political witch-hunts of the 1950s, began his downfall when a lawyer, Joseph Welch, rose to defend a colleague attacked by the senator, saying, "Have you no decency?" Groucho, a life-long liberal and hater of McCarthy, sent belated congratulations. As it turned out, the lawyer was a Groucho fan and replied in kind.

TO JOSEPH N. WELCH

MAY 31, 1957

Dear Mr. Welch:

Those immortal words in the April *TV Guide* were said by your correspondent who, incidentally, has been an ardent fan of yours ever since watching you permit Senator McCarthy to hang himself.

I was a little frightened when I read the imposing list of lawyers on your letterhead. There are at least forty. Over the years I have been sued by groups of attorneys on most of the minor charges—rape, larceny, embezzlement, and parking in front of a fireplug—but none of the legal documents received at my residence ever had more than four names on it.

How do you all get along in the office? Do you trust each other? Or does each one have a separate safe for his money? Isn't there some danger that you and one of your many partners could both be in a courtroom representing opposing clients, and not be aware of it until you faced each other before the judge? Do you have one community storage room for your briefcases—or does each one sit on his own case?

Someday, if I ever get to Boston, I would like to come in and gaze upon this vast array of legal talent at work—or even at play.

No, I'm not rich. I'm rich enough, however, to know that inflation is knocking hell out of what I have.

I hope that you are well and enjoying the Harvard football team.

Cordially yours,
Groucho Marx

P.S. On your letterhead, I note the name JAMES A. BRINK. Well, at least I know who HE is.

JUNE 13, 1957

Dear Mr. Marx:

You quite misunderstood this firm's letterhead. All the names below the first line are the names of our professional witnesses. They hang around street corners and turn up unexpectedly as witnesses in all of the automobile cases we try.

As to the questions you ask, I am sure they were mostly rhetorical but I list them with appropriate answers:

Q. How do you all get along in the office?
A. By leaning on each other heavily and on our secretaries.
Q. Do you trust each other?
A. In every area except money, property, and women.
Q. Does each one have a separate safe for his money?
A. Yes, except I have so much money I have two safes.
Q. Isn't there some danger that you and one of your partners could both be in a courtroom, representing opposing clients?
A. Damned if there isn't and every now and then somebody takes in a case where the client is against the client of another guy in this office and there is hell to pay and no foolin'.
Q. Do you have one community storage room for your briefcases? Or does each one sit on his own case?
A. I do not understand this question. I sit on what you sit on only I do more of it than you do.

If you ever do come to Boston and do not come to see me now that you have gone to such length in writing me, I will do all that I can to harm you. Come to think of it, perhaps the most harmful thing that could happen to you in Boston would be for you to call on me and have that fact become public. While a very choice collection of people across the country seem to think favorably of me, a highly numerous and vocal collection of people in Boston thought and still think that hanging is too good for me.

Sincerely,
Joe Welch

On December 31, 1951, Groucho made the cover of Time *for the second time (the first was on August 13, 1932, when he and his brothers were pictured in* Horse Feathers*). The occasion could not go by without a comment.*

TO JAMES A. LINEN, PUBLISHER OF *TIME* MAGAZINE

JANUARY 4, 1952

Dear Mr. Linen:

The picture of me on the cover of *Time* has changed my entire life. Where formerly my hours were spent playing golf and chasing girls, I now while away the days loitering around Beverly Hills' largest newsstand, selling copies of the December 31st issue of *Time* at premium prices.

Admittedly the picture on the cover didn't do me justice (I doubt if any camera could capture my inner beauty), but nevertheless my following is so fanatical that they buy anything that even remotely resembles me. Yesterday, despite the fact that it was raining, I made $13. This is all tax free, for I steal the copies of *Time* while the owner of the newsstand is out eating lunch.

Please use my picture again soon and next time I promise to give you half of everything I get away with.

Cordially,
Groucho Marx

P.S. In addition to Henry James, I also read the *St. Louis Sporting News.*

Groucho never took tennis very seriously—except when his son Arthur was a ranking amateur. Don Budge, a tennis champion, was diplomatic enough to tell Groucho not to bother with lessons.

TO DONALD BUDGE

JANUARY 28, 1952

Dear Donald:

As you pointed out, my game is so close to perfection that it would be sheer waste of money for me to take any additional lessons.

I must say that I envy you your vacation. It is not every man who can make a living merely by having an 18-year-old-girl on the other side of a tennis net with all of her equipment bouncing up and down. Since you are still young enough to jump over the net I predict you will spend many a happy afternoon, particularly if your wife is out of town.

I hope you prosper in your new venture.

Regards,
Groucho

Alistair Cooke, American correspondent of the Manchester Guardian *and television host, was used to getting his way with celebrities. Most of them were only too happy to appear on his programs for minimum pay. That was before he met Groucho.*

TO ALISTAIR COOKE

JULY 8, 1957

Dear Mr. Cooke:

I was a little disappointed on receiving your rather lengthy letter, to find no mention of money. I am, of course, an artist, with my head in the clouds. And I was very happy to be invited to appear, gratis or there-abouts, on *Meet the Press, The Last Word*, the City Center Theatre in New York, two all-night telethons, etc. But my business manager, Mr.

Gummo Marx, has a passion for money that is virtually a sickness. I am constantly being embarrassed by it. Still, he is my brother, and rather than upset him, I have to bow to his wishes.

I hope you and your charming wife are happy and as gay as the weather permits; and that this note will not end our fragile friendship.

Regards,
Groucho

COVERING GROUCHO

Groucho made the cover of Time *magazine twice, once in the company of his siblings, and some twenty years later as a soloist. In 1932 the Brothers were saluted as the stars of* Horse Feathers. *The biography was brisk, humorous, and inaccurate (the Marx grandfather, Opie Schoenberg, for example, did not live to be 101). It is also filled with attitudes of the period: Groucho is considered "the prototype of Hebrew wisecrackers." Nonetheless, the piece did wonders for the Brothers, as well as their incomes. Long after the act had broken up Groucho continued to star, this time as the emcee of the quiz show* You Bet Your Life. *In 1951, saluting the comedian's "unsquelchable effrontery,"* Time *was again brisk, humorous, and inaccurate, this time describing its subject, a desultory if ambitious reader, as an "expert in the novels of Henry James." No matter; the praise more than compensated for a subsequent neglect, when Groucho's death was reduced to a handful of* Time *lines in order to make room for the obit of Elvis Presley, who died the same week in 1977.*

Horse Feathers

(*Time*, August 13, 1932)

If the trustees of Princeton or any other U.S. university which lacks a president had met last month to choose one, they would surely not have chosen Groucho Marx. He lacks the manner, the appearance, the erudition, proper to the post. Nonetheless, at the beginning of *Horse Feathers* (Paramount) it becomes clear that the trustees of Huxley College have been so haphazard as to select Groucho, thinly disguised under the pseudonym of Professor Wagstaff, for this honor. He is discovered on a rostrum where the retiring president of Huxley is addressing the faculty and student body. Attired in a mortar board, with a tailcoat over his arm, Groucho is shaving his false mustache in a portable mirror while puffing a stogie. The retiring president asks him to throw away the cigar. Groucho Marx casts a look at the faculty of Huxley and says: "There'll be no diving for this cigar." He goes on puffing. Carried away by his own address to the students, he breaks into a song called "I'm Against It," leads the faculty in a soft-shoe dance.

Harpo Marx's profession in *Horse Feathers* is somewhat more appropriate than his brother's—Harpo is a dog-catcher. He has a large lamp post to attract large dogs, a small lamp post for lap-dogs, nets of various sizes. Running wildly about the town, he presently arrives at a speakeasy where Groucho Marx is trying to find a pair of professional football players to improve the Huxley team. Chico Marx is associated with the speakeasy as bootlegger and he-man. In the speakeasy, Harpo plays the slot machine with buttons, tries to enlarge his winnings by dropping coins in a pay telephone. He bowls grapefruit at bottles on the bar and when he hears someone say, "Cut the cards," does it with an axe which he carries in his pocket.

Incompetent Groucho Marx hires Chico and Harpo to play football for Huxley, gives them each a contract. When Groucho wants a seal to make the contracts official, Harpo produces a live one. Presently, all three go to a classroom where Groucho gives a lecture on geography and anatomy. Says he: "The Lord 'Alps those that 'Alps themselves." Harpo and Chico stop clawing at pretty female classmates long enough to blow spitballs at Groucho. Groucho dismisses the class, blows spitballs back.

Like other Marx Brothers pictures (*The Cocoanuts, Monkey Business*) this one is distinguished by an irrationality which is only vaguely challenged by romantic episodes concerning Zeppo Marx. This time Zeppo is attached to a blonde Miss Bailey (Thelma Todd), the college widow. Groucho, Chico, and Harpo also attempt to become familiar with Miss Bailey. She tries to steal the signals of the Huxley football team from President Groucho by taking him for a ride in a canoe. Groucho lets her paddle, throws her a candy lifesaver when she falls out. Presently, Chico and Harpo go to kidnap the two best players of the rival football team. The football players kidnap Chico and Harpo. Harpo and Chico saw their way out. Half naked, they drive to the game in a perambulating garbage can that resembles a chariot. After Harpo has made one touchdown by scattering banana peels in the way of the opposing team, all four Marx brothers ride up the field in their refuse wagon and put down several balls for several more touchdowns.

As everyone knows, there are really five Marx brothers. They are descended from a Hanoverian magician and ventriloquist named Lafe Schoenberg, who toured Germany for fifty years, carrying his scenery, tricks, wife, and three children in a roofed wagon. Mrs. Schoenberg played the harp between Lafe Schoenberg's tricks. In 1860, the Schoenbergs emigrated to the United States. Lafe Schoenberg died in Chicago in 1919. He was 101. One of his sons, Al Schoenberg, a tailor's assistant who was frequently discharged for his habit of organizing noisy quartets, took to singing on the stage. He chose the name of Al Shean, became famed with the late Ed ("Oh, Mister") Gallagher. Al Schoenberg's sister Minna was a Manhattan fur and lace worker. She married an Alsatian immigrant named Samuel Marx who frequently sat up all night playing pinochle in his tailor shop. Mr. and Mrs. Samuel Marx had five sons: Leonard (Chico), Arthur (Harpo), Milton (Gummo), Julius (Groucho), and, ten years later, Herbert (Zeppo).*

It is preposterous that in *Horse Feathers* Groucho should be cast as a college president and Zeppo as an abnormally stupid undergraduate who has spent twelve years in one class. Zeppo is the only Marx who has

---

*The four older Marx brothers received their nicknames at Galesburg, Illinois, in 1915, from Art Fischer, vaudeville monologist, who was playing poker with them. Groucho was glum, Harpo played the harp, Chico liked chicken, Gummo wore rubbers. Zeppo's nickname, selected by Groucho, means nothing.

enjoyed the advantages of a high school education. Mrs. Marx, eager to train her children for the stage, saved money for Chico's piano lessons. Soon he was able enough to play in cheap cinema theaters. Harpo, two years younger than Chico, looked exactly like him. He could play two tunes on the piano. They enabled him to defraud theater managers who had hired Chico. He went to work in jobs that Chico had secured, four times received a week's wages before he was discharged. The fifth theater manager, forewarned, recognized Harpo by a wart on his nose. Harpo was thrashed.

While Chico and Harpo were playing pianos, Groucho was developing his soprano voice. Confirmed in the Jewish faith at thirteen, he became a choir boy in a Manhattan Episcopal church, quit when punished for puncturing the organ bellows with an alto's hat-pin. He learned to tap dance. His mother persuaded her friend Ned Wayburn to get him a job in a Gus Edwards act (where famed Eddie Cantor, George Jessel, Georgie Price, Walter Winchell received their histrionic training). When Groucho was fourteen, he went to Denver to be a boy soprano in a trio. Soon after he arrived his voice changed. He got a job driving a grocery wagon in Cripple Creek, Colorado, saved enough for a ticket home and ten dollars to pay for his food. He lost the ten dollars. An old lady who had a basket of fruit fed him on oranges and peanuts.

By the time Groucho returned to Manhattan, his brother Gummo had shown signs of talent. Mrs. Marx hired a girl soprano, got up an act called the Three Nightingales. They performed in Atlantic City in a beer garden on a pier. Underneath the pier were fishnets. The manager of the beer garden fed the Marxes only fish, because it was cheapest on his menu. Next season, Mrs. Marx thought that Harpo also was fitted for her act. She recalled him from the Seville Hotel in Manhattan where he was a bell-hop. Unable to think of anything for Harpo to say, she had him try some of his grandfather's tricks. When the Marxes were performing in Waukegan, Illinois, they were surprised to hear, in the orchestra pit, the piano playing of their brother Chico. He had been touring the country as a piano player and wrestler. At Waukegan, Chico, Zeppo, Gummo, and Groucho made their closest approach to an academic career in an act called "Fun in Hi-Skule." On the Sullivan-Considine circuit they toured with Charlie Chaplin, gave him good advice about taking a hundred-dollar weekly contract with the Keystone Cinema Company.

In Chicago, Harpo Marx bought an old harp. He tuned and played it to suit himself. The harp became so dilapidated that when his train was wrecked at Mobile, Harpo claimed and received $250 on it although it had been unhurt. With the money, he purchased a new harp. He was amazed when a music store offered him $150 for his old harp, amazed further when the music store sold it for $750 as an antique.

In 1917 the Brothers Marx discovered the proper way of performing. Outside a theater in Nacogdoches, Texas, where they were playing, a mule ran away and smashed a store. The audience deserted the Marx Brothers to watch the mule. When the audience returned, the Marxes, indignant, burlesqued their act. By the time they reached Oklahoma City they were rich enough to stay at a hotel.

In 1918, the Marxes toured U.S. training camps with their first show, *Mr. Green's Reception.* When influenza caused the barracks to be quarantined, Gummo and Harpo enlisted. Groucho and Chico joined organizations for entertaining soldiers. Harpo reached France with the Seventh Regiment. He worked as a reporter for the *Stars & Stripes*, like Editor Harold Ross of *The New Yorker*, Columnist Franklin Pierce ("F.P.A.") Adams, and Alexander Woollcott. With them he helped form the famed Thanatopsis Club for poker.

After the war, Gummo entered the raincoat business. He now has a prosperous ladies' wear establishment in Manhattan. Zeppo, just out of high school, joined the act. Soon it was a great success. At Manhattan's Palace Theatre, Harpo fell into the pit. In London the Marxes were first booed, then applauded. In 1923, they bought and disorganized a musical comedy called *The Thrill Girl* (renamed, *I'll Say She Is!*), ran six months in Chicago, eight months in Manhattan. Their next plays were *The Cocoanuts* and *Animal Crackers*. Their first cinema was an adaptation of *The Cocoanuts*. A year later, they made *Animal Crackers*, then *Monkey Business*, their first "original" screenplay. Mrs. Samuel Marx, who stopped touring with her sons just before the war, later changed her name to Minnie Palmer, opened a theatrical agency in Chicago. She died just after the first Marx Brothers cinema was released. Father Samuel Marx, sleek, young-looking, happy, still addicted to pinochle, lives with Zeppo Marx in Hollywood.

Zeppo Marx, married to Marion Benda (*Love 'Em and Leave 'Em*), acts straight juvenile roles. He does it poorly enough not to detract from the antics of his confreres. Chico, married to Cinemactress Betty Karp, is differentiated from other Italian dialect comedians by his ability to play the piano, by a certain irrelevant vehemence which makes it seem that he is chagrined by something but has forgotten what it is. Groucho Marx, married to Ruth Tyrell, a dancer, is talkative, cool, depraved. The prototype of Hebrew wisecrackers, he rattles off disgraceful puns (invented for him in *Horse Feathers* by Harry Ruby, Bert Kalmar, S. J. Perelman) in tones of nasal nonchalance.

Far more depraved than Groucho, more irrelevant than Chico, more implausible than Zeppo is Harpo Marx. He never speaks, he does not need to. His appalling brain expresses itself in a language more disastrous than words. He pursues women with the abandon of a satyr and the stamina of Paavo Nurmi. Sofa and tables are his racetracks and it amuses him in *Horse Feathers* to coax dogs away from their masters into his flea-bitten equipage which has two canary cages in place of sidelights. His harp (which he still tunes and strums in utterly unorthodox fashions) is all that he apparently admires. On it he plays superbly with grace and sumptuous gestures. Having completed *Horse Feathers*, Harpo Marx took it into his head to visit Russia. Last week, leaving his animals (dog, cat, monkey) in his brothers' care, taking with him harp, red wig, and Max Reinhardt, he set out from Hollywood to act in pantomime for the Moscow Art Theatre.

Personality

(*Time*, December 31, 1951)

To some Americans, the name Marx summons up a bearded prophet of social doom, but to most it means a zany tumble of brothers. Groucho is the zaniest and most durable of the lot. In his long career as a comedian, he has met and mastered three mediums: movies, radio, and now television.

Professionally, the other Marx Brothers haven't worn nearly so well. Harpo, once the rage of several continents, has just finished a series of television commercials for a milk company; Chico does his hoary piano routine and Eyetalian dialect around nightclubs; Gummo, who quit the act for good to become a World War I doughboy, is his brother's agent; Zeppo, now out of show business altogether, manufactures airplane parts.

The middle Marx brother in age, Groucho (whose real front names are Julius Henry), now sixty-one, is at the height of his powers in both radio and television, with an annual income of $400,000 before taxes. Fairly dignified bodies of medal pinners have voted him Best Comedian of the Year (1949), Outstanding Television Personality (1950), Best Quizmaster, et cetera.

His quiz program (NBC, Wednesday, 9:00 P.M., EST; TV, Thursday, 8:00 P.M.), *You Bet Your Life*, is now well into its fifth season. When one of the contestants, a pretty and shapely high-school math teacher, explained that geometry is the study of lines, curves, and surfaces, Groucho gave his celebrated leer and panted, "Kiss me, fool!" The audience reaction threatened to blow the back out of the broadcast theater. [Another time], he asked a tree surgeon on his program, "Tell me, Doctor, did you ever fall out of a patient?"

With Groucho, delivery is almost everything. An old line of his, "The air is like wine tonight," used to make audiences choke with laughter a couple of decades ago. When he would simply say, "I think I'll go out and get a cold towel," then start for the wings with a queer, buzzardy shuffle he used for a walk, it would leave the audience strangling. Because nowadays he seldom moves from the high stool he sits on during broadcasts, the buzzardy shuffle is gone. But the rest of the delivery is still there, as good or better than ever; the perfectly timed twitch of the brows; the play of the luminous brown eyes—now rolling with naughty thoughts, now staring through the spectacles with only half-amused contempt; the acidulous, faint smile; the touch of fuming disgust in the voice ("That's as shifty an answer as I ever heard"); above all, the effrontery.

Unsquelchable effrontery has always been Groucho's chief stock in trade. During his stage and screen career, he played a succession of brazen rascals: fraudulent attorney, flimflamming explorer, dissolute college president, amoral private eye, cozening operatic entrepreneur, horse doctor posing as fashionable neurologist ("Either this man is dead or my watch has stopped"), bogus Emperor of France—using such aliases as J. Cheever Loophole, Captain Spaulding, Professor Wagstaff, Detective Sam Grunion, Otis B. Driftwood, Wolf J. Flywheel, and Napoleon. Whatever the alias or whatever the rascality, he was always the same rascal, the con man who made no bones about the disdain he felt for the suckers he was trimming.

A good deal of this disdainful effrontery Groucho employs in private life, at least in his casual dealings with his fellow men. At a function presided over by Governor Frank Merriam, one of the stuffiest governors the state of California was ever afflicted with, Groucho, summoned to the platform to be presented to His Excellency, dragged two friends up with him. "Governor," he said, in a voice for all to hear, "I want you to shake hands with a couple of degenerates."

There were countless times in his childhood, youth, and early manhood when Groucho needed all the effrontery he could muster. Born in a tenement on Manhattan's Upper East Side, he was the third son of an Alsatian immigrant tailor whose attributes were loving kindness, great charm, and a genius for failure. As a boy, Groucho loved reading and dreamed of being a doctor, but the family was always behind with the rent, and his mother, the celebrated Minnie, had him traveling with one of Gus Edwards's kid acts when he was four or five years away from long pants. Zeppo, the youngest, was the only Marx brother who ever reached high school.

The brothers' act finally attained vaudeville's Mecca, the Palace, but the way there for more than a dozen years was gritty and grisly. Billed variously as the Four Nightingales ("The Four Vultures would have been more like it," Groucho says today), the Six Musical Mascots (when Minnie and Aunt Hannah joined the troupe), and Fun in Skool (a warmed-over kid act), they played whistle stop and tank towns on the smallest-time circuits. They performed in sinkhole theaters and fetid saloons, dressed in alleys and rat-infested cellars, slugged it out with rustic hoodlums laying in wait for them at stage doors (Groucho carried a small sack and brass knuckles), ate in coffee pots and greasy saloons, suffered baggage seizures by inexorable boarding house landladies, were fined incessantly by managers for brawling and horseplay, and now and then literally walking the railroad ties.

Once when a harassed conductor informed Minnie that her half-fare "children" were smoking cigars, chasing girls, and playing three-card stud in the coach ahead, she beamed at him and explained, "They grow so fast." After the Marx Brothers had gained fame and fortune from three musical comedies (*I'll Say She Is!*, *The Cocoanuts*, and *Animal Crackers*), Groucho lost $240,000 in the crash of 1929. Anybody who could survive such a life would always have effrontery to burn.

Groucho's other superb professional asset is his lightning ability to ad-lib jokes. His mind is like a panful of popcorn kernels with heat underneath: one ad lib bursts, and the air is filled with popcorn. *You Bet Your Life*, his current show, simultaneously tape-recorded for radio and filmed for television, is not exactly a simon-pure ad-lib performance. Contestants are chosen in advance, made to fill out questionnaires about themselves, and coached for an hour and a half before facing Groucho. But Groucho is still a better field shot than any other ad-libber, and shows it by shooting from the hip at these clay pigeons.

Married and divorced twice (two children by the first marriage, one by the second), he lives with a pair of servants in a fifteen-room Beverly Hills house. He does all the shopping. Afternoons, he works on the two dozen fruit trees that stand on his back lawn; he is a martyr to what Robert Benchley described as dendrophilism, which might be described as tree-tickling. Groucho takes excellent care of himself; he plays golf, never has more than two drinks at a party, and always leaves at midnight, even parties where he is the host. His only excess is cigars. One of his favorite occupations is sitting for long hours in his den strumming Gilbert & Sullivan (at which he is an expert) on his guitar. He is also an expert on the novels of Henry James. Having had hardly any formal education, Groucho, by dint of greedy reading, has made himself a well-read man. His friends are endlessly amazed at his mastery of the contents of magazines which they regard as highbrow (*Atlantic, Harper's, Saturday Review of Literature,* et cetera).

Those who know Groucho best insist that beneath his brash exterior lies a shy, thoughtful and kindhearted man. "The guy doesn't mean to be insulting," songwriter Harry Ruby says. "It's an involuntary motion with him, like a compulsion neurosis." When Groucho won the Peabody Award for being Radio's Best Comedian of the Year, it turned out that he had never heard of the awards or of the late George Foster Peabody, in whose honor the award is named. "It's a good thing the guy died," Groucho ad-libbed, "otherwise we couldn't have won any prizes." From Bob Hope, Jack Benny, Fred Allen, or Ed Wynn, such a crack might have seemed outrageous. From Groucho it was merely funny.

The Play in Interview

(The New York Times)

At the age of forty-nine, in 1939, Groucho let it be known that the Marx Brothers had decided to break up the act. Brooks Atkinson, theater critic for The New York Times *and a fan from way back, interviewed the comedian on the subject of retirement. The piece is notable not for any disclosures but as evidence that Groucho's approach was so infectious that even a sobersided journalist took on a jaunty, iconoclastic tone.*

~

GROUCHO MARX CONFIRMS THE RUMOR THAT HIS KNOCK-ABOUT TEAM OF FOOLISH BROTHERS HAS BROKEN UP FOR GOOD— TO ACT IN OWN SHOW SMOOTH SHAVEN

By Brooks Atkinson

An ugly rumor has been going around the country. People say that the Marx Brothers have broken up their slap-stick team. *Rialto Gossip,* which hears all evil and tells a good part of it, printed a melancholy confirmation of the rumor signed by Groucho Marx a fortnight ago. But this column believes the worst slowly, reluctantly, and skeptically, for show business is an asylum of fraudulent rumors. Since Groucho had secluded himself in an anonymous hotel at the corner of Sixth Avenue and Fifty-fourth Street, directly across from the Ziegfeld Theatre (Suite 17E), this column trotted up yesterday afternoon to make inquiries at the source.

Groucho was stalking about the living room in what would have been his shirt sleeves if he had not been wearing a ducky little sweater cutely buttoned at the neck. Gray pants, cut rather high, supported chiefly by suspenders. Over the back of the chair hung a casual sports jacket of cultivated pattern. Bushy hair, thin at the forepeak, but flaring with considerable bravado astern, and rimless spectacles of dynamic design. Except for the resonant voice which has shot a lot of impudence into theaters and films and except also for the panther style of walking, you would hardly have recognized the illustrious Flywheel who has been playing low comedy in the grand manner for more years than any of us likes to think about.

"Come on, Groucho, how about it?" the interview began. "Are these rumors on the level or not?"

"Absolutely authentic," he growled as he sullenly turned off the radio. "Right from the feedbag. Part of the historical truth."

"You mean, never again?"

"I mean I'm never going to put on the prop coat again as long as I live," he said decisively.

"You mean, in the pictures, don't you?"

"I mean pictures, theater, airplane, submarine, jeep-car and pogo-stick," he said. "I'm never going to get behind that phony mustache again. I'm through with the whole racket."

Well, probably the boys would be on the radio from time to time as a unit.

"No radio units, I'm telling you," he said, "and, I know what you're going to say, not in television either. I wouldn't go through that stuff again if they could inject it into your arm with a hypodermic needle."

So long, Groucho, the sardonic buffoon. At the age of forty-nine Mr. Marx of stage and screen may go on the radio in a personal program. He has a soft spot in his heart for studio audiences because they laugh at him without the mustache. But he has just come East with a play that he and Norman Krasna have written, and if his friends do not think too badly of it he may appear in it in New York this season.

"It's about a guy who is, you know, trying to fix things up when things, you know, get sort of this way and that," Mr. Marx explained. "He comes in in the first act and he runs into this situation which, of course, puts him on the par and he sees all these lugs and dames around there and then he kind of dives in and goes on from there the best way he can."

"Fine," this department responded with some swift reflection. "Comedy?"

"Uh-huh, comedy. Still, some drama, you know, here and there the way things are," said Mr. Marx to fill out the outlines of the picture.

"You figure on playing it straight?"

"Just get that grease-paint mustache out of your mind, will you?" he interjected with a flash of temper. "The mustache is out for good."

Mind you, this department wholly sympathizes with Groucho's situation. He and Harpo and Chico have worked at the same trade all their lives with nothing but a fortune to show for it. They have covered about as much comic ground as three fantastic characters with separate personalities are able to do without bogging down in formula. Formula removes the spontaneity from clowning, and this department understands perfectly.

"Now, in this play you say you have written, although no one seems to have seen it yet," the interview continued, "would it be entirely out of character—we'll say in just the last scene—for you to come in smoking a cigar and wearing, for instance, a black cutaway?"

"Well, now that you mention it," Mr. Marx said thoughtfully, "it wouldn't be absolutely impossible. Nothing is impossible, as my grand-father, who lived to be over a hundred, used to say."

"Now, let's get one more thing straight. Did I hear you say you are going to pay smooth shaven?"

"Look here, chum, the mustache is out," Mr. Marx said irritably. "You take the mustache. It would be an improvement."

FREELANCING

*Groucho was never able to live on the proceeds from his writing, but the size of the payments never stopped him from trying. From the 1920s to the 1970s he wrote or co-wrote eight books; in addition, magazines and newspapers published scores of his articles. Most of these pieces were solo efforts, but on occasion he was known to use the discreet help of his friend, the gagwriter Arthur Sheekman (*Shyster, Flywheel, and Shyster*)*

Up from Pantages

(*The New York Times,* June 10, 1928)

"Up from Pantages" was published just as the Marx Brothers were getting ready to release their third Broadway show, Animal Crackers. *It would be an even bigger hit than their two previous smashes,* I'll Say She Is! *and* The Cocoanuts.

There is no denying the fact that I am getting old, particularly if you take a look at me. Although I believe I still have a few years to go, I have reached the point in my career where I can look back at what is known among show people as My Twenty Years Before the Footlights, which is equivalent to Gerard's Four Years in Germany, and the time is rapidly approaching when I will be known, if at all, as Groucho Whiffen Marx, the grand old man of musical comedy.

After this, of course, will come a dinner at the Green Room Club, with possibly a bust of Joseph Jefferson from the class of *Uncle Tom's Cabin*, then oblivion, and a few years later the inevitable book of memoirs called, in this case, *The Gus Sun Also Rises*. This book will have its usual phenomenal sale, and may even hit the hundred mark. Seventy-five copies of this masterpiece will be purchased by the author as birthday gifts for his immediate family, and the other twenty-five will be used to keep the window in the attic from falling down.

Looking back twenty years, I can remember playing a movie and vaudeville house in the business section of Jacksonville, Florida. It was a long, dark, narrow hall, filled with folding yellow chairs, the kind that are used by undertakers to make the mourners more uncomfortable, and by politicians for their preelection rallies. It wasn't really a theater, but a gents' furnishings store that had been converted into a theater simply by removing the counters, shelves, and some of the rubbish, and by installing an electric piano.

There was no stage. There was, however, a long, narrow platform about as wide as the scaffolding used by painters and stonemasons, and it was on this precarious ledge that most of the performance was given. If the act involved dancing, acrobatics, or anything strenuous there was a brief intermission to enable the performer to jump to the floor for that part of the act.

The dressing room was large and roomy and had perfect ventilation. It was, in fact, a trifle too roomy, as it comprised the whole backyard and was shared alike by a grocer, a butcher, and a blacksmith. It was not much for privacy but great for congeniality and comradeship. One had for companions a crate of chickens, three pigs that were about to be slaughtered, some horses waiting to be shod, two girls who later became known as the Dolly Sisters, and a covey of the largest rats that ever gnawed at an actor's shoes.

The program consisted of four turns. At least that was the manager's contention, but actually there were only two acts. The manager built up the bill by advertising the mechanical piano as an act, and also a reel of the most flickering film that ever ruined an audience's eyes.

The first performance began at noon and then every hour on the hour until midnight, or longer if the business warranted it. The manager was a Greek who had been in the theatrical business only a few months—just long enough to master such a childish profession—and he had therefore set himself up as critic, censor, master of ceremonies, stage manager, ticket chopper, and, frequently, bouncer.

We had named ourselves the Nightingales, a title that certainly bore no relation to our singing, but it promised much and, in those days, bookings were made on promises. The opening performance Monday found us Marxes singing lustily to what we imagined was a spellbound and enraptured throng. We had just arrived at the point in the chorus where we hit the big harmony chord, the chord which was supposed to put the song over with a bang, when we heard a terrific noise, which might have come from a wild bull, but which turned out to be the manager running down the aisle, waving arms, head, and hands, shouting: "Stop it! Stop it, I say! It's rotten. Hey, you fellers, you call that singing? That's terrible. The worst I ever heard. My dog can do better than that. Now you go back and do it over again and do it right or you don't get a nickel of my money, not a nickel."

Embarrassed and red-faced, we slunk to the side of the stage, too dazed to utter a word of defense. We were certainly the saddest-looking nightingales that ever chirped a song. While we cowered in the corner, the Florida Belasco announced to the audience which was entirely too sympathetic to suit us that these hams—pointing to us—could sing rotten in Tampa, could sing rotten in Miami, and, if they so desired, could sing rotten in St. Petersburg, but when they sang in Jacksonville, the biggest and best town in the state, they would have to sing on key or they wouldn't get any money. Ordering us back to the stage, he jumped off the ledge and ran up the aisle to hearty applause and vocal encouragement from the local music lovers. Apparently there was no more than the usual amount of discords on our second attempt, as there were no interruptions, except the customary jeers and catcalls which always accompanied our musical efforts.

In Orange, Texas, we lived at a wormy-looking boardinghouse run by a landlady who looked like a cross between one of the Whoops Sisters and a coach dog. Her rates were five dollars a week—a little high, she conceded, but she set a grand table, easily the best in Texas.

If it was all the same to us, she would prefer her money in advance. We held out for four and a half apiece, and after much general haggling we compromised on four seventy-five, this to include laundry.

For our first meal, which she announced as lunch, we had chili con carne, bread, and coffee. This was not an unusual lunch for Texas and we thought nothing of it. The chili was good—everybody makes good chili down there—but the coffee was terrible. It may have been good to the last drop, but I never got that far; the first drop was awful. That evening for dinner we had chili and a depressing-looking vegetable which we finally agreed to call okra, and for all I know may still be known by that name. The following morning for breakfast we had bacon and chili, and for lunch we each had a big bowl of steaming chili.

What the baby of song and story is to its mother, what the saxophone is to a jazz band, what Gilbert was to Sullivan—those were all nothing to what chili was to this landlady. It was her pièce de résistance, her monument to Mexico with a low bow to all of Central America. By Thursday, despite the fact that we still had a healthy equity in the four seventy-five we had paid in advance, we had retreated to the general store in the village and there rounded out the week on canned goods, dried fruits, brick cheese, and Coca-Cola.

Later on that season we played an open-air theater in Gulfport, Mississippi. It was just a short way as the wind blows from the swamps of Louisiana, and was set in a clearing in the woods. It had the appearance of an early frontier fort and we later discovered it was just about as safe. The wind had been blowing steadily from the marshes all day and by show time that night the air was black with blood-hungry mosquitoes, which, if they had been labeled like asparagus, would have been known as the giant variety extra size. The dressing room had sides and a floor, but a thrifty management, knowing the actor's love for the great outdoors, had decided that a roof would be superfluous, and had therefore taken that lumber and with it built a few extra benches for the customers. This was fine for the manager and the customers, but hard on the performers. The makeup lamp on the shelf acted like a village church bell calling the faithful to the meetinghouse, and these faithful fell on us, hook, line, and stinger. Like thousands of miniature monoplanes they swooped down, while we, armed with towels, socks, rolled up newspapers, and fans, tried vainly to repel them. It was like trying to stop a cyclone.

Stung beyond endurance, our screams of anguish finally brought the manager on the run, and we told him, between slaps, fans, and curses, that, wedded as we were to our art, we would have to abandon it for the time being unless something drastic was done in the way of relief. The manager promised us that he would return in a few moments with a remedy that he had used for years, a remedy that had never failed. Then, leaving us, he rushed out to mollify an audience that was threatening to tear down what theater there was, unless the promised and advertised entertainment was forthcoming.

In a few moments he was back with a half dozen smudge pots filled with pitch and pine, and which when lit quickly drove out the man-eating insects. We got dressed and went out on the stage, puffed and swollen, but still the Nightingales and still singing off-key.

While singing our opening song we smelled smoke, and were happy because of it, figuring the more smoke, the less mosquitoes. But by the time we came to our third song we noticed a certain warmth in the rear that we realized could not be entirely due to the Southern climate, and when we came to our last song, we saw the audience rushing out of a theater that was entirely in flames. We rushed after them, happy that we had lost the mosquitoes. But we also had lost our wardrobe and our trunks, and we later discovered we had lost the manager with what salary was coming to us.

The Return of the Four Mad Prodigals

(The New York Times, April 21, 1929)

The Return of the Four Mad Prodigals *marked the Marxes' reappearance at the Palace Theatre in New York. Essentially, it was a reprise of* Animal Crackers, *which had closed only a week before. The Brothers were always crowd pleasers, but this time*

*out they were guaranteed seven thousand dollars a week, the
highest paid act ever to play the Palace.*

~

It doesn't seem possible that it could be merely a coincidence—the day
after the Palace announced "The Triumphant Return of the Marx
Brothers for a Limited Engagement," Radio-Keith-Orpheum stock
dropped ten points.

Be that as it may, it was with great delight that I realized that, after
eight years on what has been whimsically called the legitimate stage, the
Marx Brothers were returning to vaudeville. I expected to find things
greatly changed during that period. But some things were the same as
ever:

There are still as many children running up and down the aisles in
vaudeville shows as there were eight years ago. During tense dramatic
scenes, especially, games are considered quite the thing by the younger
set.

Then, there are the same old jokes that were sprung eight years ago,
and they are greeted with the same laughter by the same audiences.
Why, when we were breaking in our act a week ago Saturday at the
Madison Theatre in Brooklyn I actually heard a team pull a brand-new
joke which began like this: "Who was that lady I seen you with?" And it
got a pretty good hand, at that.

Seriously, I hadn't been playing in the Palace ten minutes before I
noticed one thing about vaudeville audiences. They get the point of a
joke much sooner than do musical comedy audiences. They laugh
much quicker. And also stop much quicker.

I also observed that the members of the acts and the leader of the
orchestra will twit one another with the same extemporaneous dialogue
that has been carefully rehearsed three hours before the show.

And the same speeches when the act gets a couple of encores. "How
can we ever thank you? It's so good to be back at the Palace." But the
best speeches the audience never hears. These are made on the way to
the dressing rooms when the act doesn't get its two encores.

Some things, however, are radically different from the days when the

Marx Brothers were sensations in such sketches as "On the Mezzanine," "Fun in Hi Skule," and other problem plays. Among the changes I have noted in vaudeville are:

The performers dress much better today than they did eight years ago. Instead of wearing a pair of spats, they wear two pairs.

And they talk differently. In the old days they'd grab you and tell you what a riot they were in Findlay, Ohio, and how they wowed them in Des Moines. Now, all you hear is, "We don't know what to do—Vitaphone wants us to make a short but Movietone is after us to do a full length."

The nature of the acts is a little different today than formerly. No longer do bills open with acrobats in white tights. They still open with acrobats, but they come out in evening clothes and the only indication that they are acrobats is the resin marks on their trousers. Nobody suspects they are acrobats, except the entire audience.

And what has happened to the trained seals? I met a seal backstage whom I hadn't seen since we were playing Pantages time. As Walter Winchell says, he immediately slipped me a fin and told me how disgusted he is with the profession. All that seals can do now is to hang around waiting for Yuletide, when they can dig up a little trade acting as Christmas Seals.

One thing I dislike about the Palace is the fact that the stage door is so narrow that we have to bring Heywood Broun[1] in the front, like a baby grand piano.

After the show, in the old days, the actors used to rush to the nearest one-arm lunch for a load of ham and eggs. Now they all rush to Reuben's to find out how many sandwiches have been named after them.

In conclusion, it certainly is wonderful to be back with our old friends at the Palace. What a welcome I got from the stagehands, especially one fellow with a remarkable memory. Think of remembering a small sum like ten dollars for eight years!

---

[1]New York newspaper columnist and certainly the largest member of the Algonquin Round Table Crowd. Ed.

Holy Smoke

(*College Humor*, February 1930)

Groucho and his cigar are inseparable in the public mind. In fact, the panatela was more than just a prop; Groucho actually enjoyed a good smoke and would have been appalled that his home state of California forbids smoking in his favorite places, movie theaters and restaurants. Holy Smoke was written in early 1930, while the Marx Brothers were performing Animal Crackers in Chicago. It is one of five pieces Groucho published in the then-popular College Humor.

Smoking was originated by the American Indians, who settled all their arguments by smoking the pipe of peace. Their system was simple and effective: when one tribe was sore at another, they'd invite the rival *mispocha* over for a tobacco klatch. After the hostile tribe had spent several evenings smoking the pipe of peace, the home team found themselves with enough coupons to secure a dozen Indian blankets.

Through the ages, this system has been preserved almost intact by American businessmen, who use the same method to settle their disputes. When they have an argument on hand, the rival magnates get together, light cigars, and blow smoke in each other's faces.

Smoking was introduced in England by Sir Walter Raleigh, who was taught by the Indians how to blow rings. He returned to England and blew rings for Queen Elizabeth, who was so impressed that she immediately promoted Raleigh to the post of Chief of Room Service. In this capacity he continued to blow rings—one ring for ice water, two rings for bed linen, et cetera.* The system is still in vogue in the palace to this day.

Pipe smoking made its appearance in Ireland in 1066, the same year that clay was discovered. In 1067, every Irishman above the age of twenty-one was telling the gag about the advantage of a clay pipe—

---

*And one Ring for Lardner.

when you dropped it, you didn't have to bother about picking it up. By 1068, all England was laughing at the joke.

Twenty years later smoking was introduced in Scotland. The Scotch, true to their tradition, not only smoked their pipes but also played them.

Since these pioneer days there has been a great development in the art of smoking. Some years ago, ex–Vice President Marshall got himself famous,* and many boxes of cigars, by stating that what this country needed was a good five-cent cigar. Conditions have changed radically since then. What this country needs today is a good five-cent cigar with a twenty-cent filler.†

Briggs afterward immortalized this idea with his cartoon, "When a Filler needs a Friend."

During the Civil War, smoking gained in popularity because of Ulysses S. Grant, who was devoted to the weed, as tobacco is often called (but not by cigarette manufacturers).

If Grant had lived today,‡ he would find himself greatly in demand.

His picture would be used in all the magazines, a blindfold over his eyes, accompanied by this sort of testimonial:

I'll fight it out with this cigar if it takes all summer!

During the winter of 1864, I noticed that many of my soldiers were coughing. This is serious in wartime, as it gives the enemy a good idea of your position, to say nothing of your health. I passed out a fresh supply of smokes and soon there wasn't any more coughin' in the camp.**

(Signed) Ulysses S. Grant

These testimonials apply not only to the army, but also the navy. Nowadays a sea captain can't get his papers until he passes his blindfold test. Think of the opportunity missed by the cigarette manufacturers by not having Captain Lawrence say in type: "Don't give up the ship—I left my ciggies in my cabin."

---

*And was the only vice president who ever did.
†My address is Great Neck, L.I.
‡There would be no Grant's Tomb.
**He probably meant there wasn't any more coffins in camp.

Moreover, if the testimonial hounds had been on the job in the good old days, posterity would be richer by pictures of Lincoln freeing the slaves between puffs and Eliza crossing the ice, accompanied by a pack of greyhounds and a pack of cigarettes.

Some twenty years ago the highest honor actors could hope for would be to have a cigar named after them. But in this effeminized day, actors, alas, are well satisfied to have sandwiches named after them.

In the last ten years, the smoking situation has undergone a decided revolution. Old fetishes and shibboleths have been overthrown: a new order of smokers rules the land.

Smoking has always been the greatest problem American men have been called upon to face. For years they have waged a fierce campaign, a campaign to convince their wives that ashes are really good for the rugs. For years we men have been struggling in vain to remove the tobacco crumbs from our overcoat pockets. A friend of mine, also a Scotchman, has the right idea. He lets the crumbs accumulate for three years—as who doesn't? At the end of this time, he cuts out the pocket and smokes it.

The matter of accessories is another tremendous problem which smokers have to face without flinching. No man is free from this evil. If he hasn't a smoking jacket, he has a pouch;* if he hasn't a pouch, he has a lighter; if he hasn't a lighter, someone is sure to give him one.

Smoking jackets quietly disappeared when lighters were invented. Only a millionaire can afford to own a smoking jacket and maintain a lighter. The upkeep of a lighter is terrific. In the first place, lighters quickly get out of style, to say nothing of getting out of order. Lighters, in the good old days, were substantial. A good two-pound lighter was the order of the day and men had to have leather pockets built in their suits.

These heavy models grew passé, however, and nowadays the latest lighters tend to slender lines and beveled ruching. A man would be as embarrassed to pull out a 1924 model lighter as he would be to carry around one of those gold toothpicks which were all the rage some years back.

In the gay 'twenty-twos and 'twenty-threes, lighters went in for fancy

*The pouch was introduced in Australia by the kangaroo.

initials. In the blithe 'twenty-fours and 'twenty-fives, futuristic designs were de rigueur. In the carefree 'twenty-sixes and 'twenty-sevens, wind protectors reared their ugly heads. And in the frolicsome 'twenty-eights and 'twenty-nines, lighters completed the cycle by again reflecting the utilitarian motif.

I can still remember the days when lighters were primarily lighters. Now they are primarily wardrobe trunks. No self-respecting lighter is complete without a watch, a mirror, a nail file, a compass, a calendar, a corkscrew, and a can opener. The latest models, I am informed by Poiret, will also have toothbrush holders. They will also once more have the small wick which was finally retained by the fashion experts after a heated argument.

It has been pretty generally accepted that bachelors are behind the great increase in smoking. Several years ago, smoking fell off considerably and bachelors scurried about in great alarm, holding conferences and appointing committees to do something about the decrease in smoking. This struck at the very roots of bachelorism. For if there was no smoking, how could bachelors have reveries? And if there were no reveries, what would be the fun of being a bachelor?

Happily, however, we can report that smoking is more popular than ever, and as a consequence, the Field Secretary of the United Bachelor Brotherhood tells us that 1929 will be a bumper year for reveries.

Be that as it may, smoking isn't what it used to be. In the days of my youth, if Father caught little Willie stealing a smoke behind the woodshed, he'd caress him with a hairbrush or a razor strap. Nowadays, when he catches him, he merely grabs the kid's coupons.

Which brings us finally to the greatest evil in present-day smoking— coupons. Coupons represent a tremendous departure from the day when beautiful reproductions of actresses were enclosed in each package of cigarettes. These pictures, beyond all question, constituted Early American Art. Each man was a collector and didn't need Sir Joseph Duveen to tell him when he had a real masterpiece. Coupons can never take the place of the good old cigarette pictures.

Nowadays they don't give art studies with cigarettes, but they give everything else, except tobacco. You can get a good gift from the coupons but you can't get a good smoke from the cigars. In fact, most of the cigars are so bad these days, it would be much better to save the cigars and smoke the coupons.

~

My Poor Wife

(*Collier's*, December 20, 1930)

In this tongue-in-cheek appraisal of his first marriage, Groucho revealed more than he intended. "The curse of my profession" was a constant need to be funny, on and offstage. Ruth Marx disliked being the butt of her husband's jokes, and her "beautiful patience" soon wore thin. Although the marriage endured for two decades, the couple's disagreements grew less and less amusing as she sought solace in alcohol.

~

The lady—a new acquaintance—tittered as she was leaving our house. Turning to my wife, she said: "If laughing makes people fat, how do you manage to keep your figure? Why, you must spend most of the time in hysterics, having a comedian for a husband."

My wife smiled, or rather tried to smile, and I felt ashamed. I knew how many times Ruth had heard the jests, wisecracks, and puns that I had uttered during the evening, and I wondered how long her beautiful patience could last.

How often (I couldn't help thinking), how often she must have wished she had married a plumber or an undertaker, who, although he might talk shop at home, would hesitate to work at it after hours! I had seen my wife wince when I told the story (again) about the Scotchman who painted red stripes on his son's thumb so the child would think he had a peppermint stick. She had heard the story five (possibly six) times before, even though it was, I still hope, new to our guests. She had even laughed a little during the second and third recitals of the anecdote. And the second time she had actually directed the conversation to small talk about thrift.

But there are limits to human endurance. . . . Oh, I know that a theater usher has to hear the same jokes as often as two and three hundred times a year (when the show's a hit); but then that's the usher's job. And I doubt that my wife could have been happy as an usher.

Then why, you ask (and it's about time you were taking an interest in what I'm saying), why do I tell and retell these trifling japes and nifties? Why don't I become a quiet, unclownish husband like Mr. Smith, the grocer, or Mr. Jones, who delivers our coal?

Dear, dear reader, you are now going to hear about the curse of my profession. When a man is in the comedy business, people expect him to be comical at all times. A violinist can leave his fiddle at home; a pianist can forget to bring his music; but a comedian has no excuse. If he isn't conspicuously funny, he's regarded as a rather dull and disappointing fellow.

Let a stage clown go to a party and completely forget his profession, and people will say: "Oh, he's all right behind the footlights, but isn't he uninteresting when you meet him? I suppose he just isn't a natural comedian." Whereupon the poor man develops a first-class inferiority complex and begins slinking down alleys for fear that a mad critic will bite him.

There are, of course, a few men—men braver than I—who are in the business of being funny and yet will not hesitate to indulge in a quipless evening, no matter how many eager auditors are around them, hopefully waiting for something to laugh at.

Ring Lardner, for example, is one of the wittiest men in America; certainly he is the most humorous. But when away from his typewriter, Ring is content to be as solemn and unfunny as a New England preacher dedicating a new funeral chapel. I have spent evenings with Lardner when he didn't say one funny thing. I have spent evenings with him when he didn't say anything at all.

George Kaufman is another of America's First Wits; and he, too, is considered a grave gent by people who meet him for the first time. "Great playwright," they say of George, "and a funny writer, but he didn't say one amusing thing all evening."

And I ought to cite Ed Wynn, too, among the heroic gentlemen in the comedy business who can (when away from the theater) puff at their pipes and ask whether Radio [RKO] is likely to go up a few points during the next day and how do you think the Giants will hit the old apple around next season?

Courageous men, Lardner, Kaufman, and Wynn. How my wife must envy their wives!

Not, of course, that she wasn't sufficiently warned before our marriage. Ruth was a dancer (I might add, a good dancer; in fact, I'd better add, a good dancer) in our vaudeville act when we met; and, although I tried to keep her from hearing me repeat my offstage comedy in our courtship days, I wasn't altogether successful. You see, we were almost constantly together. And I was weak. I couldn't always resist making fresh use of a good anecdote, or what I considered a snappy bit of repartee, whenever there was a new listener to hear it.

The wedding itself might have changed Ruth's mind, but it didn't. It was the only comical wedding I have ever attended.

We were married in Ruth's home in Chicago; and of course my brothers (also in the comedian business) were present. Harpo was in a particularly mirthful mood.

Just as the clergyman—he was a most dignified old gentleman—began to say the words that were to make Ruth my wife and permanent audience, he coughed and made a funny noise with his throat.

Unfortunately, it was just such a sound as that which served as a signal for a comedy bit in our show. On the stage, when the straight man did an "er-r-r-r," Harpo would pretend to become frightened and would quickly fling himself under the carpet.

Yes, it happened at the wedding. The clergyman had no sooner cleared his throat than Harpo was under the carpet; the wedding became giddier than any skit I have ever seen in the revues. Everybody but the clergyman laughed.

As Harpo left his hiding place under the rug, Chico began wishing me luck in Italian dialect, and Zeppo asked the preacher if it would be bad taste for him to sing a little ditty about his yearnings for Alabammy.

I, of course, had no part in these monkeyshines. It was my wedding, a solemn day in my life. A day of dignity. And it's only because Ruth's memory isn't as good as mine that she says I answered the preacher in Moran-and-Mack fashion.[1] Oh, I might have walked up to the altar doing a modified fox-trot (I was rather proud of my dancing in those days) but I did not—I most certainly did not talk like Moran and Mack.

For my part, I can only wish that my comedy during our married years had been easier for Ruth to bear. To be sure, she has never once complained. More often than not, in fact, she has encouraged me.

I can remember (with no pride at all) remarking that I could tell the age of a chicken by the teeth. "But a chicken has no teeth," Sam Harris—I think it was Sam Harris[2]—said, and I replied: "No, but I have." There was a round of laughter in the room.

Personally, I thought this a pretty terrible crack, but the Marxes believe that the customer is always right.

The next time we had chicken for dinner, and a few friends at the house, I found myself saying once more that I could tell the age of a chicken by the teeth. And it was Ruth—Ruth herself—who said, "But a chicken has no teeth."

But to be perfectly honest with you, I must confess that I brought up the subject of a chicken's age three or four days later. . . . And it was four months before my wife served chicken again. She said she had grown tired of poultry, but down in my heart I knew.

It is with honest humility that I am citing my worst offenses in after-working-hours comedy, because I want you to know the extent of my wife's grievances. I can remember when Reigh Count—or was it Man o' War?—won the Kentucky Derby in the rain, and the papers referred to him as a good mudder. And I said, "And does the mudder eat his fodder?"

Well, George White,[3] who was present at the time, had won a few nickels on the horse. Consequently he was in good humor at the time. He laughed. And you can't guess how laughter can spoil a comedian.

The next night, when Reigh Count was mentioned again, Ruth said—very slyly I thought—"He's an awfully good mudder, isn't he?" Dear, dear Ruth! That, I knew, was my cue. So quick as lightning—as though the thought had just struck me—I went into my little joke.

Four days later, when Eddie Cantor mentioned the Kentucky Derby, Ruth neatly changed the subject. Nothing was said about mudders and fodder.

Then there was the time when we went fishing in Long Island Sound and the man who rented the boat and fishing equipment said the bait would cost us eleven dollars. I said it would be cheaper to cut up the children for bait; and Ruth became annoyed. She said it wasn't a nice thing to say; the man might take me seriously; and . . . anyway, I knew she was right. But my objection to the remark was it had fallen pretty flat. The boatman merely stared at me and held out his hand for the eleven dollars.

I am not, to be sure, always weak. Only a month ago when the grocer talked about the "pesky kids" who swiped cherries from in front of his store, I restrained myself from asking if a pesky was a skeleton key in Russia. And never—may I never hear another laugh if I'm lying to you now—have I said that the best way to tell a bad egg is to break it gently.

Because I wear a painted mustache and a comical costume on the stage and in the movies, I seldom am recognized by strangers. Which is quite a handicap (or maybe a blessing) for some of my offstage comedy.

You see, people are always a little quicker to laugh at a professional funnyman than they are at a person in another profession or business. When we moved to Great Neck, I went to one of the village confectioners and asked for some candy for the children.

"Just a few dainties to make the kiddies sick," I told the clerk and he gave me a frigid stare—and the candy.

A month later, after the confectionery man had learned that I was a comedian, I happened to drop in for more candy.

"The kiddies want to get sick again," I said, and the clerk shook the counter with his laughter. Surely this wasn't a funny remark. Certainly it wasn't any more amusing than when I had said a similar thing before. But the fact that I was a comedian made a difference.

Now this confectioner chuckles when I merely walk into his store. He has, I think, a frustrated yearning to be some comedian's "straight man," or foil.

Ruth has no such wish.

For ten years she has been listening to my oft-repeated flippancies; she has heard me say the same things again and again—serious things as well as skittish.

Even all this—all that I have been telling you—Ruth has heard before.

I'm sorry for my wife.

[1]George Moran and Charlie Mack were a popular vaudeville minstrel act who performed in blackface and affected stereotypical black speech. Ed.

[2]Sam Harris was a prominent theatrical producer whose many hits included *The Cocoanuts* and *Animal Crackers*. Ed.

[3]George White was a vaudeville dancer, writer, and producer. Ed.

Bad Days Are Good Memories

(*The Saturday Evening Post*, August 29, 1931)

Like most comedians, Groucho had a trying childhood. Like most comedians, he looked back on those early days through a scrim of nostalgia. While he and his brothers went through the travails of vaudeville, they had a litany of complaints, from bad hotels and hostile theater managers to inadequate rundown theaters in the sticks. Some twenty years later, every failure was good for a laugh—and for some money from magazine editors.

"And what," asked the young newspaper reporter, as he took a chair in my dressing room and set fire to his pipe—surely tobacco could not have given off such an aroma—"and what is the happiest memory of your life?"

"The happiest memory," I said, "is of a time when I was a boy actor, stranded in Colorado, hungry and broke."

"And did you actually enjoy being hungry and broke in Colorado?" the gentleman of the press wanted to know.

"It was dreadful," I assured him. "It was misery. That's why the memory is such a happy one."

And before I could explain the paradox, the reporter laughed. Not, of course, that he was amused by the remark; he wasn't in the least. His chuckle was merely a gesture of courtesy; a bow to my years as a professional comedian.

But I was in earnest. It only happens about once in twenty years—well, twice if you're going to quibble—that I want to talk about memories, and here was one of the times. When I tried to point out why I delight in remembering the least agreeable experiences of my life, the reporter only laughed again. Then he promptly changed the subject. Did I think the talkies would ever replace the stage? Well, that was a pretty personal question and I'd have to talk it over with my wife. Did I plan to play Hamlet? No, we couldn't think of playing any town under a hundred thousand—not with road conditions as they are. And thus the conversation was dragged away from the subject of memories. Now don't think I'm going to be so easy this time. You may laugh if you like, but you're not going to change the subject. I'm here to talk about memories, and nothing—except possibly a hurricane, or maybe the editor—can stop me.

For me, a happy experience does not necessarily mean a happy memory. On the contrary, I am sometimes jealous of my past.

If I enjoy recalling the days when my diet was regulated—and oh, how rigidly!—by my purse, it is because such recollections add a zest to such a simple thing as a well-cooked, well-served dinner. On the other hand, if I get no pleasure in remembering how I once was able to consume, with ecstatic gusto, four or five hot dogs at one sitting, it is because I can't do that anymore.

No, the eating of five consecutive hot dogs is not a particularly important accomplishment—I mention it only as an easy symbol, as the first example that comes to mind; and because I still feel rather ill from the effects of one handsome frankfurter eaten at lunch two hours ago.

What I'm trying to say is that boiled mutton is pretty poor stuff to a man with caviar memories.

I'm not one who looks back with a wistful yearning at the good old days of the theater. When I think of my early years as an actor, I think mostly of tawdry boardinghouses; jobless weeks—even months; wages that barely paid for the simplest requirements; and of theater managers who thought nothing of bringing your act to distant towns, then canceling you after the opening performance.

Canceling was the dread of every small-time performer. It meant that after you had traveled miles, at your own expense, for three or four days' employment, you were likely to be dismissed after the very first show. For in those days the manager was the czar of his theater. If he didn't happen to like your songs, or jokes, or the way you combed your hair, he could cancel without a moment's notice.

In the dressing rooms—where there were dressing rooms; I can remember changing my clothes in a yard back of a theater—we would come across signs like this: DON'T SEND OUT YOUR LAUNDRY TILL THE MANAGER SEES YOUR ACT.

But canceling wasn't the manager's only prerogative. If your work displeased him during any performance, he assumed the right to fine you any amount that struck his fancy. When you were found smoking in your dressing room, that usually meant a fine of five dollars—and a fight on payday, because actors never accepted the fines very willingly.

The actors' associations, and the improved contract laws, have put an end to the powers of despotic little theater men. Now, when an act is engaged for a week, it gets paid for a week. It is the booking man's duty to know what it is he's engaging before the contract is signed.

But I'm wandering a little from my subject. . . . Here are the ten happiest memories that occur to me—heartbreaking little experiences that have done something to make my later years more pleasant.

1. Sometimes when the audience likes our performance and there is laughter and maybe applause, I like to think of that night—that horrible night—we were known as the Three Nightingales: my brother Gummo, who has since quit the theater to become a manufacturer and if business doesn't improve, he'll soon quit being a manufacturer; a soprano; and myself. Harpo, Chico, and Zeppo had not yet gone on the stage.

I know now, as I faintly suspected then, that the Three Nightingales were not very good. At any rate, the managers seemed to agree that we did not belong on the two main programs which were given each day in the leading vaudeville theaters. We were among the beginners or second-raters—or both—who appeared, four times a day, on the fill-in programs which kept the theaters going from one o'clock to eleven at night.

When the Nightingales came out to sing, there was seldom anyone in the audience, for apparently our reputation had preceded us. So it was very depressing, singing our snappy ditties and amorous ballads—songs we had rehearsed for hours—to a dead silence. Did I say silence? Well, I was thinking only of applause. The house wasn't actually silent, because we could always hear—even when we sang—the footsteps of the boys who walked up and down the aisles putting chocolate in the slot machines that were attached to the back of the seats.

"Love me," I'd sing out very coyly at our soprano, and there'd be a loud, disconcerting clunk as another empty candy box snapped open, ready to be refilled. It was most discouraging.

But finally our Big Opportunity came. One of the two-a-day acts had failed to arrive and the manager of Keith's Boston Theater—it was then known as the Cradle of Vaudeville—told us we were going to be used in this main evening performance. If we were good, it meant that we'd be two-a-day players from then on.

It was 8:10. The audience was in the theater. I think it was the first audience we had seen in about six weeks.

"It's a cinch," Gummo said to me, and I shook his and the soprano's hands.

She patted us both on the shoulder, and I could feel her hand shaking nervously.

Well, the orchestra struck up the introduction, a thrilling sound; the soprano walked on the stage alone, to sing the verse of "Love Me and the World Is Mine." And Gummo and I, taking turns looking through the peek hole at the side, could see that the audience was at least interested. When the verse was finished, Gummo and I, slickly attired in white yachting outfits, with artificial flowers in our lapels, marched in from opposite sides of the stage to join in the chorus with our trick harmonies and barbershop chords, which we thought were pretty hot.

The chorus of "Love Me and the World Is Mine" jumps from B flat to C, and the soprano inadvertently leaped to E flat. And she leaped alone; for Gummo and I had rehearsed the chorus in C, and no soprano was going to get us to change.

The audience laughed—more at our comic nervousness than at the botching of the song—and we went on singing, vaguely hoping that a bolt of lightning would suddenly appear to strike us all dead, or that our soprano would change her mind and return to the key of C.

Never before had I known such anguish; for, besides the humiliation of being laughed at—even the musicians were laughing—we knew that our chance to become two-a-day players was being tossed away by a note and a half. It was sad, bitterly sad; because if there is one talent that young people have in common, it is a talent for suffering.

And so the next week found us at the Howard Theater in Boston, where the second-rate variety acts went on before, between, and after the burlesque shows. For that week, the manager had booked the Jeffries–Johnson fight films and, because there was no other place for us on the program, it was decided that we were to do our singing during the showing of the films.

We were—let's face it—the vocal accompaniment for a prizefight picture. And while the audience was yelling at the fighting gladiators on the screen the three broken Nightingales were chanting, "How'd you like to be my sweetheart?"

2. What success we have had with our screen comedies has been all the more gratifying because of that unhappy venture, years ago, when we decided to produce a picture of our own.

Chico, Harpo, Zeppo, and I each contributed a thousand dollars; and similar amounts came from the author, Jo Swerling, and two friends who would rather be nameless, although their names are Al Posen and Max Lippman. To be sure, the art and business of making movies were profound mysteries to all of us, especially to Jo, who, maybe because of this, has since become a celebrated Hollywood author. But our lack of knowledge and experience did not keep us from going ahead. And go ahead we did—to Fort Lee, New Jersey, where somehow or other the picture got itself finished.

I was the old movie villain, Harpo was the Love Interest—and these weren't the only things wrong with the production, which, I'm rather ashamed to say, was called *Humor Risk*.

So the seven cheerless producers gathered in the projection room with notebooks, cigars, and heavy hearts. None of us was very hopeful about the proceedings, but we said, without really believing our words, that, "you can't tell until an audience sees it. We'll get the thing previewed in some theater around New York and then we'll know if we've got a picture or not."

But we knew what we had, and so did the managers who viewed *Humor Risk*. Not one of them wanted the picture shown in his theater. We even offered to pay a small rental, but the managers seemed to be too considerate of their audiences. It was Chico—it was always Chico— who found a weak-willed exhibitor in the Bronx who was willing to let us show our picture in the afternoon, when the audience consisted mostly of backward children.

The Marx Brothers in *Humor Risk*. . . . The title was flashed on the screen, and the seven producers were seated in their chairs, waiting for the verdict of the children. "Children," we told ourselves, "have instinct for drama."

It must be true, because never before—or since—have I seen so many screaming children run up and down the aisles. When the picture began Benny, in the fourth row, would recognize Sammy sitting in Row L, and the two would shout hellos, and then join in running up and down the aisles. Unless it was wholly imagination on my part, I think that the manager ran with them.

And so the preview was over. The producers, actors, author, and director walked out of the theater, saying not a word.

"What'll I do with the film?" said the weak-willed little manager, who was now man enough to be ashamed of his weakness. "What d'ya want me to do with the film?" he repeated, when he heard no answer.

I think he was being polite, for he knew very well what to do with the film.

And so, silently and sadly, we walked out into the afternoon and—for several years—out of the movies. We tried to forget *Humor Risk*, but it remains one those memories.

3. No, I'll never forget the humiliation of that night in Washington Courthouse, Indiana. My brother Harpo had become an actor, joining Gummo and me in the Three Mascots, which was heralded as one of the Three Big Acts on the local bill.

Besides the Mascots, the Three Big Acts consisted of a lantern-slide troubadour and an unmanned player piano, which performed its entertainment when the manager put a nickel in the slot.

Not surprisingly, the lantern-slide singer became temporarily drunk, and the manager hurried backstage to ask if one of us could take his place. I was about to volunteer, when Harpo, who had never sung a solo note in his life, stepped in ahead of me.

It was an embarrassing spectacle. The song was of the 'neath-the-old-cherry-tree-sweet-Marie school, and it might have been all right if Harpo had known either the words or the tune. Bur perhaps the mellowness of years makes me exaggerate in Harpo's favor. The performance would have been sordidly frightful even if Harpo had known the words or the tune, because Harpo happened to be possessed of the worst singing voice I had ever heard.

When the song was finished, the manager came backstage and fined us five dollars for Harpo's work. "It'll take six months to get the bad odor out of this house after that song," he said, quite frankly.

We refused to pay the fine; but when payday came around, the manager held out five dollars of the seventy-five dollars due us—salary for the Performers, who were required to pay their own railroad fares out of this allotment. My mother sent for the chief of police, who turned out to be the theater manager's brother-in-law. He fined us another five dollars for disturbing the peace.

The ten dollars in fines amounted to the surplus we would have had after our expenses were paid. So it was a week before the Mascots had any spending money.

4. It had every indication of being a perfect week. For one thing, there was six days' work ahead of us—three days in one Pennsylvania town, and three in another, a town about eight miles away. And to the strolling small-timer, six days of consecutive work was something pretty close to a week of paradise.

The first town began as a pleasant engagement. To be sure, nobody actually agreed with the ads, which described our act—now called Fun in Hi Skule—as An Artistic Screamingly Funny Howling Masterpiece;

still, on the other hand, the manager hadn't canceled us and the audiences refrained from throwing things.

Then the blow fell. It was on the night before we were to leave town; an epidemic of smallpox had been discovered, and no one was permitted to enter or leave the town. Here was a problem. The epidemic was serious, but so was our need of work. Besides, we were still too young to regard a quarantine as reason enough for depriving the good people of the next town of Fun in Hi Skule. We decided that we'd get to that town if we had to walk, with baggage in hand—and that's precisely what we had to do. When the town was sound asleep, we sneaked out of our boardinghouses and hiked the eight miles to our next theater.

I can remember our mood of high triumph as we entered the theater—I think it was called the Bijou, because in those days most of the smaller variety theaters were called Bijou. We were still weary from the walk when we gave our opening performance, with the manager sitting in the first row, glowering at us.

When the act was over, the manager came backstage and told us we were through, canceled, unwanted. After we had walked eight miles with our baggage—through the mountains too!

We were too disappointed to argue, too amazed to protest, and much too tired to fight. Finally I managed to say, "Well, you've got to pay us for this one performance."

"Say," he said, "you're lucky not to get run out of town."

And now, as I recall the jokes and antics in Fun in Hi Skule, I think that maybe he was right.

5. From there we went to Asbury Park, New Jersey—completely broke. After our week's board had been paid in advance—six dollars for each of us—there was not a nickel—and I mean that literally—in the troupe.

Oh, the things we wanted to buy as we walked along the boardwalk from our boardinghouse to the theater! There were ice-cream cones; rich, juicy hot dogs, and popcorn—beautiful molasses-covered popcorn!

It was the molasses-covered popcorn that cast the most powerful spell.

For three days I walked by the popcorn stand, each time pausing for a look. On the fourth day I had not the strength to walk by.

I went through my pockets, although I knew very well that my only treasure was a fountain pen, which had been given to me on my thirteenth birthday. I adored this pen; it was the first gift I had ever received. As owner of this pen, I was envied by all the youngsters in Gus Edwards's act Kountry Kids, which was appearing on the bill with us.

I examined the pen; I looked again at the popcorn. The choice was not easy to make. Still, a choice had to be made.

"I'll give you this fountain pen for some popcorn," I heard myself saying to the man who presided over the stand.

"Can it write?" he asked. And I, resenting a little the impertinence of his skepticism, showed him that it could. I wrote my name on a paper bag, and how beautifully the ink flowed!

"All right, here you are," he said. I watched the pen leave my hand. There was still time to alter my decision. But my will remained weak. Besides, there already was a handful of popcorn in my mouth. It was food for the gods; it was ambrosia for a child actor. I ate it slowly.

But that night I was far from happy. I missed the fountain pen. And even now I would give anything to have it back.

6. My first experience on the stage was, I think, my saddest. I was fifteen years old when I saw an ad in the *New York World* saying a boy singer was wanted for the LeRoy Trio. Well, I had done some choir singing; my uncle, Al Shean—later of Gallagher and Shean—was an actor, and I was ambitious.

So I walked the four miles from Ninety-third Street to a tenement near Second Avenue and Twenty-eighth Street to display my qualifications before Mr. LeRoy. These consisted of a slightly changing voice and the rudiments of tap dancing.

Mr. LeRoy led us job seekers to the top of the tenement, where we sang and danced for him on the tin roof. Johnny Morris, an actor now in Hollywood, was immediately hired for his buck dancing, and LeRoy was considering me for the third member of the Trio. He liked my voice.

"Know any ragtime?" he asked, and I didn't quite know what he meant. I knew that ragtime had something to do with singing, so, snapping my fingers, I sang "The Palms," which I had just learned in the choir. And I was hired, with a salary of four dollars a week and board.

LeRoy hadn't told us that our first jump would be to Denver, and that we'd have to sit up for three nights in day coaches. But we didn't much care. It was worth a few discomforts to become an actor. Nor had LeRoy told us that we were going to be female impersonators.

Still, four dollars a week was four dollars a week, and even female impersonating was acting. We were now professionals; we were now of the theater, and we actually liked LeRoy's curious whim which required Johnny and me to have LeRoy Trio printed on our hatbands.

The Denver engagement was the first and last of the LeRoy Trio at least so far as Johnny Morris and I were concerned. It began unfortunately. On the opening performance Morris missed a few steps of his buck-dance routine, and the manager fined the act twenty dollars, which was about half of what LeRoy got for himself and his company. Remember, LeRoy had paid our railroad fares, and his own, too, to Denver.

At the end of the week there were no more bookings in sight. There was no money in the troupe. So, without saying good-bye, LeRoy left town. Johnny was able to leave too; but I was without money—alone and discouraged and without a friend for hundreds of miles.

I was no longer a professional with LeRoy Trio on my hatband. I was now a child, and I think I cried.

The next day I was lucky enough to get a job driving a grocery wagon from Victor, Colorado, to Cripple Creek. By saving most of my salary— three dollars a week—and the few nickels I earned by singing illustrated songs here and there, I soon collected enough money to buy a ticket home, with ten dollars additional for meals. The money was tucked into my grouch bag—a chamois bag that many actors used to wear around their necks—and I said good-bye to Colorado.

On the way to the train I lost my grouch bag. I thought of three days without food, and I thought of myself being carried home starved—a deceased member of the inglorious LeRoy Trio. But fortunately there were kindly old ladies on the train. There are always kindly old ladies on the trains—I think they must be provided by the railroads. From these benevolent travelers I obtained large quantities of bananas and peanuts, with an occasional sandwich too.

I returned home despondent, penniless—and with a mild rash from the excess of peanuts and bananas.

7. I remember, too, the day when my son Arthur—he was seven years old at the time—walked out on our first successful movie, *The Cocoanuts*, because the picture contained no shooting. It depressed me—not so much because he didn't care for the movie, but I was afraid he was going to become a critic when he grew up.

8. Then there was the time in Ohio when a woman came backstage and asked me if I wouldn't entertain at a little party she was giving in her home. I felt flattered. Besides, I had heard of actors who were paid handsomely for entertaining at parties.

When we got to the door of the woman's house, I heard a man's voice. "Get away from here!" he shouted. Then I heard a revolver shot, and it seemed that a bullet was whizzing by my head.

I was terrified as well as surprised. While running for the theater, I naively supposed the man was a maniac. And from one of the stagehands I learned that he was a maniac, but also a husband whose wife had a habit of meeting actors by telling them she wanted them to entertain at a party.

9. As the Four Marx Brothers, one of our first productions was a tabloid musical show called *Mr. Green's Reception*. And when I think of *Mr. Green's Reception*, I think of that mournful afternoon in Battle Creek, Michigan, when we gave our entire show with only four patrons in the audience, in a theater that seated close to three thousand.

10. I can never look at fish without thinking of that cheerless week in Atlantic City when the Three Nightingales were singing in the Atlantic City Garden. The salary for the act was forty dollars a week with board. And, while the board was certainly plentiful, it consisted of nothing but fish.

That wasn't because the theater manager—he also owned the boardinghouse—regarded fish as brain food and healthful. He happened to keep a huge fish net right below my bedroom window, and at night I could hear my breakfast, lunch, and dinner swimming into the net.

By Wednesday I detested fish. I wanted meat. By Thursday I was spending all my leisure hours in front of a roast-beef counter, sniffing at the luxurious meat which I could not buy. I began to feel something like a cannibal. I could have eaten children, or even the two unappetizing midgets who were on our bill. But instead I ate cod, halibut, and floun-der—cod, halibut, and flounder.

On the following week I ate nothing but roast beef.

I can remember when—but hold on a moment; my young son, Arthur, is coming in with a bag of molasses-covered popcorn, and I can no longer interest myself in the past.

I say, "How's the popcorn, son?"

"Pretty good," he answers.

Pretty good! . . . As though molasses-covered popcorn could be any-thing but perfect! For a fraction of a second I wonder if it would be wise for me to take away Arthur's fountain pen so that he, too, will have a happy memory when he grows up. Or should I—should I take away the popcorn? No; he knows how much I like it myself.

So I resolve to tell Arthur about that day in Asbury Park when I gave up my only treasure for the delicacy that he calls pretty good.

And while I decide that I never want him to have experiences like those, I wonder if he won't miss them a little.

"Arthur, here's a dime. Go out and get me some popcorn like yours."

Our Father and Us

(*Redbook*, March 1933)

When Groucho's affectionate memoir was written, the Marx Brothers were in rehearsal for Duck Soup, *their last film for Paramount, and Zeppo's final performance with his siblings. Much had been written about the Marxes' legendary stage mother, Minnie, but little was known about their father, Sam—*

the man the boys called Frenchy. As usual, the writer's timing
was impeccable. Less than three months after this piece was
published, Frenchy died suddenly on May 11, 1933.

He is seventy-two years old now, but his hair is still thick and black; his mustache is still trimmed in the sprightly Menjou manner, and his gay Chesterfieldian wardrobe remains the envy of all his five sons—Chico, Harpo, Gummo, Zeppo, and I.

Ever since we've been children, we have regarded him as a sort of sixth brother. We've called him Frenchy—partly because he could speak only French when he first came to this country form Alsace-Lorraine, and partly because of his passion for dancing, lively neckties, and good cooking.

I sat looking at my father at dinner the other night, when the entire family was gathered at my house. Frenchy was the most dapper man at the table; there was scarcely a wrinkle on his face, and his appetite was better than mine. We talked about things theatrical, and business conditions, but Frenchy was only mildly interested. He was wondering which of us boys would take him on for a game of pinochle.

"Darling," he said to Chico, "maybe after dinner we get out the pinochle deck, huh?"

Chico, now the business manager of the family, smiled; he had an important engagement. He was going to play bridge.

"But maybe," he suggested, "Groucho would like a game."

"Groucho is no good at pinochle," said Frenchy rather sadly—much as Joseph Conrad might have sighed, "My son cannot write." To Frenchy, my own shortcomings at pinochle have been one of the minor disappointments of his life.

However, Chico put off his appointment for an hour, and Frenchy was elated. Chuckling as he shuffled the cards, he winked at me to indicate that he was going to give Chico the trimming of his life. I looked on, without paying attention to the game. I was thinking of the extraordinarily picturesque life the Old Man has led.

His story, I thought, is the story of a happy pinochle player—a philosophic fellow who has looked at life from behind a deck of cards, and when the cards were running, found life very pleasant. Depressions have come and gone—gone and returned—during his lifetime; but Frenchy has only worried when his partner was melding four aces and a hundred and fifty in spades.

Not that pinochle has been Frenchy's only career. He has been a tailor, a salesman, a manufacturer, and—what is vastly more important—a cook and housekeeper, looking after the feeding of a large flock of stagestruck sons, while his wife served (far better than anyone else could have done the job) as their manager.

During our early years in the theater, when my mother was camping in the booking managers' offices, informing anyone who would listen that her sons had got a lot of laughs in Aurora, or that they had taken four bows in Freeport, Frenchy was at home preparing a dinner.

There was a perfect understanding between my mother and my father. When it was definitely decided that our work (when we could get it) was in the theater, a field completely foreign to Frenchy's experience, my mother became our manager. She had come from a theatrical family; her parents had been strolling magicians and musicians in Germany, and her brother Al (Al Shean, later of Gallagher and Shean) was already in vaudeville, and something of a success. So Frenchy looked after the cooking; it was his own suggestion.

And what a cook he was! His Kugel (plum pudding, our favorite dish) became the talk of the booking offices—and the talk wasn't only ours.

There were times when that Kugel got us work. For when a booking manager was only half-sold on the potentialities of the Marx Brothers, Mother would invite him over to dinner. And as he sat purring over the ambrosia that was Frenchy's pudding, Mother found her job easy. Before the dinner was over, she usually got us the assurance of a few weeks' work.

When we were living in Chicago, and playing (now and then) the five-a-day houses, Frenchy would come into our dressing room after the final matinees, with a big basket of food. There was scarcely enough time to go out for dinner, and even if there had been enough time, there probably wasn't enough money. Anyway, no restaurant could provide roast chicken or Kugel like Frenchy's.

After dinner was over and it was again our turn on the stage, Frenchy would pack his basket and rush out into the audience to provide his "prop" laugh, which nearly always proved infectious. He spent most of his spare hours in our theaters, roaring at our jokes, which he knew quite as well as we did. The prop laugh was designed not only to lead the rest of the audience to laughter, but also to fool the managers, who unfortunately soon became as familiar with Frenchy's mechanical merriment as we were.

So, at Mother's suggestion, Frenchy began hiring "boosters." A group of boosters, as they were called in those days, was a paid claque— theatergoers brought in to applaud and laugh at their employer's entertainment.

The players had to buy the tickets for the boosters, and sometimes pay them an additional dime for their time. I can remember when our act opened at the Majestic in Chicago. It was our Opportunity, our first experience on the Big Time.

"I'll go out and get some boosters," Frenchy volunteered at the dinner table.

"Get fifty," my mother said.

This large order astonished Frenchy, but he saw the wisdom of it. Furthermore he was rather proud of his proficiency in hiring talented boosters. He hoped we had forgotten the sad afternoon when he brought in those six boosters who, mistaking an earlier act on the bill for ours, yelled and stamped their feet to express approval, and remained perfectly silent when we were performing our antics. That time our act was canceled after the opening matinee. Maybe even the boosters couldn't have saved us—but Frenchy blamed himself. Later he was more careful in instructing his professional laughers and hand clappers.

So Frenchy brought in the fifty boosters, and such laughter and applause I have never heard since. And we remained on the Big Time.

It was, my mother used to say, Frenchy's Kugel that got us the job; and his boosters that kept it for us. . . .

Dinner at home—it was always something of a festival. While Frenchy was in the kitchen getting ready the dessert, my brothers and I would be gathered around the piano, rehearsing. We would try out new jokes and sing new songs, under Mother's direction.

And Frenchy, hearing a tune that he liked, would come out of the kitchen in his apron, and perhaps carrying a large spoon that always managed to leave a few drippings of whipped cream on the carpet. He would offer a gag for the act, knowing perfectly well that it wasn't going to be accepted. But he didn't mind. Let others provide the family's comedy, so long as he could supply its Kugel.

If Harpo remarked, at dinner, that he had had a good luncheon at the White Front Restaurant, Frenchy was faintly resentful. He disliked hearing anyone else's food commended. It seemed like a subtle affront to his own culinary accomplishments. He would sit down at the table, and while eating a plentiful meal himself, would glance out of a corner of his eye to see how the dinner was going. True, he delighted in hearing that someone had praised our act, but he liked also to hear a nice word for his pot roast and potato pancakes. Above all, he liked to see all the food consumed; and invariably it was.

Then followed the hurried business of clearing the table and doing the dishes, a chore in which my mother always assisted. If Frenchy raced through the job as though he was being timed by a stopwatch, it was because a Mr. Hempelmeyer, next door, was coming over for a little session of pinochle. And if Mr. Hempelmeyer or another crony couldn't come over, one of us boys would be expected to stay in for the game. Chico and Harpo were Frenchy's favorite opponents. Gummo and Zeppo were too young for the game, and I (may Heaven forgive me for it!) could not get pinochle through my head.

I was too occupied with learning the current popular songs, and their parodies. Wasn't I the tenor of the act, and hadn't that booking man promised Minnie Marx that her sons would be given a route if Groucho would learn a few new parodies?

Once, in touring small-time houses around Chicago, we were to play in the old Pekin Theater, on South State Street. This was a colored neighborhood house; and I, unfortunately, had forgotten to alter my principal parody, which had something to do with the approaching Johnson–Jeffries fight. In my ditty I had been vocally assuring my listeners that Mr. Jeffries would knock the tar out of Mr. Johnson, a prediction that was not altogether accurate.

Well, here we were, going into the Pekin Theater, and Jack Johnson was going to be in the opening audience. That meant a busy morning for me. I had to rewrite the parody, to predict that it would be Mr. Jeffries who would have the tar knocked out of him, and not Mr. Johnson.

I can still see Jack Johnson, a big ebony hulk of a man, sitting in the front left box, in a white silk shirt, with huge muscles bulging out of sleeves that were rolled up. Frenchy was in the audience with a half-dozen colored boosters, who laughed even before we said our jokes.

As I finished the first chorus of the pugilistic prediction, the phony applause of the boosters was completely unnecessary. The house shook like thunder, and Johnson, his face a large grin, was turning around, bowing to the audience.

But I had been careless; I had neglected to change one line of the second refrain. And as I approached this line, I grew panicky. How I had overlooked it during my morning's rewriting, I don't know. Anyway, there I was, about to utter a bit of sentiment to the effect that the heavyweight crown would remain on Jeffries's head. The rhyme made it impossible for me to transpose the names. So I stood there, silent and confused, while the orchestra went on playing.

Frenchy knew I was in trouble. He signaled to his boosters, who were sitting with him, and they started their bedlam of applause and cheering, which went through the house like a hurricane. Johnson was applauding too. There was no need for me to go on. I made a little speech; Jack Johnson made a little speech, and the act was "in," so far as the Pekin Theater was concerned. . . .

It was when we were very young, and living in New York, that Frenchy was in the tailoring business. He was not a particularly distinguished craftsman, because, as I have said, his heart was in pinochle and in cooking.

Occasionally he got customers, and occasionally these customers paid him for the clothes he made—but not often. Sometimes when Frenchy went out to collect some money that was due him, the delinquent customer would give him a pinochle game instead of cash; and Frenchy would feel that the trip had not been altogether in vain.

Poor collections was not Frenchy's only problem. For, what with one thing and another, Chico (the oldest of us boys) was becoming in need of funds. And unfortunately for the tailoring business, Chico had learned that, if you took a new pair of pants to a pawnshop, a man would lend you two dollars and fifty cents.

After that, Chico made frequent trips to the pawnshop.

Obviously Frenchy had to regain the pants. So Chico would be given a whipping, and the two dollars and fifty cents necessary to get trousers out of hock. Chico didn't really care for the whippings; but he was no coward, and two dollars and fifty cents was two dollars and fifty cents in any man's pocket.

Pants hocking became one of the major problems of Frenchy's tailoring establishment.

Later my father began to make suits with two pairs of pants—one for the customer and one for Chico to hock. That, I believe, was the origin of the two-pants suit in America.

Frenchy has always fancied himself a businessman. There were times when he convinced himself, usually with unfortunate results, that he had just as much talent for commerce as he had for cards and cooking.

Once he opened what was meant to be a fashionable tailoring shop at Fifth Avenue and Fifty-first Street in New York. The shop might have been successful if a bakery hadn't been opened across the street—a bakery with fancy white ovens, where you could look through the window and watch the bakers at work. This spectacle fascinated Frenchy.

We knew that if we didn't find him in his tailoring place, he would be across the street, looking in the bakery window. We knew that, but Frenchy's customers didn't. That is, if we can assume that there would have been customers. . . .The first crowd to come into Frenchy's shop were the men who came to take away the counters, the sewing machines, and the showcases.

In Chicago, Frenchy was persuaded (by a gentleman who wanted to go in business with him) to open a suit-pressing shop. For four hundred dollars they could buy a machine that would press twenty suits in an hour. So the place was opened, and the proprietors spent the first hour experimenting with the machine. They pressed the same suit of clothes twenty times, and were happy to find that the apparatus was all that the salesman had said it would be.

But it so happened that the partner, like my father, had an avocation. His was crapshooting, just as Frenchy's was pinochle. The partner used to leave in the morning with a pair of dice in his pocket; a few minutes later my father would saunter out to the cigar store nearby, where a pinochle game was always available. It was only three weeks later when a man came to call for the pants-pressing machine, that the firm was unceremoniously dissolved.

After that came other business ventures. There was, for example, the cafeteria that Frenchy opened in New York—and closed in Dallas, two weeks later. (The rest of the family was touring the Texas towns of the Interstate Circuit, and Frenchy was becoming lonesome. So he joined us in Dallas, and from there he closed the restaurant by mail.)

In making this deal, Frenchy felt (as Bernard Shaw would, too) that he had earned one thousand dollars; because the loss was only one thousand dollars, and he had expected to lose twice that much.

As a businessman his success was something less than sensational, but what of that? There is probably no one in the world who can produce Kugel or biscuits like Father used to make. And I know of no one—not even Chico—who can make a better score at pinochle.

That Marx Guy, Again

(*Variety*, August 23, 1934)

After being hammered and praised by critics in the early 1930 Groucho got his own back by mocking the Variety *reviewer wh had tracked the comedian to the backwaters of Maine. Ther he was appearing in summer stock.*

Editor *Variety*:

There are only two things that ever make the front page in Maine papers. One is a forest fire and the other is when a New Yorker shoots a moose instead of the game warden. Last week, however, they not only had a story that made the front page, but overlapped right into the sporting section.

The story was Groucho Marx had entered the legitimate, and sans mustache, black eyebrows, and insults to a dowager, had stepped into the Oscar Jaffe role in *Twentieth Century*, and created a furore that hadn't been equaled since Mansfield played *King Lear* in Portland.

When *Variety* arrived at the grocery store in Skowhegan, I quickly snatched it out of the grocer's hand (he was looking through the routes for the address of a fan dancer who had promised him one of her fans as soon as the season was over) and hastily thumbed it for the review. Well, sir, you could have knocked me over with a copy of *Harrison's Reports*. There wasn't a line about it. To be sure there were many items of interest. There was a little gem that someone was optimistic and would try burlesque in Pittsburgh, there was a piece about a girl trapeze artist that had sprained her elbow in Kansas City, and a back page telling the world that Joan Blondell always uses Lux after she has removed her cosmetic. But the important fact that I was keeping the drama alive in the Maine woods wasn't even in the obit column.

I realize that you boys are busy making book, but if you want to keep the theater breathing it might be advisable for you to occasionally get up out of those barber chairs and inject some theatrical news into that so-called trade paper of yours.

Don't forget, gentlemen, Groucho Marx in the legit is an important theatrical event and certainly rates as much space as the review you gave to the opening of a cafeteria in Cedar Rapids.

In conclusion I want to say that on my opening night in *Twentieth Century* the audience cheered for twenty minutes at the end of the first act, but for some reason or other never returned for the next two acts.

Respectfully Yours,
Groucho Marx

My Best Friend Is a Dog . . .

(*This Week*)

On occasion Groucho would imitate the offhand, self-deprecating style of Robert Benchley, The New Yorker's *resident humorist.*

*Benchley liked to take the standard props of modern life and
weave essays around them. For Groucho, then based in Long
Island, the most obvious symbol of suburban life was in his
canine, Bowser.*

A man in my position (horizontal at the moment) is likely to hear
strange stories about himself. A few years ago they were saying that I
made a pig out of myself drinking champagne out of Miss Garbo's slip-
per. Actually it was nothing but very weak punch.

And now they say I am not a dog lover. Not a dog lover indeed!

Why, if I have a friend in the world it's my Great Dane named
Bowser. We have been absolutely inseparable for years. The only reason
he didn't come with me when I went to New York recently was that he
didn't have money enough for a railroad ticket.

Meanwhile, New York is a very lonely place without my dog. Actually
so lonely that when I see a girl with a pretty dog in a hotel lobby, tears
come into my eyes and I invite the pup into the lounge for a drink.

Maybe I'm a sentimental old fool. My wife says I spoiled Bowser by
letting him sleep in my bed at home, while I slept in the doghouse outside. But I'd do the same thing again. To turn a Great Dane out of my
bed would take a harder heart than mine, and stronger muscles.

In the eight years we've been together, Bowser and I have never quar-
reled. I don't spend any more on his wardrobe than I do on my wife's,
but he has never once asked for a new collar just because Archie Mayo's
dog across the street dresses better.

Bowser has never sat in a nightclub with me and whined that George
Raft is a wonderful dancer. Just because George is light on his toes, does
that make me a heel? Let's not have a hasty answer.

I give you my word that Bowser has never said, "Dear, why don't you
take a few dancing lessons? Really, nobody does the Bunny Hug anymore."

Well, *I* do the Bunny Hug. Is it my fault that I'm crazy about rabbits?

Don't misunderstand. I am not suggesting that dogs should replace
wives in the home. That is something every man will have to decide for

himself. Personally I don't see why a man can't have a dog *and* a wife. But if you can afford only one—

Well, to help you decide, I might point out that a dog already *has* a fur coat. It lasts a lifetime. And if you and your dog ever split up, he doesn't go to court and ask for ten bones a week more than you earn.

Only once has a dog disappointed me. That was the time I took Alonzo, a big Saint Bernard, home from the studio. He had been working in a picture, earning twelve dollars a day, and he seemed lonely. I would have been even happier to get a dog with the spirit of the late Rin-Tin-Tin, who used to bring home fifteen hundred bucks a week.

However, Alonzo was a very intelligent beast and his habit of running off with our brandy was, I suppose, typical of Saint Bernards, although many of my two-footed guests have done the same thing.

I was a little annoyed when Alonzo refused to eat our food, preferring to take his meals at a nearby delicatessen. (Not that the food at our house is good; I don't want people to get that idea.) But I kept my trap shut. After all, Alonzo was earning twelve dollars more than I was getting at the time.

After he had been with us a week, I had the shock of my life. On a Saturday night, just as I got through marking the liquor-level on my brandy bottles, a little man stuck his head out of Alonzo's skin and asked for his salary—twelve dollars a day!

Of course I should have suspected that something was wrong the day my wife came into the living room with the cat. Instead of chasing the cat, as a dog should, Alonzo chased my wife.

Possibly it was this incident which gave rise to the ugly rumor that I was not a dog lover. People stopped inviting me to their homes—just as they had once before (1907 to 1940); ladies walked by without troubling to curtsy, and even my barber cut me. That hurt. Nevertheless, to me it was enough that my dog kept faith in me.

My overwhelming affection for dogs does not mean, of course, that I have no love for other pets. All my life I have had animals of one kind or another around the house, even if it was only a small distant relative, or a termite.

Once, when I was a child, I was given a pair of guinea pigs which, with only a little difficulty, I learned to love like brothers. (Learning to love my brothers wasn't easy either.)

Well, the guinea pigs settled down in our cellar and one afternoon I found the cellar floor literally covered with pets.

In those days my heart was smaller than it is now and I was able to love, at the most, no more than thirty or forty guinea pigs. I was in a quandary. Did you ever spend the afternoon in a quandary with ninety-six guinea pigs?

"Sell them," my brother Harpo suggested.

"If that," I replied, "is all you have to say, you ought never to bother to speak again."

And to this day Harpo has remained silent, and I can't tell you how pleased I've been.

Another brother, Chico, came into the cellar and he, too, said, "Sell them." (When I suggested that he, too, remain silent from then on, he compromised by offering to speak in broken English, which he, too, does to this day.)

Anyway, being overruled, I went out with Chico to a nearby pet shop and offered to sell ninety-six fine guinea pigs for twenty dollars.

"I'll do better than that," the dealer said. "I'll give you one hundred guinea pigs for nothing."

For a good, all-year-round pet, I don't believe there is anything to compare with a simple, unpedigreed chorus girl. Like the Maltese cat, the chorus girl becomes attached to any man who feeds her. But there the resemblance ends.

For, whereas you can take the Maltese cat to the basement for a saucer of milk, the chorus girl insists on eating on the roof, where there is dancing and a nine-dollar cover charge.

Not a poor man's pet, the chorus girl. But I am saving my money.

Mackerel for Xmas

(*Variety*, January, 1, 1936)

Throughout his long life Groucho had a distaste for fish. It came from a vague recollection of unpleasant meals on the road, and from one specific holiday when he expected feathers and got scales instead.

Here I am sitting at home Xmas day, clutching the swag presented to me by admiring friends and relatives. Pajamas and briar sets, sets of books, costly wines, and a year's subscription to the [Hollywood] *Reporter* (I dare you to print it).

What a racket. I have two cars, two kids, two servants, two suits of clothes, two overcoats, and two pictures to make under our present contract.

I remember a Xmas day twenty-five years ago with Mother, Harpo, Gummo, and myself. We were playing Passaic, New Jersey, at a theater called the Bijou, Majestic, or Family, and we were living at a boarding-house which had been highly touted to us by the Empire Comedy Four, and Pipifax and Panlo, boardinghouse epicures of no mean standing. The place was conducted by a lady called Mrs. Abernathy, who had sus-piciously red-streaked hair, a tightly corseted figure, and giant and phony earrings. The rates were a little higher than we usually paid — eight dollars a week double and nine dollars single American plan. But it was Xmas week, we had been working pretty steady, so what the hell.

Our first meal, breakfast, was around 11:00 A.M. and it wasn't bad. Choice of fruit, half orange, or prunes, griddle cakes, and a composition that the landlady swore was coffee. We inquired about Xmas dinner. Would it be around one or after the matinee? Mrs. Abernathy said she always had it after the matinee as the actors were then more in the mood. We gave two shows a night and, as we didn't go on until about 8:30 for the first performance, we felt that after the matinee would be perfect. It would give us plenty of time to gorge and recuperate before we panicked Passaic with that classy act known as The Three Nightin-gales.

Mrs. Abernathy had two dining rooms. One was for the townspeople (mostly bachelors, with a sprinkling of schoolteachers and clerical work-ers) and the other was for the actors. This was necessary as the actors had been known to throw food at each other in discussing material priority. Some of the boarders didn't like their food served that way. Personally we didn't care how our food was served, as long as they served it.

All through the matinee we thought of nothing but the turkey, cranberry sauce, and pumpkin pie that awaited at Mrs. Abernathy's. At five o'clock we were up and down the halls in eager anticipation of that pungent Xmas dinner. At 5:10 we were all at the table discussing routes, layoffs, agents, and Albee. At 5:30 a big dish arrived and on it was a huge baked mackerel and a dish of cranberry sauce. At first we suspected Mrs. Abernathy of having turned comic for the moment and that pretty soon this offensive dish would be removed. But there sat the mackerel and there sat us and for five minutes neither the fish nor the actors moved. And then with a bitterness too deep for violence we realized that the turkey was for the regular boarders.

The local theatergoers must have been slightly bewildered that Xmas night to see and hear five acts give a complete performance about mackerel. I doubt if a more hysterical and insane performance has ever been given in the history of vaudeville.

After the show we returned to the boardinghouse and sneaked into the kitchen, broke into the icebox, and found the carcass of a cold turkey and cranberry sauce. So there we sat, five vaudeville acts grouped on the floor of a cold dark kitchen, ravenously eating a belated Xmas dinner.

Night Life of the Gods

(*Variety*, January 30, 1940)

Like many another comedian, Groucho had highly mixed feelings about the Hollywood that made him famous and then pushed him to its margins — until he proved to be a major radio and TV star. His look at the town's manners and mores is lighthearted but contains more than a drop or two of acid.

When one considers the setup, it seems to me that this local bull pit called Hollywood has considerably less scandal than it is entitled to. Here is a town teeming with beautiful ingenues, marble-chiseled juveniles, low-priced vintage wines, and half-priced bedroom suites; it has a desert moon, a neighboring ocean, and dozens of lovely, lonely mountaintops, yet, despite all this, its Sodom and Gomorrah Crossley is lower than any hinterland cow town.

What is the reason for all this? Is sex going the way of the horse and buggy? Is a well-turned ankle less important than a well-turned phrase? Not that it matters—but where is the next generation coming from? Be calm, my friend, love is still alive and kicking, but Hollywood is too wrapped up in its groups and sets, its cliques and intrigues to bother about that little thing called love.

To begin with, there is the young whippersnapper group. This is the sixteen to twenty-one crowd. The studios pair them up like horses at a state fair and they are instructed weekly with whom they are to go and when to announce their engagements. They are usually snapped with their current fiancés, holding hands at a nightclub, sharing a nutburger at a drive-in, or gingerly holding a tennis racket at El Mirador. The fact that they have never played tennis has nothing to do with it. It gives them a chance to pose in shorts, and besides, there's a sort of unwritten publicity law that all young starlets (as they are revoltingly called) must be photographed at some time in their young careers brandishing a tennis racket. If the lenser is particularly ingenuous, he poses them peering coyly through the gut. This is tops in photography, as it combines both sex appeal and sport! This crowd also goes in for mass bowling, serenading each other on roller skates, and officially greeting visiting Washington Congressmen. . . .

Then there is the gambling group! They bet on anything—a card came, a roulette wheel, whether their next kid will be a boy or a girl, local and national prizefights, the horses, African golf, the market, baseball, and most of all, football. The football chatter usually starts around July in the studio commissaries and ends up the following January at the Rose Bowl. They bet on punchboards, lotteries, high and low scores, and have even been known to make book on how many collective pounds a team will shed in one afternoon. These boys go in for plenty of check kiting and financial legerdemain and their mornings are usually spent in a bank trying to square things with a brace of vice presidents.

Then there is the cultural or white-tie-and-tail crowd. They spend half of their lives running to the Philharmonic to hear lectures, concerts, symphonies, to see dancers from Bali and Monte Carlo, and, in fact, anything that promises a high-hat opening. They take French and Spanish courses at the local universities; they specialize in first editions and Old English plate; they rush over to Pasadena for Maxwell Anderson and Shaw, and will entertain any visiting lecturer who can be induced to stop over for dinner or cocktails. They won't attend a preview unless there is a canopied awning in front of the theater, a red-carpeted sidewalk of at least four hundred feet from their limousines to the main entrance, and a grandstand of not less than three thousand admiring yokels. In addition to this, the theater manager has to guarantee in writing that when the show is over the carriage starter will bellow their names in an English accent for not less than five minutes.

The busiest and most voluble group, however, are the social-conscious kids. They go to a meeting every night—any kind of a meeting will do. If it's a cause that they agree with, so much the better; but their theory is, any cause is better than none. At the drop of a hat, they'll boycott anything. It's a night lost when they don't issue an official white paper, denouncing something. They have you slaphappy signing papers, petitions, and protests. It's all very confusing and frequently you find yourself sending money to both sides of a great cause. Unless you are exceptionally strong-minded, you eventually belong to more organizations than an insurance agent soliciting the Sons and Daughters of I Will Arise.

And now we come to the final crowd—the old guard! Somebody once said: "The old guard dies, but never surrenders!" Well, this crowd has done both. They are known as the low blood pressure group. They all have minus thyroid, leaping arthritis, and droopy eyelids. Their idea of a ducky evening is to sit around and discuss their symptoms. Insomnia is their favorite topic and, at the slightest provocation, they will reel off hours of evidence to prove they haven't slept a wink in weeks. They subsist largely on a diet of aspirin, vitamins, and shots in the arm. They swallow tablets all night to put them to sleep and chew benzedrine all day to keep them awake! They are easily recognized on the street—they all walk with a little jerk and a slight toss of the head like Lionel Barrymore in his last five pictures. They see their dentist twice a year and their doctor twice a day; they take daily messages and scalp treatments and spend more money on X rays than they do on jewelry.

So you see, love staggers along out here under many handicaps. It's doubtful if even Tommy Manville[1] would thrive under these conditions, and that, gentlemen, is the acid test! So if you think the scandal from the Western Front is a bit on the dull side, don't blame it all on Vine Street.

[1]Other than his wealth, Tommy Manville, heir to the Johns Mansville asbestos fortune, had only one claim to fame: he married thirteen times. Ed.

What This Country Needs

(*This Week*, June 16, 1940)

Groucho was never known as a political comedian, but as Franklin Delano Roosevelt prepared for a run at a third term, there was much speculation about the president's choice of running mate. To mock the many trial balloons being floated, Groucho whimsically added his own, then popped it.

I want to say at the outset that I am not a candidate for anything. The Marx-for-Vice-President boom never had my support, nor did it ever get very far. It was launched by an obscure Californian who was politically inexperienced and, incidentally, very drunk.

The whole thing was nothing if not spontaneous. I was at an obnoxious little dinner party the other evening, talking about world affairs, when this fellow said suddenly, "Let's run Groucho Marx for vice president."

Naturally I was touched, but only for five dollars, and that came later. At the moment, I asked why I should be singled out for this honor; why should my friends want me to be vice president?

"Because," snarled my sponsor, "the vice president generally keeps his mouth shut. It might be an interesting experience for you."

So you can see that the boom didn't get a good start, which is just as well because, as I say, I'm not a candidate for any office.

But don't get me wrong. This isn't any false modesty. If somebody wants to start another boom, the vice presidency is right up my alley, although I'll admit it might take a little time before I could manage to listen to the Senate every day.

I remember that about twenty years ago a vice president made himself famous merely by announcing that what the country really needed was a good five-cent cigar. Now that's more in my line. As a matter of fact, I've been making a few notes about what the country needs and, regardless of politics, here they are:

Frankly, I don't believe we need a thirty-dollars-every-Thursday plan, because Thursday is such a bad day. In the first place, the maid is out; Junior has the car, and—but there's no point to rehash a measure that's already in the ash can.

But the nation does need, for one thing, a good ham sandwich. I refer to the simple, old-fashioned (now obsolete) single-decker ham sandwich which was a national institution until the druggist, with his passion for mixing things, ruined it for us.

As an experiment, I went into a drugstore yesterday and ordered a ham sandwich.

"Ham with what?" the clerk asked.

"Coffee," I told him.

"I mean," he said, "do you want the ham-and-tuna combination, the ham-sardine-and-tomato, or ham-bacon-and-broccoli? And will you have coleslaw or potato salad?"

"Just ham," I pleaded. "A plain ham sandwich, without even tomato or lettuce."

The young man looked bewildered, then went over the drug counter to consult with the pharmacist who glowered at me suspiciously until I fled.

That's the sort thing the country is up against.

Another of our direst needs is a coat to carry tobacco without making it necessary to carry a bulky, bulging pouch. It has been suggested that tailors make suits out of tobacco so that, if you wanted to fill your favorite pipe, you would merely have to tear off a piece of the material and plug it into the bowl.

This is unsound on the face of it, because a suit, with its lapels smoked off, would be highly impractical. Where would you wear your campaign button or elk's tooth?

My suggestion is that only the *vest* be made of tobacco, because the vest is an otherwise useless garment. It isn't ornamental and it doesn't give much warmth. I believe that a nice mild, Burley-cut vest, trimmed with Turkish, would add a great deal to the comforts of the American man.

In designing this outfit, some enterprising tailor could also supply another need: A pair of pants that would automatically hide at night so that your wife couldn't possibly know where you were caching your bankroll.

Making your pants vanish may sound a trifle visionary, but I have been making quite a bit of progress with the idea. I've already succeeded in making my shirt disappear, merely by sitting down at the bridge table with my wife. I know a fellow who bid two hearts with only three quick tricks in his hand, and his *wife* disappeared.

That, of course, solved his problem. He could then hang his pants out in the open at night. But this solution is not to be recommended generally, because I believe that wives have a definite place in the home. They're invaluable as mothers, and also for keeping you informed when the lady next door gets a new car, or a fur coat, or is taken out dancing. Wives are people who feel that they don't dance enough. Give them their way and you won't have to hide your pants at night, because there'll be nothing in them to conceal.

The country also needs the old-fashioned corset which was laced up in the back. It's simply ridiculous to say that the present-day girdle serves the same purpose, because it doesn't. Why, thirty-five years ago, the wasp waist meant something to a man. It gave him his daily exercise, tightening up his wife's laces. But now the girdle is here and we're becoming a nation of softies.

(My wife has just informed me that the old-fashioned, laced-in-the-back corset *is* here, so disregard the whole paragraph. On second thought, I feel that the American man exercises too much. He doesn't get enough peace and repose.)

We need two oxen in every garage. *There!* I've said it. Not that I don't realize it will mean a political break with the automobile industry (I need any kind of break I can get), but because I wouldn't be worthy of a vice presidential boom if I didn't have the courage of my convictions, both of which were for parking forty minutes in half-hour zones.

That's the problem: parking! With oxcarts, our great-grandfathers had nothing to worry about. Although it took them an hour to drive six miles to the downtown shopping district, they could immediately pull up in front of any store they chose. And, while we can drive the same distance in ten minutes, it takes an hour to find a place to park. That gives the ox a clear ten-minute advantage over the automobile.

Of course I realize that no ox is as good-looking as one of the 1940 sport models (the yellow, snappy job): also that it might be a little inconvenient trying to buy hay at a filling station. But we cannot overlook the fact that ten minutes saved every day amounts to 3,650 minutes a year, or sixty hours and fifty minutes. And that time, properly used—say on the radio by Charlie McCarthy—is worth approximately $250,000. And while $250,000 ain't hay, it would feed a lot of oxen.

Another national need is laundries that will send you a sheet of pins with every shirt, instead of making you pick the pins, one at a time, out of the collar; or (if you don't see them in time) your neck. My own laundryman and I have an understanding. Every time he sticks me with a pin, I stick him with a bad check. His cries of anguish can be heard from Culver City to my bank in Beverly Hills.

We need, too, a vacuum cleaner that won't scare the daylights out of you by whining like a Boeing bomber wherever you try to snatch a brief four-hour nap in the afternoon. At considerable expense and bother I've managed to solve the problem in my own home but, as you will readily see, it is far from the ideal solution.

I've placed land mines around my bedroom door. (Neutrals, of course, have been warned.) Thus, if a cleaner zooms within twenty feet of my room, it'll be a good joke on our maid. The only disadvantage is that, after a direct hit, you have to get a new vacuum cleaner. And of course a new maid.

Another of the country's needs—a project nearest to my heart—is a federal school for lovemaking. Under GMP (Groucho Marx Plan), girls would be taught to sigh like Garbo, smile like Myrna Loy, and pout like Ginger Rogers; and men to moon and roll their eyes like Charles Boyer.

I'd been practicing the eye-rolling business at home, but under a serious handicap. My wife asked me to stop, because it was frightening the children. So I've resigned myself to remaining the Gary Cooper type (with spectacles). Although the resemblance between Gary Cooper and myself is often commented on, I believe he's a little too tall and has too much hair on his head. And yet I feel that he is even more the Gary Cooper type than I am.

In the theatrical world I feel that we need a chain of movie houses where there are no movies, so a housewife can get her free dishes and turkey without delaying dinner. It's getting so that some women, not having time enough to sit through two pictures, go to department stores for their crockery. This is hurting show business. Now I'm not suggesting that movies be done away with. They could very easily be shown in the dish stores and poultry markets.

I would like to see a call bureau established, so anybody who wants a fourth in bridge can get immediate satisfaction. I don't know why it is, but bridge players have a habit of convening in threes; and there is nothing in the world so futile and bitter as three bridge players.

They'll call you up and, although you insist you can't play, that you loathe the game, and that you're in bed with a fever which the doctor says has a good chance of developing into pneumonia, they become savage and accuse you of trying to ruin their evening. They keep phoning until, out of desperation (and perhaps your mind) you put on woolen underwear and a mustard plaster and get to their table.

Then, after your first card is put down, your partner immediately winces. You've betrayed him. He had wanted you to lead a spade. He takes it for granted that you're an expert in mental telepathy who is maliciously lying down on the job. He assails your character, and intimates that to call you an idiot would be flattery. Why didn't you go up with your King, instead of your fever, doubled and redoubled? So you write out a check for $12.70 and trudge home to bed where the doctor smiles, very pleased with himself. His prediction has come true. You've got pneumonia, which means you won't have to be a fourth again for at least three weeks—or ever, if that call bureau is established

One thing more. The country needs men's hats that can be neatly folded and put away in your pocket so you won't have to buy them back from the hatcheck girl. In fifteen evenings out, I have paid $3.75 (at two bits a night) for the return of an old fedora that originally cost only $2.95, and for which no haberdasher would now give me thirty cents. Obviously that's bad business, and what we need in Washington are businessmen. See what I mean? . . .

"Folks, go to your neighborhood politician and ask for a nice, warm, mellow Groucho Marx for vice president."

Sh-h-h-h!

(*This Week*, November 23, 1941)

In the belief that many a truth is told in jest, Groucho wrote a lighthearted piece about sleeplessness. It disguised a deep concern; he suffered from chronic insomnia and never did find a cure. That was one reason why he was so well read: many nights were spent perusing the classics in the vain hope that they would make him drowsy.

There are few subjects of conversation that will keep a mixed crowd interested for any length of time. If you touch on baseball, business, or the likelihood of an increase in the price of long underwear, most of the women will yawn and slink over to the punch bowl. If the subject turns to facials, salad dressings, or whether the new winter hats will be worn over the eye or over the hook in the closet, most of the men will start pitching pennies or wrestling with the host's Great Dane.

However, there is one subject that both sexes enjoy discussing: insomnia.

Just let someone casually groan that he didn't sleep a wink last night and guests who have been dozing for hours blink back to life again;

eager, bloodshot eyes begin searching the room for sympathetic listeners.

The insomniacs are a weird breed. They may quarrel about politics, movie stars, and the potency of vitamin capsules, but they unanimously agree that there is nothing as deadly as those long hours between midnight and morning—and they'll eagerly spend the rest of the night proving it.

I don't claim to be the top man of this eerie clan but, as an involuntary owl of many years' sleeplessness, I have acquired a mass of information that may be helpful to those upstarts who have been plucking at the coverlets for a mere eight or ten years.

To begin with, what keeps *you* awake at night? Is it a leaky faucet, your income tax for 1938, or your children bounding in around 3:00 A.M. from a triple feature at your neighborhood theater?

If it's a leaky faucet, you might as well toss in the sponge. There is no one alive who can fix a leaky faucet. My bathroom tap has dribbled for eight years and in that time hundreds of plumbers and master mechanics have clumped their way into my bathroom to peer at its relentless drip. They all prescribe the same remedy—a new washer. So a new washer is installed—a nickel for the washer and $8.35 for the labor. It works perfectly all that day, but next night, as I am drifting into space, the familiar *plop-plop* of the leaking tap jerks me back to consciousness.

A certain comely matron living in the outskirts of Zanesville, Ohio, thought she had solved the leaking-spigot problem. One night, before going to bed she hammered a crab apple into the dripping nozzle. Unfortunately her nine-year-old son, Grunion, had seen her do it, and in the middle of the night, when all was still, the sly youngster sneaked into the bathroom and cribbed the crab apple. Later that same night the matron concluded that the leaky spigot was less of a disturbance than Grunion with the colic, so she threw the whole scheme out the window.

Not all insomniacs are alike. Some midnight bed-tossers are in agony if the night is noisy, while others require all sorts of gruesome sounds to keep their eyes shut until morning.

A friend of mine, a retail dealer in provender, and a poor sleeper to boot, has worked out an idea he claims is unbeatable. Through a series of canny trades and shrewd purchases, he acquired two chronometers, three grandfather's clocks, an infernal machine, and a basketful of assorted alarm clocks. These he has planted in various parts of his room—all ticking furiously. He admits that the racket is terrific but explains happily that it keeps him from hearing the radio next door.

Now, dear reader, the bed you sleep in is important. Do you use a soft bed, a hard bed, or sleep on the floor like the Chinese?

Sleeping on the floor when half-crocked is a common practice, but how many of you have tried it when sober? It has many advantages—to begin with, you save the cost of a bed; then, there is nothing to fall out of unless you are near an open window. Also, the floor has no lumps, if it has been carefully swept. The danger of getting your foot caught in a mousetrap can be easily avoided by simply wearing overshoes—or by having a good-sized tomcat crouching in a corner of the bedroom. I'm sure I don't have to tell you how terrified mice are of tomcats.

Some people find a bath very helpful in inducing slumber. It's also an excellent way to get clean—but that's the chance you take. A friend of mine who, for some unaccountable reason, hasn't been able to sleep since the market crash in 1929, found out that if he sat in a hot tub for thirty minutes before retiring, he would quickly fall asleep. The trouble was that he always fell asleep in the bath and on three different occasions his family had to send for the emergency squad to fish him out of the water and roll him over a barrel.

Sleep is an elusive minx, and care must be taken not to frighten her away. If you pursue her too aggressively, she will turn tail and scamper off.

A girlfriend of mine has a husband named Hal who hasn't slept since they were on their honeymoon. She has tried to help him by hypnotism, reading aloud to him out of the Congressional Record—but he is stubborn and insists on using his own methods, though they fail him night after night. Now, that doesn't mean the remedies he uses are all worthless. Of course not. But some are downright dangerous. Particularly if used all in a bunch.

One evening, while playing chemin de fer with his wife, I watched Hal prepare for bed. This particular night, he tried Formation F-2: hot noodle soup, a mustard bath, three aspirins, earmuffs, and a black mask.

The following morning, weary after a sleepless night, he staggered into the living room where his wife and I were still at our game. I had forgotten about Hal and his sleep remedies and when this masked figure appeared, I thought it was a stickup. Instantly, I whipped out a derringer and shot him.

He has not forgiven me to this day.

Have you tried snaring sleep with mental games? Have you tried outwitting insomnia by trickery? Good sleep-inducers are radio announcers and counting sheep. It is best to have the sheep in your bedroom, if possible. However, if you are allergic to wool (and most of the sweaters I buy seem to be) you can also court sleep by counting panthers. In many ways panthers are preferable to sheep—it is common knowledge that sheep bleat and frequently stumble as they walk; panthers, on the other hand, tread the floor silently and are smart enough to keep their mouths shut. Of course, there is some danger that the panthers may eat you, but if you have insomnia, that is really the best thing that can happen to you.

So far, we have discussed only the physical, the less aesthetic side of sleep. But what is your frame of mind and mental condition? What thoughts are you thinking as you prepare for nightie-night? Is your mind composed and at rest or is it shooting sparks and flying off into space?

If you are married, and your wife snores and looks like a windblown witch, you unquestionably have a problem confronting you. Let's say Ann Sheridan is your dream girl—this is just a hypothetical assumption as mine happens to be Priscilla Lane—but let's say you are thinking of Ann Sheridan. Now there is nothing wrong with that. Millions of American youths are doing that all the time. But before you go to bed, you must pull yourself together and say, "Man" (or whatever your name happens to be), "this is folly. I'm married to a loyal wife, a wife who has been a staunch helpmate and provider and who has stood by my side through fair weather and foul. I have no right to be thinking of Ann Sheridan or even Priscilla Lane."

If this doesn't work, the best thing to do is to take a hot footbath and a cup of cocoa every two hours and, as soon as day breaks, hop out of bed and grab a train for Reno . . .

Let's see, there's an 8:45 train for Reno. It arrives at Stockton at 8:20

and leaves there at 8:21. This train doesn't carry a diner, but has a bowling alley and a Turkish bath. Then there's the 3:53 train that arrives in Reno at 4:42 A.M.—or is it P.M.? Gee, I'm getting sleepy. I haven't felt like this for years. I can hardly keep my eyes open.

Say! Maybe I've stumbled on something that will make insomnia as old-fashioned as a flannel petticoat. Try it sometime. Just prop yourself up in bed with half a dozen timetables and—and—ho, hum—I just can't keep my eyes open. Good night, folks—pleasant dreams!

Many Happy Returns

(*Saturday Review*, January 24, 1942)

This was a short version of Goucho's second book, published in January 1942 by Simon & Schuster.

March used to mean the beginning of spring; now it's the end of your bankroll.

That is when you have to answer the government's quiz program, a costly little game played by mail. You answer thirty-two questions concerning your public life—such as how much money you earn and where the hell is it? The only difference between this and other quiz programs is that you don't get paid for giving the right answer.

But, somewhat like the program called *True or False,* you do take the consequences for giving the wrong replies.

Having answered all the questions on the quiz, you run madly through office buildings looking for a notary public. This is a gnome with a green eyeshade and a rubber stamp who will testify to practically anything for two bits. Although he has never seen you before, he'll swear on anything from a stack of Bibles to flapjacks that you are the man you say you are, although secretly you know you're not half the man you used to be.

You're probably saying to yourself, "Why do I have to pay an income tax? What does the government do with my money?"

This is a pretty dull routine and I'd advise you to change it if you expect to get anywhere with yourself. What do you think the government does with your money? Spends it on a woman? Gets drunk? Or plays the ponies? That's what you might do with the money, or, if you have to get personal, what I do; but I can assure you that the government is not just out for a good time. It has a job to do in Europe and Asia.

Why does the government need money? Well, a steam engine will run only if you throw coal into it. Wouldn't you run if someone was going to throw coal into you?

Here is a picture* of the governmental train shooting down the track.

Now, to go a step further, I want to explain what happens to your tax dollar. Your tax dollar goes right to Washington, where, contrary to popular impression, it is not thrown across the Potomac River and caught by a dollar-a-year man who bites it to see if it is counterfeit. Nobody bites your dollar. The bite is put on you.

It has a fully equipped dining car with a full crew onboard. The President is the engineer. Members of Congress, the cabinet, the FBI, and a lot of other swell fellows are the crew. The revenue collector is the fireman who pours your coal into the engine; the Secretary of Agriculture is the dining-room steward; the Vice President is the Vice President; and Wendell Willkie is the fellow who missed the train, but is going right along with it anyhow.

You will notice the smile on Mr. Willkie's face. He is in a position to throw things at the engineer, but he doesn't because this is a democracy, which is you and I and the farmer in the Iowa cornfields, and the George Washington Bridge. Mr. Willkie merely comments constructively on the track. Is it muddy? Fast? Clear?

That is why the government needs money. And I haven't begun to list the incidental expenses, such as two Thanksgiving days, which means a double order of turkey at forty-six cents a pound, not to mention the extra cranberries.

There are two methods a government can use to get money. One is by

*Publisher's Note: What picture?
G.M.: The one I gave you.
P.N.: That one? You should be ashamed of yourself.

taxes, the other is printing. To print money requires very expensive paper (otherwise you can't use cheap post-office ink) and to buy expensive paper you have to have money. That, again, means taxes.

Besides, the printing of money means inflation, which I shall explain very briefly.

Suppose you take a gallon of whiskey and pour three gallons of water into it. Or perhaps it would be better to pour three gallons of whiskey into a quart of water. Any kind of water will do, but be sure to use hundred-proof whiskey.

Perhaps this is an even clearer explanation. Take a small glass; pour in a hooker of rye whiskey, drop in a piece of ice (unless you have your skates on), a lump of sugar, a dash of bitters, a cherry, and a slice of pineapple. This isn't much of a drink, and you would have to drink an awful lot of them to get crocked, but it makes a wonderful fruit salad. And even this is better than inflation.

I have prepared a chart showing what happens to this dollar of yours. Technically it is known as a pie chart, the dollar pie chart. The fifty-cent pie is apple, peach, or coconut custard. Just as the dollar pie shows what happens to your money, the fifty-cent pie shows what happens to your stomach.

Obviously there are a few governmental expenses I had to omit—the cost of the war, for example—because the pie was so small. Even as it is, it comes to $1.08*

You can see, though, that the government is not making a nickel on you. The government is not out to make money. If it were, would it be owing $60,000,000 to every Tom, Dick, and Harry?

I have no hesitation in saying that every government nickel is accounted for. Can you say as much for your own nickel?

*Publisher's Note: Who's counting?
Treasury Department Note: We are!

Yes, We Have No Petrol

(*Variety*, November 25, 1942)

During the early 1940s, whenever people complained about
shortages on the home front they were greeted with the reply
"Don't you know there's a war on?" That didn't stop Groucho
from his primary avocation: griping.

～

HOLLYWOOD, NOVEMBER 24

I have no desire to evade the gasoline visitation that is about to descend upon us, but don't you think the law is a little unfair to the unfortunate few who happen to own large and well-upholstered automobiles?

Back in the comparatively lush days of '37, a beady-eyed and persistent salesman cajoled me into purchasing an automobile that was considerably longer and heavier than what I originally intended buying. He told me, as he fondly stroked the fender of this shiny monster, that here was a job (they were all called jobs in those days) that would ride like a Pullman. As I wavered, he added as a final clincher, "Brother, this job has class!" And, from the look in his eye, it was quite evident that this was a commodity he didn't think I had a great deal of. At any rate, dazed by his eloquence and flattery, I soon became the owner of a luxury super-eight.

The salesman didn't lie—it did ride like a Pullman—but he didn't tell me that it was almost as heavy as one and that it sopped up gas as though its insides were lined with blotting paper. A good deal of my time was now spent at gas stations, steadily pouring fuel into this iron camel. It was quite expensive but still not particularly tragic. I had money and gas could be bought at almost every corner.

Then the blow fell—the Government decreed that nonessential workers (and no description ever fitted me so accurately) would be allotted four gallons a week—enough to propel the average motorist sixty miles in any direction. Gargantua or the Frankenstein Eight, as it was now called, laughed heartily at this estimate. He said that if I were to equip him with new spark plugs, adjust his timing, give him a downhill shove and a favoring wind, he might possibly eke out twenty-eight miles on four gallons—but sixty miles! Ridiculous! Who did I think he was—Alsab?

So here I am, stuck with an iron horse and twenty-eight miles a week while my poor but fortunate friends, who were lucky enough to buy small cars, have practically unlimited mileage. I ask the Government not to discriminate against me. It is unfair and un-American to penalize me because I once was a member of the privileged classes.

This is not a complaint—this is a plea for justice! I willingly drink chicory for breakfast, eat broiled kidneys on meatless Tuesdays, wear cuffless trousers, have my salary frozen in the dead of winter, send my cook to Lockheed, and play dead for the local air raid warden; I buy War Bonds, stamps, entertain at the Service Camps, and know the second stanza of "The Star-Spangled Banner." In return, all I ask is a fair measuring stick for my ancient ark. If I can't get that, I hereby petition the authorities to revise the local zoning laws so that I can legally stable a pair of mules in my living room.

How to Build a Secret Weapon

(*This Week*, November 7, 1943)

Censorship is anathema to today's Internet users, but during World War II it went on unquestioned. Overseas, and sometimes even stateside, the mail that GIs sent home was carefully screened for mentions of troop movements or other information that might fall into enemy hands. Groucho lampooned the whole process by blacking out his own prose.

It has recently come to these shifty old eyes that the U.S. Army has announced the Bazooka as an official weapon in World War II. That pleases me moderately because the inventor of this lethal instrument is my friend Bob Burns.[1] It seems that this Bazooka shoots rockets at enemy soldiers, and if that doesn't do the trick, it plays a few choruses of the "Arkansas Traveler" for the coup de grâce—that's French for those who care for French.

Now, I'm not one to belittle such a great achievement. But truth compels me to announce that Bob Burns's Bazooka is already obsolete! It's as out of date as a porterhouse steak. You hear it from my own lips—I who have invented the Super-Bazooka. This amazing new weapon operates on exactly the opposite principle from the old one. Briefly, where Bob Burns's Bazooka shoots rockets at Nazis, my Super-Bazooka will shoot Nazis at Bob Burns. This doesn't have much to do with winning the war, but it seems like a good idea in general.

But then, the Super-Bazooka is merely one among countless other inventions of mine. For example, Marx's Military Dice. These cubes are equipped with cleats on each face and are especially adapted for use in rocky terrain. Pull up a bayonet and sit down and I'll tell you the whole gripping story of my rise to obscurity as a secret-weapon genius.

In 1937, by popular demand, I decided to retire from public life and seek what had always been my true goal—Contentment. "A loaf of bread, a jug of wine . . ." That's how Omar Khayyám put it. As far as I'm concerned you can switch the wine for a bottle of beer (you know what kind!). And while you're about it you can switch the bread for a fat blonde.

Ah, Contentment!

But soon the bugles of war aroused me from my lethargy. In rapid succession, I was rejected by the Army, the Navy, Marines, Wacs, and Waves. I even tried to enlist in the Spars as a Sparring partner, but they said I was too feminine.

In desperation I offered myself to the Wags. However, at the induction test, I proved gun-shy and also bit a technical sergeant as he was examining my dewlaps.

For weeks I was utterly crestfallen, but one day I looked myself straight in the eye—not an easy trick with bifocals. "Am I a man or a mouse?" I demanded. (Readers are invited to send in their votes. All ballots marked Rat will be discarded unless there is cheese attached.) Anyway, I boarded a train and after three days on the road I arrived in Washington and went straight to the War Department.

"Lafayette, I am here!" I announced. They threw me out. I then buttonholed Secretary Stimson or General Marshall—I forget which one it was, but whoever it was, he told me that they were pretty well filled up at present. "Who are you anyway?" he asked.

"Who am I?" I parried. "Why, I'm America's greatest living inventor. God, sir, have you never heard of Marx's Dropped Living Rooms for Fallen Arches?"

"Why, naturally!" he cried. "And the fact is, Mr. Marx, we have an opening for an inventor."

The opening proved to be a window on the twelfth floor. In less time than it takes to tell, I was dusting off my pants on the sidewalk.

Let me skip the next three months and also the next three paragraphs. Let us take up the story again as I enter my private laboratory one dark evening in March. The reason it's dark is that I neglected to pay my light bills during those three months we skipped. I am now gainfully employed as a secret-weapon designer on a piecework basis—$22.50 per dozen secret weapons—10 percent off to wholesalers. This particular night I have been assigned to an especially difficult problem: how to fit three lieutenants and a light Howitzer into an upper berth. Howitzer like to try that?

I worked into the wee small hours, drinking Scotch and a certain brand of beer. Beads of perspiration started on my forehead and trickled down my face to my neck, forming a rather unbecoming bead necklace. I knew I was getting close but I attributed this to the Scotch. The first fifteen attempts brought nothing at all. The sixteenth produced a formula by which high-octane gasoline could be manufactured from old shoelaces. I tossed it aside with an impatient frown. My seventeenth attempt was also a failure. But finally—finally on the eighteenth attempt, I captured the magic formula! Mad with excitement I flung up my hands. One hit the ceiling and the other landed in a wastebasket. I could scarcely believe my great good luck. Rushing out of my laboratory, I ran through the house in the frenzy of joy.

"Eureka!" I shouted. "Eureka!"

Eureka is my wife. She came tripping down the stairs in her nightdress and almost broke her fool neck. After she regained consciousness, I whispered the secret to her.

Here it is in a nutshell, the famous Marx Upper Berth Theory:

▬▬▬▬   ▬▬▬▬   ▬▬▬▬   ▬▬▬▬   ▬▬▬▬▬
▬▬▬▬   ▬▬▬   ▬▬▬▬   ▬▬▬▬   ▬▬▬

I'm sorry, the censor from the War Department has just arrived. (Here, keep your fingers out of that humidor, Hawknose!) However, I'll try to give you an idea of some of my other recent secret weapons, in spite of him:

No. 387KL44Y—A double-pistoned ▬▬▬▬ for ▬▬▬ and ▬▬▬▬ which facilitates ▬▬▬ in emergencies such as ▬▬▬▬ but on the other hand ▬▬▬.

No. 58396X2D—A turbine-driven ▬▬▬▬ for the purpose of ▬▬▬▬ ▬▬▬ and in the same operation to ▬▬▬ regardless of ▬▬▬.

Well, what's the use of going on further? I'm sure this gives you a pretty fair idea of my work. It also gives you a pretty fair idea of the censor.

My greatest invention of all, though—my chef d'oeuvre—if you don't mind a little restaurant French—is as follows:

1 jigger of ▬▬▬
▬▬ of brandy
▬▬ of lemon
Dash of ▬▬▬
Ice well and ▬▬▬
Serve with ▬▬ in tall glass.

I call it the Marxotov Cocktail, and my plan is to lob it over into enemy trenches in individual thermos bottles. If this secret weapon affects Nazis the way it affects my friends, all our boys will have to do is march over their prostrate bodies.

I've only known one person who was strong enough to down a Marxotov Cocktail without batting an eye: it was the champion steamfitter of Los Angeles County, a Miss Diana Tiffin. It's interesting to see women emerging as the tough sex after all these centuries. It sounds incredible, but I know a man who recently married a furniture mover.

On second thought, that isn't so incredible. All women are furniture movers. A friend of mine married the most violent furniture mover I

ever saw. Once I visited their home and on the third day became so confused I sat down in a potted begonia and put my feet up on the French
maid.

After demonstrating the Marxotov Cocktail to a Secret Military Commission I was deluged with honors from the Government: I received the
Order of the Purple Heart, the Order of Distinguished Service, and an
order from the Collector of Internal Revenue to pay up my income tax
or else.

Shortly after this, I received a commission to solve the vital question
that is uppermost in every American's mind today, briefly: When the war
is won, what shall we do with that dirt so-and-so in Berlin by the name of
Adolf ■■■■■■■■?

(Aw, shucks, I thought that censor had dozed off. I'm sure everyone
else has. And why can't I mention ■■■■■■■ anyway? Oh, well, censors
are all a little queer. I'll just call ■■■■■■■—something else—for
instance, Willard M. Schickelgruber.)

I'll tell you what we'll do with Willard M. Schickelgruber. We'll say,
"Now look here, Willard M. Schickelgruber, we're going to let you go
back to your old job. For the next fifty years you're going to paper the
new Pentagon Building in Washington. You can start on the first floor
and paper it with paper from *Mein Kampf* and old German commu-
niqués. When those run out you can paper it with paid-off United States
War Bonds. And then, Willard M. Louse, if you can get through with
the first floor before fifty years have elapsed, you can start the second
floor!"

How's that for a peace plan? My motto is, "Buy a Bond and Keep
Willard M. Hitler Hanging!" (Let's see you censor that, Hawknose!)

[1]Bob Burns, "the Arkansas Traveler," was a radio comedian who played an odd, noisy
instrument he called the Bazooka in honor of the Army's cylindrical antitank
weapon. Ed.

Your Butcher Is Your Best Critic

(*Variety*, July 14, 1943)

*Radio was never very profitable to Groucho until he hit upon
the quiz show format. Despite his praise of the medium in 1943,
it took another decade for him to achieve in it the phenomenal
success he had enjoyed in vaudeville, theater, and film.*

There are many reasons why I prefer radio to any other kind of show
business. The advantages are obvious and numerous. To begin with,
there is no traveling, no daily application of greasy makeup, no memo-
rizing long strings of frequently dull dialogue, no early morning set calls,
and no living in bum hotels—or even good ones. In addition to this, all
the sponsors are solvent.

It has, however, one disagreeable feature that can never be eliminated
and, because of this, a radio comic is a fugitive and furtive character,
constantly exposed to insult, humiliation, and, on occasions, even danger. What I am referring to is the avalanche of gratuitous criticism that
descends upon him as soon as he has completed a broadcast. This is a
condition that I never encountered in the legitimate theater. True, there
was criticism and it frequently was poisonous, but if the show was a hit, it
was quickly forgotten. Once you got past the critics, the theater could do
you no harm. The audience was composed mostly of coupon clippers,
racetrack touts, and landed gentry and, unless you frequented Wall
Street or Lindy's, you rarely encountered them.

Radio, on the other hand, is the poor man's theater. The price of
admission is a few good tubes and a check-mailing acquaintance with
the local utility company. With this meager investment, Joe Blow (Mr.
Average Man to you) automatically becomes a composite Huneker,
Brooks Atkinson, and Nick Kenny.

For example—consider the butcher. We all know how difficult it is
these days to buy meat. It requires money, coupons, and infinite
patience. Yet the steak I buy is directly affected by the butcher's reaction

to my last air show. As he chips away most of the meat, leaving me a snappy piece of suet to lug home, he explains to me what's wrong with my program. This particular bloody Casanova has a yen for Virginia O'Brien and her singing, but especially for Virginia. He says, "There's a dame with sex. Boy, would I leave my wife in a minute for her! She's got what it takes! Marx, the trouble with your show is you talk too much." I have an answer for that but I need that meat desperately so I keep my trap shut and eventually slink out of the shop with my gristle under my arm.

The gas attendant, on the other hand, is a frustrated operatic star. His idea of an ideal program is about twenty minutes of *Carmen* with Donald Dickson singing all the roles. If the program hasn't enough Donald Dickson, he either gives me the wrong kind of gas or absentmindedly fills my battery with steel shavings.

My barber, an ex–boy fiddler from Long Island City, wants more of Bobby Armbruster. Waving a hot razor at my neck, he says, "Mr. Marx, you've got a big, swell orchestra there. Why don't you use it? The Philharmonic plays an hour and a half of symphony music every Sunday and they don't use no jokes either—and they're doing all right. Why don't you get wise to yourself?"

At the broadcast, the local representative of the brewery stirs uneasily in his seat when I am up there on the stage sounding off. He is mad about commercials and smiles only when our spieler is tossing his beer pitch at the audience.

I can tell how my washerwoman likes the show by the way my woolen socks are washed. If, at the end of the day, they dangle happily on the line in their original size, she liked the program. If I see them hanging there shrunken to the size of babies' booties, she has notified me in sock language that she wasn't at all amused.

And so it goes. My critics are not Hammond, Woollcott, and Atkinson[1] anymore. My critics are now the local tradespeople and they have me in their power. If I don't click with them, they can deprive me of the necessities of life. I don't know what the solution is but if it continues, I'll either have to disguise myself as an old biddy when I do my shopping or hang a market basket on my Great Dane and send him for the groceries.

I know one thing—until I get a 20 Crossley, I'm going to steer clear of my dentist.

[1]A reference to Percy Hammond, Alexander Woollcott, and Brooks Atkinson, New York newspaper critics who had befriended the Marx Brothers early in their Broadway career. Ed.

Groucho Marx Gives Kidding-on-the-Square Pitch for Hosp Shows

(*Variety*, August 23, 1944)

As the war wound down, Groucho offered his reminiscence of USO shows. Nearly every entertainer did them, in gratitude for the sacrifices made by wounded veterans. As usual, he refused to allow any sentiment to creep into his prose.

The first of July under the auspices of the War Department I left for the poll tax section of America. These were all one-nighters and included many cities that hadn't seen me in the flesh since I was a starry-eyed juvenile.

There were four of us. Fay McKenzie, known throughout the San Fernando Valley as the Panther Woman, supplied the beauty and allure. Fay was well equipped for this junket. She was born in a theatrical trunk in Sioux City and lived in it until she was seventeen years old. Then one day her folks opened the trunk to get out some clean handkerchiefs and, to their surprise, they discovered little Fay nestling there, reading *Lady Chatterley's Lover* (the unexpurgated version). She then had four years at the Pasadena Playhouse, four years at U.S.C., four years at U.C.L.A., and three years as a cheerleader for the Green Bay Packers. Fay is a normal, healthy girl. She is crazy about marshmallows toasted over a Girl Scout, and sleeps in her pajamas.

Then there was Harry Ruby, the mad composer and mediocre ballplayer. Alec Woollcott, in describing Ruby, said, "He looks like a dishonest Abe Lincoln." Ruby doesn't look that good and never will, for along with his other eccentricities he has lately taken to wearing a rain-coat that is a replica of the one worn by Hitler during the Brown Shirt Riots in Vienna. Despite his looks, Ruby has composed the music for many successful musical shows and his song hits are played wherever there is a dead mike.

The fourth member of this moth-eaten group was a Brazilian guitarist who answers to the name of Jose Olivera and practically anything else. I was curious about his early life and how he became such a wonderful guitarist, but whenever I questioned him he closed up and would only emit a series of South American grunts. One night, however, I plied him with reefers, and as the room thickened with smoke, he suddenly broke down and told me everything. It seems that he had spent his apprentice-ship with a cluster of Latins thumping a guitar in back of Carmen Miranda and her hat, and though he liked her singing he hated fruit. Day after day, year after year, he had to watch her hat with the fruit bob-bing up and down in front of him. He was slowly going mad and vowed that, at the first opportunity, he would make a break for freedom. He bided his time and one night in Montevideo, while Carmen was writhing through a particularly intricate rumba, he slipped out the back door and fled toward the harbor. Ironically enough, he stowed away on a fruit steamer that was running bananas up the Amazon and, in less time than it takes to tell—three months to be exact—he arrived at Rio de Janeiro disguised as a fruit salad. The rest is history and can be found in any standard history.

Before I quit this nonsense, I want to say that this is not written to impress or acquaint America with our patriotism. There was nothing heroic about our tour. Where we went there was no shooting, except occasionally when they didn't like our act. But the Purple Heart Circuit means a lot to the boys in the hospitals. As the head doctor at the Leder-man Hospital in San Francisco told me, "The important thing is not that you put on a show, what is important is the psychological value the entertainment has in short-circuiting the boys' mental processes. It's a distraction of inestimable value and cannot be measured in terms of just songs and jokes. When a show is advertised to appear, it is discussed for days before it arrives, and long after it is gone, they still talk about it.

From a curative standpoint it contributes an element that no medicine can supply."

And that is why Marx's Moth-eaten Mannikins—Fay, Harry, Joe, and I—headed south for Uncle Sam.

How to Be a Spy

(*This Week,* February 16, 1946)

"How to Be a Spy" was part of the publicity for the Marx Brothers' twelfth movie, A Night in Casablanca, *a send-up of the espionage genre.*

The public may be surprised that I am able to write on the subject of espionage. As a matter of fact, the public may be surprised that I am able to write. But the truth is that my latest picture is so fraught with international intrigue that I have become an expert in that field. Thus, I decided I must write this vital article which every man, woman, and child in the nation can afford to overlook.

Let me lead you step by step from elementary code work right up to the firing squad. In the first place, you must understand that there is more than one kind of secret agent. There is, first, the General Spy, whose activities are unlimited. Then there is the man who specializes in bargain-counter and lunch-counter cases, and he is, of course, the Counter-Spy. Finally there is the Northern Spy, which hasn't anything to do with the subject except that it's good eating if you like apples

But I am getting away from my theme. I always say an article is like a lady's stocking—it's important to keep the theme straight. I knew we'd get around to women sooner or later. Aren't you glad?

On becoming a spy, you will have to learn to deal with feminine wiles. The temptation of a beautiful woman can be your downfall—if you're lucky. Of course, Marx, the Master Spy, is proof against blandishments of the sveltest brunettes and the most ravishing blondes on earth.

On the other hand, a redhead can get anything out of me in two minutes flat.

Let me tell you about my first femme fatale, that suave, bejeweled agent of Hungroslavia. Her name was Mandolin, and I shall always remember that evening in her scented boudoir on the Rue de la Strapontin-Casace. My mission was to wrest from her the blueprints of the fearsome Gatling gun.

But I am getting ahead of my story. Let me tell you how the mission first started. Our spy outfit was stationed on a secret island off the French coast. We had all been through a terrifying period: We had run out of paper clips, and we could no longer file reports in sextuplicate. We had to have clips! One panic-stricken soul among us suggested we try a clip joint, but that would have been tantamount to dealing in the black market. I was running feverishly all over the island. I was ready to drop in my tracks, except that I don't run on tracks.

Then the General approached me. "Marx," he said, "you must go to the mainland in a small, unseaworthy craft and then proceed to Paris on a small, ungroundworthy motorcycle. Once there you must wrest the blueprints of the fearsome Gatling gun from the beauteous Mandolin. May you wrest in peace."

I set out at midnight in a dory. The waves were so high that they broke over the gunwales (pronounced "gunnels"). All I could find to bail with was a funwale (pronounced "funnel"). To make matters worse, the night was black as a tunwale (pronounced "tunnel"). This kind of humor is known as beating a dead horse, so let's drop it.

Suffice to say, I eventually reached Paris and burst in upon the beauteous Mandolin. "Dear lady," I said as I took her in my arms, "I am not hemmed to fit the touch of your skirt!" (This is the way spies always talk to each other—code language.)

"Mandolin," I continued, "I have come to curry favor." I ran my fingers through her hair. "Sorry I forgot my currycomb." Then I prostrated myself before her. "Mandolin," I slavered. "I swear that your beauty has crazed me. Your eyes, how they shine! They shine like the pants of a blue serge suit!"

At the moment the plans of the Gatling gun dropped from her bodice—I snatched them.

"Monster," she shrieked. "For this night's work you shall reap dismay!"

"You've got it all wrong," I said. "I shall plow dismay—I won't be reaping till dis-august."

At that point Mandolin's lover, the Count de la Défense d'Afficher, rushed into the room. I had to swallow the blueprints quick, and I must say they were the worst I've ever tasted.

"Cochon!" cried the Count. "What are you doing in my fiancée's apartment?"

"Well, right now I'm trying to find a bicarbonate of soda."

He advanced and slapped me across the cheek with his gloves. I could not let this challenge go unheeded. I produced my card case. "Take one, Monsieur," I snapped.

He did.

"What is it?" I said.

"Queen of spades."

"Pay me—I drew the ace."

This did not satisfy him, however, so I stalked away to my motorcycle and drove off in low dudgeon—I couldn't make high on the gasoline we were getting in those days.

This whole episode goes to prove an important point: A good spy must be able to take insults and hardships in his stride. He must keep constantly gruntled—the moment a spy becomes disgruntled he is of no use to anyone. For instance, let me tell of another important case of mine. This one happened right in New Jersey.

As I sat one night swatting mosquitoes, I received three mysterious telephone calls. The first two were wrong numbers, the third was an acquaintance of mine, J. J. Fusty, who runs a large penwiper factory in Hoboken. "Come to me quick, Inspector," he pleaded.

I rushed right over. A butler ushered me into the drawing room, where Mr. and Mrs. Fusty were waiting to greet me.

"Thank heaven you are here, Inspector," said Fusty. "Sit down anywhere."

I sat down in Mrs. Fusty's lap.

"Inspector," continued Fusty, "my business is going to rack and ruin.

Labor is scarce. Supply is turning my hair gray. Price is dangling a sword over my head."

"Why don't you dangle a sword over Price's head and see how he likes it?"

"You don't understand, Inspector. There is worse trouble—a suspicious character is writing me letters, threatening to hijack my trucks."

"That's right down my alley," I said. "Do you have an inkling as to the fellow's identity?"

"None at all, except that he poses as an Army officer."

"Hah," I said, "anyone with half an eye could clear up this case. Unfortunately, I don't happen to know anybody with half an eye, so I'll have to do the job myself."

Without further words I plunged out into the night. As luck would have it, I ran across a suspect that very evening. He was dressed in Army khaki, but my sharp eye noted that the insigne was not that of any Army outfit. I trailed him for three days, and his actions were most suspicious. Every day he would sneak out into the woods around town and meet up with a band of midgets. Then they would all go about setting fires.

I determined to bring my quarry to bay. So one evening as he trudged along the road with his midget band, I sprang from the bushes and confronted him. "I am Marx, the Master Spy," I snarled.

"Glad to meet you, Mr. Marx," he said. "I am Clarence Snood, Scoutmaster of the Beaver Troop."

Of course it was a bitter pill for me to swallow, but in a way I did not regret it—we all toasted marshmallows and became fast friends.

Incidentally, J. J. Fusty's business did go to rack and ruin. It is now known as Rack & Ruin Inc., and I understand the new owners are making a go of it.

What, you may ask, is the practical use of spy work? Can it be applied to everyday life? Yes, I say. Persons with sound espionage training can overcome many social problems that would stagger ordinary householders.

Suppose, for instance, that boring Mr. and Mrs. Pratt down the street are about to call on you. If you and your wife have had spy training, you will immediately turn off all lights in the house.

While your wife prepares an eerie fire of bleached bones on the living-room hearth, you will disguise yourself as a mad butler. After quickly shaving your hair off, you will insert a dagger in your chest so that a conspicuous bloodstain will spread all over your shirtfront. Then, when you welcome the Pratts at the front door, Mr. Pratt will probably laugh nervously and mumble something about not being able to stay long.

If the Pratts are difficult cases, I suggest hiding a dead Balkan minister in the coat closet (you should be able to pick one up cheap). When the Pratts are hanging up their wraps, the body will fall out at their feet. There is no need to make introductions, even though they may express some curiosity as to who he is.

The next step is to usher the Pratts into the living room, where the bleached bones are crackling dismally. Your wife will have set out phials of poison on the coffee table (these should be clearly marked with skull and crossbones or you'll get into trouble with the Food and Drug Administration).

If you can get hold of a baby-sitter to come over and clank some chains in the cellar, so much the better. But baby-sitters are hard to get nowadays.

By all the laws of averages, the Pratts should make their adieux within twenty minutes by the clock. But if they persist in sticking around, it is considered justifiable to take them out to the garden wall and shoot them down with rifles. Fastidious hosts will, of course, remember to supply eye bandages and a last cigarette.

Well, I think that just about covers the subject of spy work. If any of you have further questions, merely drop me a letter stating your age, weight, height, and sex.

I'm particularly anxious to hear from a few blondes under thirty who enjoy canoeing.

Uncle Julius

(*The Hollywood Reporter*, March 13, 1946)

During the 1940s Groucho contributed occasional pieces, often in the form of personal letters, to Irving Hoffman's Hollywood Reporter column "Tales of Hoffman."

~

Dear Irving,

Between strokes of good fortune I have been toying with the idea of making you my impending child's godfather. However, before doing this officially, I would like to see a notarized statement of your overall assets. I don't intend to repeat the unhappy experience that befell my parents late in the nineteenth century.

At that time there was an Uncle Julius in our family. He was five feet one in his socks, holes and all. He had a brown spade beard, thick glasses, and a head topped off with a bald spot about the size of a buckwheat cake. My mother somehow got the notion that Uncle Julius was wealthy and she told my father, who never did quite understand my mother, that it would be a brilliant piece of strategic flattery were they to make Uncle Julius my godfather.

Well, as happens to all men, I was finally born, and before I could say "Jack Robinson," I was named Julius. At the moment this historic event was taking place, Uncle Julius was in the back room of a cigar store on Third Avenue, dealing them off the bottom. When word reached him that he had been made my godfather, he dropped everything, including two aces he had up his sleeve for an emergency, and quickly rushed over to our flat.

In a speech so moist with emotion that he was blinded by his own eyeglasses, he said that he was overwhelmed by this sentimental gesture on our part and hinted that my future—a rosy one—was irrevocably linked with his. At the conclusion of his speech, still unable to see through his misty lenses, he kissed my father, handed my mother a cigar, and ran back to the pinochle game.

Two weeks later, he moved in, paper suitcase and all. As time went by, my mother became suspicious and one day, in discussing him with my father, she not only discovered that Uncle Julius seemed to be without funds but, what was even worse, that he owed my father thirty-four dollars.

Since he was only five feet one, my father volunteered to throw him out but my mother said, "Let's wait a little longer." She said that she had read of many cases where rich men had lived miserly lives and then had left tremendous fortunes to their heirs when they had died.

Well, he remained with us until I got married. By this time, he had the best room in the house and owed my father eighty-four dollars. Shortly after my wedding, my mother finally admitted that Uncle Julius had been a hideous mistake and ordered my father to give him the bum's rush. But Uncle Julius had grown an inch over the years while my father had shrunk proportionately and he finally convinced my mother that violence was not the solution to the problem.

Soon after this, Uncle Julius solved everything by kicking off, leaving me his sole heir. His estate when probated consisted of a nine ball that he had stolen from a pool room, a box of liver pills, and a celluloid dicky.

I suppose I should be more sentimental about the whole thing but it was a severe shock to all of us and, if I can help it, it's not going to happen again.

The point of all this is that my present wife has an uncle named Percy. She admits that it isn't much of a name but she says that Uncle Percy is a power in the South—she has been told that in Nashville, for example, it's practically impossible to go anywhere without seeing her uncle and she is sure that were we to name the child after him, little Percy would be sitting pretty. Unknown to my wife, I recently had her uncle investigated and discovered that Percy is a Southern Uncle Julius. His big business consists of retailing Oh Henry! bars at the Union Depot in Nashville. So, Percy is out!

Well, Irving, that's the story. If you are interested, let me hear from you as soon as possible and, remember, a financial statement as of today will expedite things considerably.

Love and kisses.
Yours,
Groucho Marx

Standing Room Only

(*This Week*, November 17, 1946)

*In the summer of 1946 Groucho was a stay-at-home dad, hang-
ing around the house with his second wife, Kay, and their
infant daughter, Melinda. When he was not shopping or playing, he worked on revisions of* Time for Elizabeth, *a stage comedy written in collaboration with Norman Krasna. When the
spirit moved him he contributed articles to magazines, taking
his ideas from the headlines. "Standing Room Only" battens on
the nation's postwar housing shortage.*

Not so long ago, a New York news reporter discovered a woman midget
living in a public phone booth. Her housekeeping equipment consisted
of a Sterno stove, a folding camp chair, some baby lima beans, and
a *Reader's Digest.* "I consider it a windfall," she stated. "Just think, I
not only have a home, but I have something even harder to get—a
telephone!"

If Tel and Tel doesn't object to the loss of a few million nickels a year,
this may be the beginning of a new way of life.

Now, I realize that there are probably more phone booths than
midgets, but I think with practice taller people too can adjust themselves to such surroundings. Of course, you'd have to learn to sleep
standing up, but that isn't so hard. Even horses can learn that.

There are many other possibilities for gracious living besides telephone booths.

One friend of mine has found refuge in a municipal gas tank. The
family has to wear respirators, to be sure, and the man's wife won't let
him smoke indoors. But at least he has a roof over his head—about 240
feet over his head, to be exact.

Another fellow keeps bachelor hall in a cement mixer. He doesn't
even need an alarm clock: when the workmen start the mixer revolving
in the morning, it wakes him up without fail. However, he does com-
plain that it's hard to dress on a dead run.

Have you thought of a barn? Half the people I know were brought up in a barn, and they're making big money today.

Out in California, people have more elaborate ideas for finding homes.

They are buying streetcars and converting them into bungalows. The latter come complete with kitchenette, bathroom, and a fine bell system for summoning the butler, if you have a butler. Personally, I prefer a French maid. However, my general feeling is that you'd best forget the immobile streetcar and settle down in one that is still going places. Your natural answer will be—you may not get a seat. Just as I thought—you're the kind who wants to sit down and loaf for the rest of your life. But let's not argue about it. The trick is to get to the car barns early in the morning. For a nickel—or seven cents, if you live in Cleveland—you've got a home for the day. I realize that you'll get bumped around a little, but, in exchange for that, you'll see a lot of new faces, and I might add that most of them will be an improvement over yours.

Living in a streetcar has many advantages. There is a constant change of scene; if you are too stingy to buy a paper, you can wait for a passenger to throw his on the floor. If the streetcar goes through a rich neighborhood, you may even pick up some magazines. And, who knows—if you are a woman, after a few years you may marry the motorman.

Another possible home is a cage at the zoo. I don't recommend this for married couples, since, frankly, there isn't much privacy in a cage; but for a single chap it definitely has possibilities.

The monkey house is probably your best bet. You might even be able to remain there permanently without anyone knowing the difference. In order not to look too conspicuous, I suggest you remove your clothes before entering their cage. Don't let's make a problem of it—if you are an ex-serviceman, there is a strong likelihood that you haven't got any clothes.

If you are one of those lucky persons who own a pen that writes underwater, you might try living in a swimming pool. You could bathe and handle your correspondence simultaneously. You will find a pool in almost any backyard in Hollywood. These pools come complete with springboard, rubber raft for story conferences, and three bathing girls who look like Jane Russell.

If you are fortunate enough to live outside California, and can't find a swimming pool, you might follow the example of a fellow I know who lives in a well. The only equipment required is a pair of hip boots and a large supply of carrots so you can read in the dark. My friend says the commutation service is fine—he leaves home by the 8:00 A.M. bucket and returns by the five-forty-five. He says the only drawback to living in a well is that the neighbors keep dropping in.

If you aren't a coward, you might solve your housing problem by renting a haunted house. The back streets of America's towns are lined with fine haunted houses that are empty simply because cravens are afraid to live in them. A homeless young couple won't hesitate a moment to move in on the wife's parents but if you suggest a haunted house to them (a far safer place in my opinion) they turn pale and chatter lame excuses.

However, if you are the yellow-streak type, I recommend a tree. A tree is absolutely safe unless you walk in your sleep, and from the top limbs you get a lovely view of the surrounding country. I would suggest a nut tree—preferably a walnut. Walnuts are large and chock-full of vitamins and the empty shells can later be used for ashtrays.

By this time, you will probably agree with me that the housing shortage can be solved. The trouble with us is that we have been allowing ourselves to get soft—our thinking is wrong, we still cling to the old-fashioned notion that man can only be happy in a house.

How ridiculous! In the rural sections, chicken coops are getting increasingly popular. The fancier coops are equipped with oil stoves, sunlamps, and mash troughs, and the addition of a few pictures and some dotted swiss will make them even homier. In order to avert suspicion, it is a good idea to start crowing promptly at sunrise. However, if the farmer is one of those trigger-happy rustics who enjoy blazing away with a shotgun, you'll just have to use your wits and outfox him. Listen for his footsteps and if you think he is approaching the coop, drop whatever you are doing, hop on a few eggs, and just sit tight until he goes away.

There are many other substitutes for homes. There are Quonset huts, drainpipes, tents, sleeping bags, and even large doll's houses. I don't recommend the latter, however, since I once had an unhappy experience in a doll's house. The doll's old man chased me out with a baseball bat.

Many people are living in the balconies of movie theaters. The loges are ideal for sleeping and so are most of the pictures. In the lobby, you can purchase popcorn, Sen-Sen, chocolate bars, and peanuts. In the rest rooms, you will find ice water, weighing machines, and poetry.

In conclusion, I say to America: "Keep your chin up—remember, we're a nation of producers—a home is what you make it."

If I had the time, I could show you many other ways to beat the housing shortage, but I have to go now and look for a furnished room. The Great Dane whose house I rented is returning from Florida and, as I always say, no house is big enough for two families.

Groucho's Column for *Variety*

In June 1947, Groucho wrote a column for Variety, *which he sent to the editor, Abel Green, with the following note:*

∩

JUNE 7, 1947

Dear Abel:

I trust this is illiterate enough even for your sheet.

Regards, Groucho

Variety, which calls itself the bible of show business (actually it's the babel of show business), recently printed a news story to the effect that for *The Jolson Story*, Al Jolson's cut—despite the fact that he didn't appear in the picture except for a brief moment—would amount to three and a half million dollars.

I have appeared in many pictures through the years (at the moment I can be seen in all my pristine loveliness in *Copacabana*), and I would swear on a stack of Bob Stacks that I have never pulled down any dough that has ever remotely touched this figure. Perhaps this is the signpost that show business has been waiting for. If a Jolson picture can roll up a ten-million-dollar gross without Jolson, how much more could it have made without Evelyn Keyes and William Demarest? Maybe the studios have been going at it the wrong way. Perhaps they should stop the present custom of bunching seven or eight stars in one movie, and eliminate all the feature names in a picture.

I can just see the marquee at the local theater. Coming next week: *I Wonder Who's Hissing Her Now*, without Olivia de Crawford and Clark Power. It can't miss. I am sure that millions of people stay away from the movies because they dislike the stars that are appearing at the local Bijou, but if they were assured that so-and-so wouldn't show his ugly kisser on the screen, my guess is they would tear the doors down to get in.

I am speaking from personal experience. In my time I have met hundreds of people who have said, "Hey, jerk, when are you going to quit the movies and get a job—" and if it's true of me, it certainly must be true of dozens of others whose talents may be even less than mine.

This system could also be applied to other fields of endeavor. I am sure that many political candidates are defeated because the public has been given an opportunity to see what they look like. The next great political victory will be achieved by the party that is smart enough to have nobody heading the ticket.

My theory is that there are too many people and too many things. Suppose you got that semiannual card from your dentist notifying you that most of your fangs are about to drop out and you had better get up to his abattoir before you spend the rest of your life gumming your fodder. Wouldn't you rush up there with much more alacrity if you were certain that this white-coated assassin wasn't there to greet you with his chisel in one hand and his pliers in the other? Imagine if horse racing had no horses—thousands of people could go to the track each day and save millions of dollars.

Years ago, there was a theory called Technocracy. Perhaps mine could be called the Theory of Scarcity. Take the actors out of the movies, take squash and rutabagas out of restaurant menus, take Slaughter and Musial out of the Cardinals, and take Gromyko out of the UN.

As for marriage, I know hundreds of husbands who would gladly go home if there weren't any wives waiting for them. Take the wives out of marriage and there wouldn't be any divorces. But then, someone might ask, what about the next generation? Look, I've seen some of the next generation—perhaps it's just as well if the whole thing ends right here

Why Harpo Doesn't Talk

(*This Week*, December 12, 1948)

Groucho's manic brother Harpo never spoke in their movies, and by the late 1930s a large part of the world's filmgoers believed that the mime act was genuine—that Harpo had been mute from birth. In fact he was an articulate and anecdotal personality, but one who realized one day that silence, in his case, was golden. Groucho was there that day and explains in detail.

It was the week before Christmas—now don't get excited. This isn't going to be a story about Santa Claus. This is a story about Harpo, Chico, Zeppo, and me.

It happened back during the wormier days of vaudeville in one of those soft-coal towns in Illinois, where if your street ensemble didn't include a small miner's lantern on top of your cap, you were eyed with considerable curiosity.

The theater was no Radio City Music Hall. It seated, uncomfortably, about five hundred people. The dressing rooms were in a damp, dimly lit cellar underneath the stage, containing very little heat and a minimum of plumbing.

Our show was a tabloid music comedy. It was advertised as a magnificent Broadway production, differing from the original only in the cost of the tickets. Actually there were other differences. Our company consisted of four men, eight girls, and ourselves. Our salary for the entire company was $900 a week, which meant that for three days we would pull down $450.

Early Thursday morning I walked in to rehearse the orchestra. Since I was the only one of the boys who didn't know an eighth note from a bank-note, I never quite understood why I was delegated for this job. In later years I realized it was because I was the only Marx Brother who could be routed out of bed before noon.

I was a jaunty sight as I walked through the stage door that morning. I had a genuine imitation diamond stickpin in my tie, a cane in my hand, and between my lips the best five-cent cigar money could buy.

As I strolled to the mailbox to see if that redheaded dame from Bloomington was coming on to see me, a burly figure appeared out of the darkness.

"Hey, you!" he shouted. "Don't you see that sign? It says, 'No Smoking.' That'll cost you five dollars."

Flicking the ash off my cigar, I replied in my iciest tone:

"Who, may I ask, are you?"

"Who am I?" he bellowed. "I'm Jack Wells, the manager and owner of this theater. We have rules here and that sign is one of them."

"What sign?" I said, a little puzzled.

"What sign!" he roared, and pointed, in the gloom, to a tiny NO SMOKING poster tacked high on the wall, almost out of sight.

"Why don't you hang the sign in a closet?" I asked. "Then you can be sure no one'll see it."

"Oh, a wise guy, eh! That crack'll cost you another five."

This repartee was beginning to run into money. Reluctantly tossing my stogie away, I left Wells and started rehearsing the music.

These were the days before actors' unions. Every theater manager was a little king, and his fines were as absolute as Supreme Court decisions. Some managers collected almost as much revenue through this petty larceny as they did through the box office.

The more I thought about Wells and that ten dollars, the madder I got, especially when I thought about the ten dollars. I was still burning when the rehearsal was over. Back at the hotel, I woke up the boys, after quite a struggle, and told them what had happened. They were purple with rage. However, I don't think they were as angry over the fine as they were over the fact that if I hadn't had the run-in with Wells they could still be sleeping.

We held a council of war and decided we wouldn't go on unless Wells rescinded the fine.

The curtain was scheduled to go up at two-thirty. At two o'clock we were all in our dressing rooms in the cellar. We donned our stage clothes, slapped on our makeup, and when we were all ready, sent for Wells.

Together we weren't afraid of him. There were four of us. We were young and full of hell, and besides, each of us carried a blackjack.

A few moments later Wells appeared. Chico, the eldest, acted as spokesman. Taking a firm grip on himself, and gulping a trifle, he said, "Mr. Wells, unless you cancel that ten-dollar fine, we're not going on."

Wells was furious. He wasn't accustomed to mutiny. He said, "Listen, you guys. I have rules in this theater, and one of the rules is *no smoking*. I caught your brother Groucho smoking, and I fined him. That's the law of this theater, and it stands!"

Chico hollered out to the company, "Okay, everybody, take off your makeup and costumes. We're not going to give a show."

By this time the orchestra had played the overture four times, and a houseful of tough theater lovers were stamping and shouting for the curtain to go up.

Wells was getting nervous. He was part of the town and he couldn't afford this. He knew we had him.

"Now, wait a minute, boys," he whined. "You can't do this to me. Those people came to see a show."

We answered, "We came to give a show, but as long as the fine stands, we don't go on. Take your choice."

We, too, were bluffing. We couldn't afford the loss of three days' salary. Then Harpo, the Neville Chamberlain of his time, spoke up.

"I'll tell you what," he said. "We'll take ten dollars and you take ten, and we'll combine it and throw the whole twenty in the Salvation Army Christmas pot on the corner."

"You can throw all your salary in the Christmas pot," said Wells, "but they don't get any of my dough."

Out front the stamping grew louder and the yells more threatening. Wells listened with alarm.

"What do you say?" Chico taunted him. "Does the Salvation Army get the money?"

Wells eyed us murderously, but rather than lose the afternoon's receipts, and perhaps his life, he surrendered and the show went on.

We were leaving Saturday night for our next jump, and by the time our last show was over we had about forty minutes to get dressed, pack, load the scenery on tracks, get to the depot, and check our baggage.

In the midst of all this confusion, two of Wells's stooges staggered in and dumped four big canvas bags on the floor.

"What's that?" we asked.

"That's your salary," one of them said. "Mr. Wells sends his regards."

Each bag contained $112.50 in pennies, but we had to make sure. We also had to catch a train, so as quickly as possible we counted one of the bags and measured it up against the other three. We could only hope that Wells hadn't loaded the uncounted bags with slugs.

We barely made the train, and as it pulled out of the depot, we stood on the track platform watching the town and theater recede into the distance.

Then Harpo, the pantomimist, raised his voice, and above the clatter of the train, bellowed:

"Good-bye, Mr. Wells. Here's hoping your lousy theater burns down!"

We thought it was just a gag, till next morning—when we discovered that, during the night, Jack Wells's theater had been reduced to ashes. From then on we decided not to let Harpo talk—his conversation was too dangerous.

King Leer

(*Tele-Views*)

Ever eager to bite the handclap that fed him, Groucho kidded the medium of television as often as possible. The opening of this piece was one of the most quoted remarks he ever made.

~

By Groucho Marx

I must say I find television very educational. The minute somebody turns it on, I go into the library and read a good book.

That's a pretty cynical attitude for "the leer" — that's me, Groucho — and now that I'm a part of television, or "TV" as we say out here on the Coast, I don't mean a word of it.

TV presents a completely new set of problems to me. In my thirty-five years in show business, I've learned the intricacies of the stage, then the movies, then radio. Now comes television. I can't even learn how to turn it on!

At first, I thought it would be simple to put our show in TV. Just me and a few contestants gabbing. That's all.

Little did I know there would be four cameras staring at me, a makeup man frowning from the wings if I raise my eyebrows, the light crew glaring from the rafters if I cast a shadow in the wrong place, my director making frantic motions if I step out of camera range, the studio audience whispering if I step out of mike range, the sponsor screaming if I forget the commercial.

I suppose I'll get used to all this. After all, television is progressing rapidly. I notice the home sets are improving all the time. For instance, the old sets used to have about thirty-five tubes, but now the sets are down to eighteen tubes. Now if they just eliminate the picture tube, they'll reach perfection.

I also notice that the television screens are getting bigger. Thank goodness for those screens. They're the only thing that keeps the stuff from crawling into the living room.

I think the ideal television sets should be equipped with two screens. Then you could use the second screen to hide the television sets.

In a nutshell, I'm happy to be plunging into television. Although frankly, I'd rather be plunging into a nutshell.

Sure, we've got a lot of problems to lick, since we're doing our show for radio and TV simultaneously. This means everything we do for television must be plain to the listener who can't see it, the old-fashioned fellow with the radio receiver. It will limit our plans for the time being, but I'm sure everything will work out for the best. I wish I could say the same for Harpo, who isn't working out at all.

As for me, I'm going to keep my cigar, my leer, and any old ad-lib wisecracks I find kicking around. My mustache is my own now. I bought it from the upstairs maid. But the frock coat and the old Groucho who chases blondes will be missing. Even the new Groucho will be missing, but that's only until I can get my spark plugs cleaned.

All I can say is this: Walk, don't run, to your nearest television set in October, tune to KNBH, and join us for our first TV session of *You Bet Your Life*. I think you'll like it.

YOU BET YOUR LIFE

(1947–1960)

Since the mid-1930s, Groucho had sought to extend his career on radio. No effort seemed to work for more than a season or two—until John Guedel watched the comedian ad-lib fluently with Bob Hope and saw a way to use the Marx touch on the air An experienced producer of game shows, Guedel devised the format for You Bet Your Life, ostensibly a quiz show but actually an opportunity for Groucho to sharpen his wit on contestants The program was not as extemporaneous as it sounded Groucho interviewed his guests before they went on mike, and a team of writers furnished him with basic one-liners to play with The emcee then added his own witticisms and wordplays. You Bet Your Life rapidly became an audience favorite and made a smooth transition to television when Groucho turned his announcer George Fenneman into the male equivalent of Mar garet Dumont. At an age when many men were collecting Social Security payments, Groucho found himself more cele brated than he had been as a movie star. His lines "Say the secret word and win a hundred dollars" and the question he asked all losers so that they would go away with something "Who is buried in Grant's Tomb?" were household phrases through the 1950s and '60s. There were bigger comedy stars in various media—Chaplin dominated film, Eddie Cantor had been the centerpiece of many Broadway musicals, Milton Berle was the dominant personality of early TV. But no other per former had scored major successes in vaudeville, theater, cin ema, radio, and TV—and, of course, no other performer eve *will. These snippets from* You Bet Your Life *give some reasons for Marx's longevity.*

THE SECRET WORD IS GROUCHO

A COMPENDIUM OF GROUCHO ONE-LINERS

To a pretty girl: You have a very good head on your shoulders, and I wish it were on mine.

To a watchmaker: Where's your business—on the main stem?

To Melba Taylor: You must be the toast of the town!

To Chief Niño Cochise of the Apache Tribe: Chief, I'm glad to meet you. You're not the chief that runs from here to Chicago in thirty-nine hours, huh?

To a cartoonist: If you want to see a comic strip, you should see me in a shower.

To a father of triplets: You've been married fifteen months and you have three daughters? This is indeed the age of rapid transit.

To a baseball umpire: And do you have any little thieves at home?

To a dealer in war surplus: How many times have you been indicted?

To a dress designer who said women dress for themselves, not for men: If they dressed for me, the stores wouldn't sell much—just an occasional sun visor.

To a meteorologist: Any little squalls at home running around with their barometers dropping?

To a pharmacist: Is it true that Rexall is a drug on the market?

To a professional gambler: Have you ever had an unusual experience— like letting a customer win once in a while?

To a tree surgeon: Have you ever fallen out of a patient?

To a skywriter: When you're up there skywriting do you ever feel that someone is looking over your shoulder?

To a pretty schoolteacher: How would you like to take over my student body?

To elderly newlyweds: I'll never forget my wedding day . . . they threw vitamin pills.

To an admiral: We're not very formal on the show, so do you mind if I call you Captain?

To a marriage broker: I met my wife on a ferryboat, and when we landed she gave me the slip.

To Gary Cooper's mother: He's a real chatterbox too . . . I've been watching him for twenty years in the movies, and I would say, conversationally he's about six words ahead of my brother Harpo.

To Fred Haney, manager of the Milwaukee Braves: This is the man who made Milwaukee famous, you know. He also made Milwaukee come in second—or was it third?

To a male contestant: So your name is John Rose—that's a simple declarative, isn't it?

To a musician: Beethoven is famous for his fifth, and he never touched a drop.

To Father Reagan: What kind of business are you in?

To Bobby Van: I know Bobby Van. You moved me into my house . . . Bobby Van and Storage.

To a pretty girl: You're quite a dish, Marie, and since I'm the head dish around here, let's start cooking.

To a muscleman: You don't have any muscles unless you take your jacket off, and I don't have any muscles until I put my jacket on.

To an English teacher: I thought homonym was a cereal.

To an Irishman: Some of my best friends are Irish . . . like Harry McRuby and David O'Selznick.

To a Vassar graduate: Were you fat when you left Vassar or did you leave Vassar-lean?

To an author: It won't do you any good to plug your book on my show, because none of our listeners can read.

To a housewife: Your husband has a very good head for business, and if you take my advice you'll have it examined the first thing in the morning.

To a poet: In other words you're out of work?

To a war veteran: Well, that's highly commendable . . . I knew his brother, Haile Selassie.

To a police officer: You have nothing on me, Copper, I've been busy every night this week at meetings of the Beverly Hills Mafia.

To a chicken raiser: How many did you raise and how high did you raise them?

To two Heidis: I'll call you Heidi-Hi . . . and I'll call you Heidi-Ho . . . and you can call me Cab Calloway.

To a fat woman: I bet you're a lot of fun at a party . . . in fact you *are* a party.

To the singing Marks Brothers: Boys, if you ever get the desire to sing again, please call yourselves the McGuire Sisters.

To a champion diver: I've been reading about your feats on the diving board for years . . . you did have your feets on the diving board?

To a cook: I tried boiling pig's feet once, but I couldn't get the pig to stand still.

To a Swiss man: Switzerland is a wonderful country . . . everyone seems so friendly . . . particularly when they clip the tourists.

To the owner of a 1902 auto: You must have it paid for by this time.

To a Chinese punster: You know, you're a bigger menace than the Asiatic flu.

To Dr. Howard Drum: Well, if you're a drum, you can beat it anytime, Doc.

To a dentist: I thought you looked down in the mouth.

To a Scottish girl: Whether you're straight Scotch or not, I'd like to be your chaser.

To a choreographer: Oh, you make maps?

To a native of Canton: I had that for dinner last night—canned tongue.

To Global Zobel: Global Zobel—that's quite euphonious . . . it's one of the euphonious names I've ever heard.

To a contestant: You say a buffoon is a clown?—I thought a buffoon is like an aspirin except that it works faster.

To an economist: I made a killing on Wall Street a few years ago . . . I shot my broker.

To a superior court bailiff: That's a good job, especially if you like to sleep in the daytime.

BRIEF EXCHANGES

GROUCHO: Do your parents live in L.A.?

CURVY GIRL: Yes, they do. My father is a meat distributor here.

GROUCHO: Your father is a meat distributor: Well, if you're any indication, he certainly knows his business.

GROUCHO: A walking race? I've never seen a walking race, with the exception of a couple of horses I bet on at Santa Anita. Well, how would a walker do against a horse?

MAN: Well, in one hundred yards, I beat a horse, and I beat a car with a twenty-five-yard handicap.

GROUCHO: Well, that's understandable. How fast can a horse drive an automobile? It'll take ten thousand dollars to sponsor you to walk across the country?

MAN: Ten thousand dollars.

GROUCHO: Here's a buck. I'm sponsoring you as far as Hollywood and Vine. From there on, you'll have to take a bus.

GROUCHO: Where do you do your teaching, Jody?

JODY: I teach for Meglin's.

GROUCHO: You teach meglins? What are meglins?

JODY: The famous Meglin Kiddies?

GROUCHO: Oh, Meglin Kiddies. Isn't that the one that teaches precocious children to become dancers and actors?

JODY: Oh, we have lots of wonderful children in our school.

GROUCHO: It's on Obnoxious Boulevard, isn't it?

GROUCHO: Is your wife of Italian extraction too?

MAN: No, she's a Slav, Groucho.

GROUCHO: Well, I'm sorry to hear that. I'm sure with a little patience you can teach her to be neater.

FENNEMAN: Groucho, we have a couple of special guests with us—

GROUCHO: Mr. Marx, if you please. Do I call you Groucho?

GROUCHO: Would you like to join me for moon gazing some night, when there isn't any moon?

PENNY: Well, thank you, but I'm very happily married.

GROUCHO: Oh. I was just checking, Penny, that's all. I was just curious to know how far a Penny will go these days. And it went about as far as I thought it would. You look pretty young to be married. Why did you tie the knot? Was he a Penny-pincher?

PENNY: No, it was love at first sight. And we've been married for four years.

GROUCHO: Well, why was it love at first sight? Was he wearing his wallet outside of his pocket?

GROUCHO: You gonna stand on your head now?

MAN: Well, I'm gonna need a little room.

GROUCHO: We'll get you a little room right after the show.

GROUCHO: Where are you from, Frankie?

FRANKIE: Brown Military Academy, sir.

GROUCHO: You were born in a military academy?

FRANKIE: No, sir.

GROUCHO: How did you arrive? Were you shot out of a cannon?

PILOT: I'm a helicopter pilot.

GROUCHO: Say, you certainly have an appropriate name for it—Eagle. That's certainly a good name for a helicopter pilot. But don't mention it quite so loud—because there are children listening. Say heck-i-copter. No, we try to be that way on this show. Every once in a while the Nice Nellie comes out in me. Tell me, what's the difference between a helicopter pilot and a regular orthodox pilot?

PILOT: Well, a helicopter pilot pilots helicopters and—

GROUCHO: I'm going to get some great answers from you.

PILOT: —and a regular pilot pilots airplanes.

GROUCHO: Well, I have a pilot in my gas stove, and it doesn't pilot anything. It's out most of the time, and so am I. I'm home on the range occasionally.

WOMAN: When a boy kisses a girl and she says, "Stop," usually she means, "Stop it. I love it." And it was sort of like that.

GROUCHO: You mean when a girl says, "Stop," she really means, "Don't stop"? Boy, the nights I've wasted. I was always so gullible.

GROUCHO: You mean when you were a young buck you traveled all the way from Washington to Arizona on horseback?

MAN: That's right.

GROUCHO: Couldn't do it today, Chief. The buck today doesn't go nearly as far as it used to.

MAN: I can tell you one joke that I gave an act when they were a little short, because another act was on the same show that used some of their gags.

GROUCHO: What do you mean the act was short? Was this Singer's Midgets?

MAN: My brother and I own a business called Up and Atom.

GROUCHO: Well, what is it? A breakfast cereal with fallout?

FENNEMAN: Well, Groucho, we've invited some railroad men to be on our show tonight.

GROUCHO: Do you keep track of them yourself? That's the tie that binds.

GROUCHO: How old are you, Jean?

JEAN: I generally say I'm one year older than Jack Benny.

GROUCHO: You mean you're ninety-seven? You don't look it.

GROUCHO: You say you have patterns that will allow me to build anything I want?

WOMAN: Yes.

GROUCHO: Well, can you send me the pattern to Anita Ekberg?

GROUCHO: Tell me, Rabbi. Do you get many actors at your temple?

RABBI: Yes, quite a few.

GROUCHO: I'm surprised you allow so much ham in your temple.

GROUCHO: You look pretty shifty to me. What sort of racket are you in?

MAN: Well, I build and wreck homes.

GROUCHO: You wreck homes? Are you the editor of one of those scandal magazines?

GROUCHO: Could you give me some idea of your age, Jeanne?

JEANNE: Groucho, that's something I don't even admit to my husband.

GROUCHO: Jeanne, if you've got a husband, I've lost interest in your age, anyway.

GROUCHO: Well, John, I've been studying you, and I think I can call your occupation. Are you an undertaker?

JOHN: No, sir, I'm a farmer.

GROUCHO: Well, farmer . . . undertaker . . . what's the difference? You're both planters.

GROUCHO: Are you interested in marriage?

GIRL: I'm a woman, aren't I?

GROUCHO: Well, even with these glasses I didn't think you were Sonny Tufts.

GROUCHO: Rock and roll is springing up in Japan?

WOMAN: Yes.

GROUCHO: That'll teach them to send us the Asiatic flu.

WOMAN: I have two locks of Elvis Presley's hair.

GROUCHO: Do you have any cream cheese to go with it?

GROUCHO: Let's see. You're Walter Knott?

KNOTT: Yes, I'm Knott.

GROUCHO: You're a Knott, did you say?

KNOTT: Knott, yes.

GROUCHO: Well, we're making pretty good time. We're making three knots an hour . . . and you say you've been married forty-three years?

KNOTT: That's right.

GROUCHO: You're the kind of knot that doesn't come untied.

GROUCHO: Wherabouts in Manhattan were you born?

WOMAN: On Riverside Drive.

GROUCHO: Oh, well. You're lucky you weren't run over by a bus.

GROUCHO: You say you write for papers all over the world?

WOMAN: Yes.

GROUCHO: And do they send them to you?

GROUCHO: Where did you get the name Crash? Was your father a stockbroker or were you born on the freeway?

CRASH CORRIGAN: No, Groucho, I was making action pictures, and of course I did some football playing. The way I used to tackle somebody, instead of fighting with them with my fists, I used to take off and dive at them headfirst. And that's how I got the name Crash.

GROUCHO: Well, I'm glad they don't name all the actors by the way they fight. Otherwise I'd be known as Kick-Them-in-the-Shins-and-Run-Like-the-Devil Marx.

GROUCHO: What's your name?

MAN: Boyd.

GROUCHO: Why don't you have a beard? Then you could be a Boyd in the bush.

MAN: I lived with cannibals in the jungle.

GROUCHO: You're lucky you didn't go to pot.

WOMAN: I have woodpeckers in my cocoa palms—

GROUCHO: You have woodpeckers in your cocoa palms?

WOMAN: That's right.

GROUCHO: Well, keep your hat on and nobody will notice.

* * *

WOMAN: Have you ever milked a soybean, Groucho?

GROUCHO: Milked a soybean?

WOMAN: Yes.

GROUCHO: I'd like to, but how do you get under it?

GROUCHO: What are your duties these days with the Air Force?

MAN: I'm commander of the 146th Fighter Interceptor Wing of the California Air National Guard.

GROUCHO: What does California need an air force for? We have no air out here.

MAN: I'm a blood analyst.

GROUCHO: Well, don't look at me unless you analyze Geritol.

GROUCHO: How many times have you been bitten by a dog?

WOMAN: Just once in the last four years.

GROUCHO: That's a pretty good record. Where'd he bite you?

WOMAN: In Encino.

GROUCHO: Why, that dirty mongrel!

GROUCHO: When did you leave Chicago?

WOMAN: When I was a little child.

GROUCHO: And where did you grow up?

WOMAN: Chico.

GROUCHO: I grew up around Chico myself. You don't happen to be Gummo, do you?

* * *

GROUCHO: Did you ever hear of a cow that just gives buttermilk?

MAN: No.

GROUCHO: What else can a cow give *but her milk?*

GROUCHO: What's your name?

SHIRLEY: Shirley.

GROUCHO: Well, Shirley to bed, and Shirley to rise.

GROUCHO: That's pretty poetic isn't it? The sea of matrimony?

WOMAN: Yes.

GROUCHO: That means you usually get sunk as soon as you leave the pulpit.

GROUCHO: Where do you go on your nights out?

WOMAN: Well, I go to showers and to—

GROUCHO: Can't you take a shower at home?

MAN: I'm from Rising Sun.

GROUCHO: I have a rising son. His name is Arthur and he usually rises around two in the afternoon.

WOMAN: After we were married, my husband enlisted in the Air Force and we traveled around for four more years.

GROUCHO: Did you ever settle down long enough to raise a family?

WOMAN: Well, no, but I had one. My children were born from one end of the country to the other.

GROUCHO: You must have pretty long children.

GROUCHO: What is it like in South Carolina?

WOMAN: Oh, it's wonderful, Groucho. Southern hospitality and wonderful folks.

GROUCHO: Well, we want you to feel at home here, Marie, so we'll pay you off in Confederate money.

GROUCHO: How did you meet your wife?

MAN: A friend of mine.

GROUCHO: Do you still regard him as a friend?

GROUCHO: Here I am again . . . all shaken up from a very harrowing experience.

FENNEMAN: Oh, really? What happened?

GROUCHO: It was terrible. I had a puncture. First one I've had in years. I ran over a whiskey bottle on the highway.

FENNEMAN: Couldn't you see the whiskey bottle?

GROUCHO: How could I see it? It was in a pedestrian's back pocket . . . He wasn't killed though. It was eighty-six proof.

GROUCHO: Well, Beverly, tell me, have you been looking for a husband?

BEVERLY: Well, not looking, but I keep my eyes open.

GROUCHO: Are you sure you've looked in the right places, Beverly? How about where you work? What kind of work have you done?

BEVERLY: Well, I've been in the Marine Corps for the last three years until recently.

GROUCHO: And you couldn't find a man in the Marine Corps?

BEVERLY: No, I couldn't.

GROUCHO: Well, the Marines aren't landing like they used to.

GROUCHO: I don't know much about French menus. Suppose I came into your restaurant. What should I order?

MAN: You just ask for me.

GROUCHO: Are you on the menu?

GROUCHO: What does a girl think when she meets a handsome boy?

COED: Oh, I imagine she thinks about the same thing boys do.

GROUCHO: You mean girls too wonder if they'll be drafted?

GROUCHO: You don't mind if I ask you a few personal questions, do you?

MODEL: If they're not too embarrassing.

GROUCHO: Don't give it a second thought. I've asked thousands of questions on this show and I've yet to be embarrassed.

GROUCHO: What were people wearing when you were a baby?

ELDERLY WOMAN: Diapers.

GROUCHO: Where did you meet you wife?

MAN: In my delicatessen.

GROUCHO: Was she pickled at the time?

PRETTY GIRL: I'm afraid you don't follow me.

GROUCHO: Even if I did, you'd have nothing to be afraid of. *(To the male contestant)* Can you follow her?

MALE: Yes.

GROUCHO: Does your wife know you go around following strange women?

LADY ANALYST: Tell me what's wrong with this sentence: Him and her went to the movies.

GROUCHO: It should be her and him. Ladies first, you know. Now tell me, what was your analysis? What job am I suited for?

LADY ANALYST: Only what you're doing now.

GROUCHO: Are you interested in matrimony?

FAN CLUB PRESIDENT: Indeed I am.

GROUCHO: Do you have any other interests?

FAN CLUB PRESIDENT: You haven't mentioned Elvis Presley.

GROUCHO: I seldom do unless I stub my toe.

GROUCHO: Is this your sister or your wife?

MAN: My wife, Groucho.

GROUCHO: Well, just checking. You know the old saying. An ounce of prevention is worth a pound of bandages and adhesive tape.

GROUCHO: How long have you been married?

WOMAN: Two and a half years, Groucho.

GROUCHO: Why are you holding on to each other? Are you afraid if you let go, you'll kill each other?

* * *

GROUCHO: How long have you been married?

WOMAN: Three wonderful years.

GROUCHO: Never mind the wonderful years. How many miserable years have you had?

GROUCHO: Do you have a job?

FATHER OF TRIPLETS: Yes.

GROUCHO: What is it?

FATHER OF TRIPLETS: I work for the California Power Company.

GROUCHO: My boy, you don't work for the California Power Company. You *are* the California Power Company.

GROUCHO: How long have you been married, Bill?

BILL: Fourteen years.

GROUCHO: Fourteen years? You've had the seven-year itch twice?

GROUCHO: How did you get to be a headwaiter, Felix? Did you start out as an ordinary burglar?

FELIX: No, I started in New York as a waiter many years ago.

GROUCHO: Well, it's a very honorable profession. I was just being facetious. What distinguishes a waiter from a headwaiter, Felix?

FELIX: Well, it depends on a lot of circumstances. And of course personality has a lot to do with it.

GROUCHO: That's right. To be a headwaiter you have to have something wrong with your personality. I'd take my hat off to you, Felix, except that it would cost me two bits to get it back.

* * *   )

GROUCHO: You're in the luau business? What do you do? You cater these things?

MAX: Yes.

GROUCHO: Well, suppose I wanted to throw one of these nightmares. What's the first thing I have to do—steal a banana tree?

MAX: No. First thing I do is go into the backyard of your house to look over the grounds.

GROUCHO: Why do you have to look over my grounds in the back of the house?

MAX: So I can dig a five-foot hole.

GROUCHO: Max, if your food's that bad, you'll have to find someplace else to bury it.

GROUCHO: You know how to make a Venetian blind?

MAN: No.

GROUCHO: Get him drunk. That's the best way.

MAN: I'd rather be a cattleman than a banker, 'cause after all, bankers never die, they just lose interest.

GROUCHO: Not the bankers I know. They'd rather die than lose any interest.

GROUCHO: What is a fur factory? I thought a live mink was the only fur factory there was.

MAN: After the mink gets through making the mink, we skin them and make them into various garments, for beauty as well as for warmth.

GROUCHO: I see. First you skin the mink and then you skin the customers.

MAN: We don't skin the customers.

GROUCHO: That's when the fur really flies.

WIFE: I spoil my husband rotten.

GROUCHO: You spoil him? Then why don't you shove him in the freezer? That'll keep him from spoiling.

GROUCHO: What's your husband's name?

WOMAN: Milton August.

GROUCHO: What's his name in September?

GROUCHO: Where are you from?

WOMAN: I'm from South Wales.

GROUCHO: Did you ever meet a fellow named Jonah? He lived in whales for a while. The middle part.

WOMAN: My father was a rear admiral in the Royal Navy.

GROUCHO: A rear admiral? You mean you never saw his face?

GROUCHO: What are you planning to do after college?

STUDENT: Be a lawyer.

GROUCHO: A lawyer. I see. Are you planning to go into politics or go straight?

GROUCHO: Would you be interested in Carol here?

RAUL: Very much so, but unfortunately I have a girl in Rio.

GROUCHO: You mean you prefer a girl who's five thousand miles away to a girl who's standing right next to you?

PAUL: Well, I'm very faithful.

GROUCHO: There are more nuts in Brazil than I suspected.

GROUCHO: Your husband is twenty, and the youngest commercial pilot in the world? How can he fly those big planes, Tootsie?

TOOTSIE: Well, he has lots of experience.

GROUCHO: So have I, but I still get dizzy . . . I get dizzy climbing up on a stool at a soda fountain. Although I was a stool pigeon for years.

GIRL: I would say it's what's upstairs that counts.

GROUCHO: Well, I have something upstairs. My upstairs maid. And that's not easy because I only have a one-story house. And the one story you're not going to hear is about my upstairs maid.

GROUCHO: Now, did you always want to be a singer?

JOHN CHARLES THOMAS: No. As I said a moment ago, I always wanted to be a surgeon.

GROUCHO: Oh, a surgeon.

JOHN CHARLES THOMAS: And I matriculated into Mount Street School of Homeopathy in Baltimore.

GROUCHO: Oh—well, I should think medicine and voice would go very well together. You could operate on a patient and then pick up another couple of bucks singing at the funeral.

GROUCHO: Is your wife listening?

MAN: Well, no . . . I don't know. She may be. But she don't like comedians, Groucho, so she may not be listening.

GROUCHO: Well, if she doesn't like comedians, there's no reason why she shouldn't watch this show.

GROUCHO: Where are you learning to be a barber? Do you go to school?

WOMAN: Yes. I go to the American Barber College.

GROUCHO: The Barber College? Must have some pretty gay blades there.

MAN: She kicked me under the table.

GROUCHO: She kicked you under the table? And did you remain there?

GROUCHO: How many times have you made a parachute jump?

WOMAN: Eleven hundred.

GROUCHO: You landed eleven hundred times?

WOMAN: That's right.

GROUCHO: No wonder you're only five feet tall. Every time you grew an inch you pounded it right back in again.

GROUCHO: Is your perfume expensive, Eddie? If it is, perhaps that's why I haven't heard of it. How much do you charge for a gallon of this stuff? Or can you buy it on draft?

MAN: No, you can't buy it on draft, but the price runs from three dollars for a purse size in Arpège, up to five hundred dollars for thirty-two ounces.

GROUCHO: Thirty-two ounces? Is that a gallon?

MAN: No, a quart.

GROUCHO: Five hundred dollars a quart?

MAN: Five hundred dollars a quart for Arpège.

GROUCHO: Well, do they get a nickel back when they return the bottle? Are there really any husbands who are willing to shell out five hundred dollars for a bottle of perfume for their wives?

MAN: Not for their wives.

GROUCHO: You don't have to explain that. I've been around. I'll bet you certainly took forward to Mother's Day.

GROUCHO: What makes a plane stay up in the air? I've never been able to figure it out.

WOMAN: The lift from the air holds the wing up. Air is very dense.

GROUCHO: What was that last thing? The air is what?

WOMAN: Dense.

GROUCHO: Well, I'd love to! Do you care to waltz or rumba?

GROUCHO: Say, you two'd make a great team. What's your opinion, Nick?

MAN: I think she's real gone.

GROUCHO: No, she's still here. But what's your opinion?

GROUCHO: He'll keep on sending flowers after he's married. All married men do that, you know. And if you're lucky, on your birthday he might even remember to send some to *you.*

FENNEMAN: Some special guests are ready to meet you now. As a matter of fact, when I heard about them, I asked them to do something we don't ordinarily do on the show—

GROUCHO: What's that? Be amusing?

MAN: We've only had one other child born to a governor and his wife while in office.

GROUCHO: Well, that is unusual. I've never seen a stork flying over the governor's mansion.

MAN: Well, uh—

GROUCHO: I've seen a lot of vultures hanging around there.

WOMAN: I just arrived from Phoenix about a month ago and—

GROUCHO: Felix? The cat?

WOMAN: No, from Phoenix, and I haven't met anybody yet.

GROUCHO: You haven't met any? How long have you been here?

WOMAN: About a month.

GROUCHO: You've been here a month and you haven't met anybody yet?

WOMAN: No.

GROUCHO: Well, where have you been spending your time? Forest Lawn?

WOMAN: Well, I know what I'd like to be.

GROUCHO: What would you like to be, honey?

WOMAN: A race car driver.

GROUCHO: A race car driver. There's the way it goes—here's a girl who's perfect for parking, and all she wants to do is racing.

MAN: Oh, it's right on the edge of my tongue.

GROUCHO: Well, stick your tongue out.

GROUCHO: What are you gonna do with your money, Colonel?

MAN: I'm gonna make my wife happy, Groucho.

GROUCHO: What are you gonna do—get a divorce?

GROUCHO: For those who don't know, a baby-sitter is someone who gets seventy-five cents an hour for watching television and cleaning out your icebox.

GROUCHO: *(To Ray Bradbury)* What kind of a job do you have, Ray?

RAY: I'm a writer.

GROUCHO: What kind of a rider? Pony Express, motorcycle, or what?

RAY: Writer. W-R-I-T-E-R.

GROUCHO: Oh, that's very refreshing—a writer who can spell.

GROUCHO: *(To a bell ringer)* Was your wife with you all this time?

MAN: No, I never married.

GROUCHO: Well, that's a shame. You've been interested in the wrong kind of bells. You should go down to the beach sometime when the belles are peeling. You know, I had to leave town one time because of a belle at Santa Monica. This was one of the belles that told at midnight. She told the police.

GROUCHO: Now, where are you from? Are you from Pasadena?

MAN: I was born right here.

GROUCHO: Right here in the studio? I realize that you've been standing there for quite some time, but I didn't think it was that long.

* * *

MAN: Well, I've traveled in a great many countries in the foreign service of the government doing personnel work, but Los Angeles is the most wonderful place in the world to live.

GROUCHO: Well, I agree, it's a wonderful city, even though I do criticize it occasionally. I'm all for it. And if they'd lower the taxes and get rid of the smog and clean up the traffic mess, I really believe I'd settle here until the next earthquake.

GROUCHO: You say it was a Tennessee walking horse?

MAN: Yes, sir.

GROUCHO: Is that the fellow who wrote *Cat on a Hot Tin Roof*?

MAN: I'm what you call a horse psychiatrist.

GROUCHO: A horse psychiatrist?

MAN: Right.

GROUCHO: You must have the biggest couch in town. I suppose you get a lot of horses whose wives are nags?

GROUCHO: *(To Liberace)* Lib, we're glad to have you here.

LIBERACE: Well, it's a pleasure.

GROUCHO: You don't object to me calling you Lib, huh?

LIBERACE: Not at all.

GROUCHO: Matter of fact, I'm a prominent member of the Liberace Fan Club.

LIBERACE: Well, that's wonderful.

GROUCHO: Last year I was voted Chief Candle Snuffer.

* * *

GROUCHO: Where you from, Lil?

WOMAN: I'm from Iran.

GROUCHO: Oh, I thought you were from Kansas City. Iran, isn't that where Great Britain had some trouble about oil concessions not long ago?

WOMAN: Yes.

GROUCHO: Well, Britain can keep their oil. You're the one I want some concessions from.

GROUCHO: Do you have any particular steady boyfriend?

WOMAN: Yes, I do.

GROUCHO: Or do you have a boyfriend who isn't particularly steady?

GROUCHO: What's your name?

WOMAN: Mimi Pill.

GROUCHO: Mimi Pill? I find that pretty hard to swallow. Imagine finding a pill like this in your aspirin bottle.

WOMAN: I like American food very much.

GROUCHO: Well, kid, I'm your meat.

GROUCHO: Are you married, Bill?

BILL: No, I'm separated.

GROUCHO: When a man gets to be your age, you have to expect to start coming apart. Maybe you've been using the wrong kind of glue.

* * *

GROUCHO: What's your name?

MAN: Mr. Cummings.

GROUCHO: Are you cummings through the rye?

GROUCHO: Have you ever been injured riding a motorcycle?

WOMAN: Many times.

GROUCHO: You have, huh? Well, they're not evident, these injuries. You look pretty healthy. Do you have any scars to prove it?

WOMAN: All over me.

GROUCHO: You have, huh? What do you mean, all over you? Specifically, where did you get these scars?

WOMAN: Well, let's see. Some of 'em were in Santa Monica, North Hollywood, and—

GROUCHO: Listen, when I want a lesson in geography, I'll speak to Rand McNally.

MAN: I was born in Brisbane, Australia.

GROUCHO: Australia, eh? You have more of an American accent than an Australian accent.

MAN: Well, there is a distinct accent, I suppose. For example, what you call a bison is a buffalo, and what we call a bison is a place where an Australian washes his face.

GROUCHO: Well, I've washed my face in Buffalo, when I was playing up there.

GROUCHO: What do you do?

WOMAN: I'm a dance instructor for Arthur Murray.

GROUCHO: You mean after all these years Arthur still hasn't learned how to dance?

MAN: I'm from County Cork.

GROUCHO: That explains why you bobbed up here.

GROUCHO: Do you manufacture beach umbrellas?

MAN: No.

GROUCHO: Awnings?

MAN: No.

GROUCHO: Venetian blinds?

MAN: No, Groucho.

GROUCHO: In that case, I apologize. I was sure you were mixed up in something shady, but what kind of a racket are you in?

MAN: At present, I'm involved in the motion picture business.

GROUCHO: Well, that's a pretty good racket. Have you produced any pictures?

MAN: Yes, one picture.

GROUCHO: You're a producer, huh? Bill Hunter. I think I saw your picture.

MAN: Oh?

GROUCHO: It was hanging on the wall in the post office.

GROUCHO: Mrs. Smith, are you in business by yourself, or are you connected with a law firm?

WOMAN: Well, I'm with Mordel, Mordel, Mordel and Smith.

GROUCHO: If you were smart, you'd get yourself a good lawyer and get out of that. Why is your name on the end?

WOMAN: I was the last one in.

GROUCHO: What, were you racing to the office?

WOMAN: I think when Philadelphia lawyers prepare a brief, their briefs are probably fifty pages long, and a brief that we would make here would be about five pages long.

GROUCHO: Well, you must remember that Philadelphia has a much colder climate and you need longer briefs there than you do here.

MAN: I did have a pretty good record before coming to Stanford.

GROUCHO: What—with the police?

GROUCHO: Imagine. Frankie Anvalo . . . Avalon on my show. Now I'm all aflutter. I can't even pronounce his name correctly. You know, it isn't every week that we get a famous celebrity up here, and I want to tell you, this is one of the biggest moments in the history of this show. This'll give you an idea of the show.

AVALON: We have four girls in Philadelphia who take care of the fan club, and four girls in New York who—that's all they do is just take care of the fan club.

GROUCHO: You have eight girls who do nothing but answer your mail?

AVALON: Right.

GROUCHO: Your staff is bigger than my fan club . . . How do you explain so many singers coming from one section of the city [Philly]? Is it because they don't produce any ballplayers there?

AVALON: I'll tell you what. Y'know, before, mothers used to meet on the street and they used to say, uh, "How's your son doing?" and they'd say, "Fine." But now they meet on the streets and they say, "How's your son's record doing?" 'Cause everybody's recording in South Philadelphia.

GROUCHO: Well, it was like that where I came from. My mother would say to another, "How's your son's record?"

WOMAN: We met at a dance in a dirigible hangar on North Island.

GROUCHO: You met him in a dirigible hangar? Was he full of hot air at the time?

GROUCHO: Ingrid Ami and Robert Crook, eh? Well, if you're a crook, you're on the right show, old boy. And you're Ingrid Ami—

WOMAN: Ingrid Ami. Yes, Groucho.

GROUCHO: Oh, well, it's the old Ami game. Are you any relation to Bon Ami?

WOMAN: No.

GROUCHO: If you were, you could clean up, you know. No soap, huh?

MAN: I was late every morning for school and finally the teacher asked me why I was late and I says, "Well there's a sign down the road says, 'School—Go Slow.' So I took my time." I didn't mind the teacher so much, it was the principle of the thing.

GROUCHO: Where did you say this happened?

MAN: In Providence, Rhode Island.

GROUCHO: Well, apparently we have very little to thank Providence for.

WOMAN: If you put the mynah bird in the cage alone and he happened to lay an egg, then you'd know that he was a lady bird, but—

GROUCHO: That doesn't mean a thing. I leave my milkman alone and he leaves eggs every morning—and he's certainly no lady. And according to my cook, he's not even a gentleman.

WOMAN: *(To a mynah bird)* Raffles, when you heard Groucho last week, did you laugh? When you heard Groucho on TV did you laugh? Did you laugh, Raffles? Raffles? What are you gonna say to Groucho? What do you say? What do you say, Raffles?

GROUCHO: Can he do anything else? Here we have a bird with a human brain, and on this stool we have a human with a bird brain.

MAN: When I was at the age of fourteen I had seven men under me.

GROUCHO: Were you working in a cemetery?

GROUCHO: Miona, what were you doing in a bar? Were you playing Parcheesi?

WOMAN: No, it wasn't a bar. It was a cocktail lounge.

GROUCHO: A cocktail lounge. Well, there is a difference, you know. When you pass out in a bar you just lie there. When you pass out in a cocktail lounge they're more refined. They shove you under a table and then they kick you.

GROUCHO: How do you like marriage, Rowena?

WOMAN: Oh, it's fine. It's very, very nice.

GROUCHO: Is it all that you anticipated?

WOMAN: Oh, yes, yes. And I don't have to feed the chickens. That's why.

GROUCHO: You don't feed the chickens anymore?

WOMAN: No, no. That's why.

GROUCHO: That's certainly a good reason to get married. It's certainly much easier to feed one rooster than a flock of chickens.

GROUCHO: *(To a man giving him a piece of the Blarney Stone)* What is this good for?

MAN: Well, it gives you the gift of gab. As a matter of fact, if you kiss it, you'll become more eloquent than you are presently, by far.

GROUCHO: When I'm reduced to kissing rocks, I'm going to cancel my subscription to *Playboy*.

WOMAN: Every woman has three ages—chronological age, a physical age, and an emotional age.

GROUCHO: That's true, isn't it, Mark? A man has seven ages and they're all lousy.

GROUCHO: How did you meet your husband?

WOMAN: He pulled up alongside me in his little white sports car and honked.

GROUCHO: What was he? A goose?

WRITER: As a matter of fact, I have a book out—*The Eternal Search*.

GROUCHO: *The Eternal Search.* Is it about a fellow looking for his car keys?

GROUCHO: When you get a flash that somebody's stranded in the snow, do you come bounding up the slopes with a keg of brandy around your neck?

MAN: No, uh, Groucho—

GROUCHO: Or do you drink it before you get there and just give him the empty keg? No, I'll tell you—you can't have your keg and eat it too.

MAN: We don't use brandy because after a shot of brandy, or after giving the patient or victim brandy, he will be colder within a half an hour than he was previous to the time that he drank the brandy. But we give him soup—

GROUCHO: After a half hour with a keg of brandy, who cares if he's cold or not?

WOMAN: I go to Los Angeles City College.

GROUCHO: You live in Guatemala and you go to school in Los Angeles? Aren't you a little rushed when you go home for lunch?

GROUCHO: What do you have to know to be a good fisherman?

MAN: Well, you have to think like a fish.

GROUCHO: You mean you have to be a chowderhead?

WOMAN: I am half Italian, half French.

GROUCHO: Well, that's a nice combination—half French, half Italian. You oughta have a lot of happy thoughts. I know a fellow who's half Scotch and half Soda, and he's happy all the time.

WOMAN: About marriage, we still have that old saying which is that women are the hind legs of the elephant.

GROUCHO: Women are the hind legs of the elephant? That's only when they're wearing slacks, isn't it?

MAN: My grandfather was in the oil business.

GROUCHO: He was in oil? Was he a sardine?

MAN: No, he delivered kerosene from house to house.

GROUCHO: You're pretty clever, aren't you. Are you married?

MAN: Yes, I'm married.

GROUCHO: Then you're not as clever as I thought you were. How did you meet your wife?

MAN: Well, I met her in the county jail, Groucho.

GROUCHO: Now you're talkin'.

GROUCHO: *(To a British woman)* Eileen, you have a very unusual accent. Do people in England ever comment about it?

EILEEN: Well, no, they all speak the same way there.

GROUCHO: Really! I'm surprised you can understand each other. No wonder you all drive on the wrong side of the road.

WOMAN: I first worked for Lloyd's of London.

GROUCHO: Oh, Lloyd's of London. I know them very well. As a matter of fact, I have a policy with them right now. If I'm torpedoed by a submarine at Hollywood and Vine, I get eight dollars a week for the rest of my life.

GROUCHO: You're forty-four and you just got married last May?

MAN: Yes, sir.

GROUCHO: Are you sorry that you marked time for such a long period?

MAN: Well, no. I didn't exactly mark time. I've done it twice before.

GROUCHO: You weren't marking time, you were doing time.

JACK LA LANNE: I swam from Alcatraz Prison to Fisherman's Wharf in San Francisco, handcuffed.

GROUCHO: Why? You crazy about fish?

JACK: Not exactly.

GROUCHO: Isn't that the way everybody leaves Alcatraz . . . handcuffed? What were you in for?

JACK: Well, I wasn't in for anything. It was just one of my birthday feats.

GROUCHO: Oh. Well, let's see the other one.

GROUCHO: Your name is Charles Snow?

MAN: Charles Snow.

GROUCHO: How tall are you, Charlie?

MAN: Five-two.

GROUCHO: That's the first time we've ever had five feet of snow in L.A.

MAN: Well, Groucho, you're a comedian . . . you tell jokes—

GROUCHO: Now wait a minute, that's debatable.

MAN: And I'm a watchmaker and I make watches.

GROUCHO: Where'd you get the notion that I'm a comedian? If your watches are as run-down as my jokes, they're beyond repair.

MAN: I'm a musician, Groucho. I play the bass viol.

GROUCHO: Well, you don't have to be so modest about it. You're probably not as vile as you think you are.

GROUCHO: *(To a woman named June)* June was always my favorite month. Usually June is followed by July, but beginning tonight, June may be followed by Groucho. Are you married?

WOMAN: Yes, I am, Groucho. I've been married a little over a year now.

GROUCHO: Oh, in that case, June will be followed by July as usual.

GROUCHO: What sort of work do you do, Ed?

ED: I'm in the investments securities business.

GROUCHO: Investments securities?

ED: Yes. We're Lester Ryans and Company. We're members of the New York Stock Exchange.

GROUCHO: You have a lot of Ryans in the fire?

ED: Quite a few Ryans in the fire.

GROUCHO: You're on Wall Street, in other words.

ED: No, we're on Hope Street. Wilshire and Hope.

GROUCHO: Eddie, everybody on Wall Street is on hope street.

GROUCHO: George, I have a riddle for you. Do you know the best way to make a coat last?

FENNEMAN: No, unless the way to make a coat last is to make the trousers first.

GROUCHO: You know, you're supposed to do the commercials. I'm supposed to tell the jokes. I'm going to give you one more chance, George.

FENNEMAN: All right.

GROUCHO: Why is George Fenneman like a boiler on a steam engine?

FENNEMAN: I guess I'd better say why? Why is he like a boiler on a steam engine?

GROUCHO: I'll tell you why—because you're both fired!

GROUCHO: You know, I've been working on this show for eleven years, and this is the first time a pretty girl has ever shown up in a bathing suit!

MISS OHIO: I think it's an honor, Groucho.

GROUCHO: Why didn't this happen eleven years ago when I was thirty years younger? Could you describe yourself for the benefit of the audience at home?

MISS OHIO: Can't they see me on the TV screen?

GROUCHO: The husbands can't. They've been breathing so hard they've fogged up theirs. So would you mind giving us your measurements? You can take them back later.

MISS OHIO: Thirty-five, twenty-two, thirty-seven.

GROUCHO: Let's see. Lumped all together you're ninety-four. That's the same as I am.

EGYPTIAN LADY: I've been married for thirty-one years to the same man.

GROUCHO: If he's been married for thirty-one years, he's not the same man. How did you meet him?

EGYPTIAN LADY: I was on a subway in New York.

GROUCHO: I thought you said you came from Egypt.

EGYPTIAN LADY: I was visiting my sister in New York and we were talking on the subway and he was listening.

GROUCHO: He was eavesdropping?

EGYPTIAN LADY: Yes, I had a very broad accent at the time.

GROUCHO: You still do.

EGYPTIAN LADY: I used to say "bawthroom" and things like that.

GROUCHO: "Bawthroom," eh? No wonder he was intrigued. I guess he was wondering how you found a bawthroom on the subway. Say, why were you saying "bawthroom" to a strange man, anyway?

EGYPTIAN LADY: It wasn't "bawthroom" that attracted him. It was my accent.

GROUCHO: Whenever you use your accent you say "bawthroom"?

EGYPTIAN LADY: No, no. When I got off, he got off and asked me, "Where are you from?"

GROUCHO: And you said, "The bawthroom."

EGYPTIAN LADY: No! He said he was fascinated. Back then, someone from Egypt was a rarity. Today there are millions of us.

GROUCHO: There's too many of you to suit me.

EGYPTIAN LADY: So then he said, "May I walk you home?" I said, "Yes." He was very gentlemanly.

GROUCHO: It wasn't that. He was just looking for a bawthroom.

GROUCHO: Where are you from, Catherine?

CATHERINE: I'm from Paris.

GROUCHO: Do you have a husband?

CATHERINE: No.

GROUCHO: That's the friendliest gesture France has made since they sent Lafayette over here. How old are you, Catherine?

CATHERINE: In France, a gentleman doesn't ask a lady how old she is.

GROUCHO: Let's get two things straight. First, we're not in France, and second, I'm no gentleman. And if you want, you can put the second first. Well, you don't have to tell me your age if you don't want to.

CATHERINE: I don't mind. I'm twenty-five.

GROUCHO: If I were twenty-five I wouldn't mind either. How long have you been in this country? Have you been here long enough to meet any American men? What a question!

CATHERINE: Since I have been here, I've been very distrustful. With American men there is an angle to everything.

GROUCHO: Any man who can find angles on you ought to have his eyes examined.

CATHERINE: Nothing much has happened, Groucho. I can't find a man who can make me tingle. It's important for me to tingle.

GROUCHO: What do you mean, "tingle"? You mean like tingle, tingle little star?

CATHERINE: No, no, no! You know!

GROUCHO: No, I used to know, but I don't know anymore. I haven't tingled since William Jennings Bryan was running for office.

OUTTAKES ACCORDING TO GROUCHO

"We now come to that section where all children should be sent out of the room: the Outtakes section. I advise this be done for a very important reason. The saucy sallies are so tame by today's standards that our kids would hoot them down, and no telling what they'd do to us. These interchanges were cut by the censors and never got out of the studio. Here, revealed for the first time, is our secret shame."

GROUCHO: Would you go with me to a movie if I promised to sleep all through it?

WOMAN: Yes! I'd be happy to. I'd even drive you there.

GROUCHO: You would?

WOMAN: Yes!

GROUCHO: Would you pay for the tickets?

WOMAN: No, I have a friend who owns a drive-in theater, so we would have passes.

GROUCHO: Oh, well, do you know what your neighbor looks like?

WOMAN: Oh, yes.

GROUCHO: Do you take your neighbor to the movies on her passes?

WOMAN: No, she's got a family, she stays home with them.

GROUCHO: Oh, you mean nobody that has a family goes to the movies?

WOMAN: Well, her kids . . . I don't know . . . sometimes they take her kids too, but she doesn't like to drive them. 'Cause she has a husband. And they just stay home.

GROUCHO: You mean that . . . what you're saying is that . . . if you're married, you don't have to go into a drive-in theater. Is that it?

WOMAN: I guess so.

GROUCHO: I'm certainly learning a lot about the younger generation here tonight.

GROUCHO: What sort of work do you do now, Karen?

KAREN: Alphabetically, or should I just rattle it off? Let me see now, I—

GROUCHO: I don't care, you can attack this any way you want.

KAREN: I'm a—

GROUCHO: And later I'll do the same thing to you.

KAREN: Promise?

GROUCHO: She may not know about Johnson being impeached, but she knows many other things which are far more important.

GROUCHO: Well, what did you do a-way up North in Tennessee, Grandma?

WOMAN: I ran a boardinghouse for the college students, and, ah—

GROUCHO: College students?

WOMAN: Yeah. And I had the boys on the first floor and the girls on the second floor, and it sure kept me busy. Lots of times I felt like usin' a broom.

GROUCHO: Why, did you want to fly around the room or something?

WOMAN: But then I'd come down.

GROUCHO: Well, I don't understand. Why did you have the boys on the first floor and the girls on the second floor? Seems to me you should've given the girls the fair preference and put them on the first floor.

WOMAN: Well, we didn't.

GROUCHO: You didn't, huh? You have no reason for this at all?

WOMAN: No, not especially.

GROUCHO: Well, what happened, why did you want to use the broom? Was it getting pretty filthy, this joint?

WOMAN: Well, sometimes you feel like it.

GROUCHO: Well, what was going on?

WOMAN: Just different things.

GROUCHO: I didn't know there *were* any different things. I'm so innocent and naive.

GROUCHO: What were you going to say about your car?

WOMAN: Well, when I go into a service station and the attendant comes over to check my battery, I don't let him.

GROUCHO: You don't let him check your battery?

WOMAN: No.

GROUCHO: I should say not. Anybody ever tries to check your battery, you hit 'em over the head with a wrench.

* * *

GROUCHO: Are you sure your husband hasn't lost some of his buttons in this laundry?

WOMAN: I don't think he ever lost his buttons in the laundry, but he lost his pants at the wedding.

GROUCHO: That's a little premature, isn't it?

GROUCHO: Now, John, are potatoes really fattening?

JOHN: No, sir. It's what you put on them that's fattening.

GROUCHO: Whaddya mean?

JOHN: Oh, butter, cheese, but if you put that on a mattress, it'd fatten you too.

GROUCHO: That's one of the few things I've never had on a mattress.

GROUCHO: Well, in what way is your husband romantic, assuming that he is . . . which I question.

WOMAN: Oh, man, have you ever been made love to by a Frenchman?

GROUCHO: Not that I can recall. This is getting like a burlesque show. What does this Casanova look like?

WOMAN: Well, he's a little fella. He's six foot five, two hundred and fifty pounds of—

GROUCHO: Pure mush?

WOMAN: No, all man.

GROUCHO: All man, huh? What makes you think that just because a man is five inches taller than six feet this makes him a man? You know it doesn't go by size. A man's size has nothing to do with his ability in any way. I'm trying to keep this on a euphemistic level, but I question very much whether I'm succeeding.

*   *   *

GROUCHO: Well, it sounds like an ideal existence. What happened to your marriage?

WOMAN: Bing!

GROUCHO: Bing? You mean you ran into Crosby?

MAN: Felt has over fifty thousand commercial uses—for ladies' apparel as well as industrial uses.

GROUCHO: Well, name one specifically.

MAN: Well, automobiles couldn't run without felt. Airplanes couldn't run. Girls in California couldn't have that new look.

GROUCHO: You mean the girls couldn't run without felt? Well, a lot of them are felt, and then run.

WOMAN: And he got a Dear John letter, and I read it to him.

GROUCHO: You got a Dear John letter?

WOMAN: Yes.

GROUCHO: Well, there's one on every floor.

WOMAN: So we got this Dear John letter.

GROUCHO: What is a Dear John letter? I don't understand. Is this put out by the American Can Company? I'm back to my old dirty self tonight.

WOMAN: My mother was a very fanciful woman. There were twelve of us in the family. We have not one John, nor Frank, nor Joseph, nor Mary.

GROUCHO: You have no John? Ah, they certainly do things differently in India.

*   *   *

GROUCHO: Is the oxygen business pretty profitable?

WOMAN: Well, sometimes it's almost too good. He's on twenty-four-hour call.

GROUCHO: He's on twenty-four-hour call and you've got ten kids?

WOMAN: He gets home between calls.

GROUCHO: Imagine if he had a job around the house.

GROUCHO: You have twenty-two children! Why do you have so many children? That's a big responsibility and a big burden.

WOMAN: Well, because I love children, and I think that's our purpose here on earth, and I love my husband.

GROUCHO: I love my cigar too, but I take it out of my mouth once in a while.